Frontiers into Borders

Frontiers into Borders

Defining South Asian States
1757–1857

Ainslie T. Embree

Edited by

Mark Juergensmeyer

OXFORD
UNIVERSITY PRESS

OXFORD
UNIVERSITY PRESS

Oxford University Press is a department of the University of Oxford.
It furthers the University's objective of excellence in research, scholarship,
and education by publishing worldwide. Oxford is a registered trademark of
Oxford University Press in the UK and in certain other countries.

Published in India by
Oxford University Press
22 Workspace, 2nd Floor, 1/22 Asaf Ali Road, New Delhi 110 002, India

ISBN-13 (print edition): 978-0-19-012106-8
ISBN-10 (print edition): 0-19-012106-8

ISBN-13 (eBook): 978-0-19-099017-6
ISBN-10 (eBook): 0-19-099017-1

Typeset in Adobe Jenson Pro 10.7/13.3
by MAP Systems, Bangalore 560 082
Printed in India by Rakmo Press, New Delhi 110 020

Contents

Preface

Mark Juergensmeyer

Shortly after Ainslie Embree, the great historian of South Asia, died on 6 June 2017 at the end of a long and productive life, I visited his wife, Suzanne, at their retirement home outside Washington DC. She invited me to go through Ainslie's papers in his study, and my eyes fastened on a remarkable thing: the draft of a manuscript typed on an old-fashioned Smith Corona typewriter, on the topic of how the uncertain frontiers of what the British called India were fashioned into the definite boundaries of today's South Asian states, largely by the political and military calculations of the colonial government.

'This is for a book that may or may not get written,' Ainslie wrote in notes for revisions and expansions of the manuscript that were found on his computer. 'But it should provide a focus for my reading and writing since I have no other large commitments,' he added in a parenthetical insertion labelled 'Note to Self'. It is not clear when he began working on this manuscript, though the Smith Corona typing would indicate some time in the 1970s or 1980s. In addition to the typed manuscript, there were a large number of pen- and pencil-inserted edits and additions. On Ainslie's computer were found several attempts at rewriting the first chapter and what appears to be a long introduction, which I have used for both the introductory chapter of this book and the concluding Afterword. The last date on which he appears to have made substantial changes and edits to the book was 2015, when Ainslie was 94 years old.

The time frame of this study changed at various places in his notes. In most versions, it was to begin in 1757; at other times 1754, 1765, or 1767. The ending date was even less certain. In some versions it was 1914; in others it was all the way up to the recent present, 2015, and would include not only the partition of the subcontinent and the creation of Pakistan, Bangladesh, and independent India, but also the border disputes with China and the continuing uncertainty about boundaries in what were the northwest and northeast frontiers. It was an expansive vision for a large project which is outlined in Chapter 1, though the next three chapters bring the reader only to 1857. In a remarkable way, however, the book is complete, since, as Ainslie argues in these chapters, all of the major parameters of the South Asian external boundaries were set during this time—the latter half of the eighteenth century and the beginning of the nineteenth.

Moreover, this was the period of Indian history that Ainslie knew best, the early British colonial years. One of the first works in Ainslie's career was also his favourite: his study of Charles Grant, one of the key players in the British East India Company from the 1760s until the first decades of the nineteenth century. In his book *Charles Grant and British Rule in India*, Ainslie scoped the historical field for the study of British colonialism in the subcontinent in the late eighteenth and early nineteenth centuries with all of its internal political intrigue, its arrogance, and its enduring impact. A return to this period of colonial rule was a natural and appropriate move for what would become Ainslie's last major project.

From the beginning of his work on this project, the phrase 'Frontiers into Boundaries' was frequently mentioned as the title, though he informally referred to it as 'the borders book'. In what appears to be Ainslie's last attempt to revise the introduction to the book, in 2015, he gave it the title *The Formation of the Modern States of South Asia: Borders, Sovereignty,*

Treaties, 1765–2015. The earlier, fully typed manuscript with four complete chapters bears two titles, *India: In Search of Frontiers,* and then below it on the same page a different title, *Frontiers into Boundaries: The Making of the Outer Boundaries of India and Pakistan.* I have chosen to go with a variant of the second title of the earlier manuscript, changing the subtitle to broaden the scope since the book talks about the borders with Afghanistan, Nepal, Bhutan, and Burma as well as defines the external boundaries of what would become India and Pakistan. Hence, my subtitle, *Defining South Asian States,* and then giving the dates that the main chapters of the book cover, from 1757 to 1857, even though the introductory chapter and Afterword briefly mention events after 1857 up to the present.

In much of the manuscript, Ainslie uses the term 'boundaries' rather than 'borders'. Most dictionary definitions regard the two as synonyms, but I suspect Ainslie's choice of terms was deliberate. The word 'borders' describes how the separation between nations appears from the ground; hence, one crosses the border to go from India to Pakistan, rather than crossing the boundary. 'Boundary' on the other hand indicates how this separation is precisely made by cartographers; so one would trace the boundaries between India and Pakistan on a map rather than tracing their borders. Since much of this book is how distant colonial administrators were debating where the lines should be drawn, the term 'boundary' is the appropriate term to use, and I have kept Ainslie's wording throughout the book. For the title, however, I have chosen the more commonly used term 'border' as Ainslie himself did in his 2015 notation of the title for the book, perhaps because he was aware of the growing subfield of border studies, for which this book provides an interesting example.

What is impressive about the research for this book is how thoroughly Ainslie mined the archives of the British colonial administration both in London and in Delhi. In addition to official reports and correspondence, he was able to tap into the personal collections of correspondence of some of the leading figures involved in this study. Because this book is about the British colonial administrators' attempts to construct India's boundaries, it is necessarily Eurocentric in its sources. Where relevant, Ainslie refers to the responses and interactions with Indian leaders and administrators, but to a large extent the book is based on English-language sources of the colonial administration.

Though Ainslie utilizes the colonial sources, this does not mean that there was by any means unanimity among their points of view. One of the fascinating aspects of the book's narrative is the degree to which administrators argued and disagreed among each other, and how in some cases the figures in India ignored or rejected the points of view of London officials. A major theme of this book, in fact, is how deeply many of the British officers in India regarded their responsibility towards India as a nation. Though London may have seen the role of the British primarily in mercantile and exploitive terms, the administrators in the subcontinent often sided with the national interests of India, and did what they thought was best for the security and integrity of the emerging nation. This gives a much richer and more textured view of British colonial rule than is often portrayed.

Perhaps because of the attention given by British officials in India to the integrity of India as a nation, Ainslie can regard one of the main outcomes of boundary creation to be nation building. As he says, many of the early nationalist leaders in India held on to the idea promulgated by British colonial authorities that India had 'natural boundaries' that destined it for national integrity. India's first prime minister, Jawaharlal Nehru, among others would refer to this idea in creating an image of a Mother India that had endured for centuries.

This quest for 'natural boundaries' was central to the British administrators' attempts to create firm boundary markers along India's frontiers. They were no doubt influenced by the European notion of nationalism that gave national status to regions defined by a common culture, and they assumed that India must have one within its natural boundaries. But such boundaries were also an essential aspect of security: determining those locations where military defence could provide protection against any possible incursions from foreign powers. For this reason, this book is primarily concerned with India's external borders, and not with interstate boundary creation. Since the issue of external boundaries was primarily a matter of land demarcation, it involves, almost exclusively, North India rather than South India. But the narrative of nation building relates to the whole of the Indian subcontinent.

In going through the manuscript, I edited very little. My main task was to decipher Ainslie's handwritten insertions, correct typographical errors, and complete unfinished sentences and paragraphs. Though the introductory chapter was not a part of the original four sections of the typed manuscript, I used most of it (omitting some redundancies with material he used in Chapter 1) for what is the Introduction and Afterword of this book. Chapter 1 of the book, 'Frontiers and Borders', replicates an article with a similar name that will be found in another of Ainslie's books, *Imagining India: Essays on Indian History*. Ainslie has, however, revised and expanded on this essay considerably, and the chapter in this book is much more substantial than the previously published essay.

The footnotes have created a special problem, since only in the Introduction, Afterword, and Chapter 1 were all of the citations fully present in the typed manuscript that we initially found in his study. After a great deal of searching through a box of Ainslie's loose papers and half-finished essays, we located—seemingly miraculously—an even earlier draft of Chapters 1, 3, and 4, some of it handwritten, but with the footnotes largely intact. Hence, I have been able to insert almost all of Ainslie's own citations for most of the chapters, though in some cases I had to reconstruct them from abbreviated notes. In Chapter 2, Ainslie indicated where footnotes were to be inserted, but we have not found the actual footnotes. What we have done in this case is to supply citations that seem consistent with the context, sources that Ainslie may or may not have had in mind. There are also a number of citations throughout the manuscript for which complete information could not be found. In those cases, we have retained whatever information Ainslie provided. With the assistance of the aptly named India Amarina, we have created a bibliography at the end of each chapter that provides full information about those works that Ainslie cited, as well as including other works related to the period that Ainslie might well have wanted to be included in a reference list. My thanks to the anonymous reviewers at Oxford University Press and others who have suggested recent works that Ainslie would certainly have wanted to include, and which I have added to the bibliographies at the end of each chapter, where relevant.

In putting this work together, I felt relatively confident that I was helping to create a book that Ainslie would want, since we worked together on two previous projects, *Imagining India* and *Utopias in Conflict: Religion and Nationalism in Modern India*, which was published in 1990 in a book series that I edited for the University of California Press. In both of these cases my task was to rummage through Ainslie's previously published articles and essays—many located in rather arcane and inaccessible venues—and through some editing and rewriting, some of it done by Ainslie and some by me, fit them together into reasonably coherent books. And, of course, Ainslie and I discussed and argued about how these books would take shape. Thus, this current book is the third project in what has been a collaborative partnership, and I have imagined Ainslie, as always, arguing with me and at times disagreeing with my choices and at times approving as I have tried to bring this volume to life.

I am grateful to Ainslie's wife, Suzanne Harpole Embree, and to their children, Ralph Thomas Embree and Margot Embree Fisher, for their enthusiastic support for this project and their help in facilitating my access to the manuscript in its various versions and providing a box of notes related to it. For help in deciphering the manuscript and retyping it for digital access, I am grateful for the labours of Ainslie's granddaughter, Sarah Langley Fisher, who retyped much of Chapter 3, and also for the work of India Amarina, who retyped much of the rest of the manuscript as well as helped with the citations. I appreciate the suggestions of the historian Judith Walsh, one of Ainslie's former students, for comments during the preparation of the manuscript, and for a mutual friend of Ainslie and myself, John Stratton Hawley, for suggesting her name. I am also grateful to the team at the Delhi branch of Oxford University Press which has shepherded the production process along. Admittedly, it has taken some of my time which could have been devoted to other things, but, in a curious way, working on this book was a way of working alongside Ainslie in a collegiality and friendship that has been 40 years old, and it turned out to be a gratifying task. It was in many ways a labour of love.

Introduction

Defining the Borders of South Asian States

The history of what is now called South Asia, but which throughout the nineteenth and the first half of the twentieth centuries
was often referred to as the Indian subcontinent or, even less
accurately as India, is usually defined as including Afghanistan, Pakistan,
India, Nepal, Bhutan, Bangladesh, Sri Lanka, and Maldives, the island
outlier. In the contemporary world, they are part of the international
community that forms the South Asian Association for Regional
Cooperation (SAARC), a loosely organized attempt to further regional
cooperation (Embree 2010, 199–200). None of them existed as independent modern nation states before 1947, but their contemporary status as
nations, including their boundaries, were determined by the creation of
the British Indian Empire and by the process of decolonization.

The time frame for this study is the hundred years following 1757,
since by 1857 many of the major territorial boundary claims by the
British had been made. By the Treaty of Allahabad in 1765, the British,
more properly the East India Company (henceforth referred to as the
Company), had established the lines of its rule by 'force and fraud',

to use an expression often used for the process. More recently, 1914 is the year of the last great exploit of British imperialism in drawing borders by its arbitrary declaration that the McMahon Line along the Himalayan ridges was the boundary line between British India and China. But the basic framework had been established a century before.

The word 'India' itself is not of Indian origin, but comes from Persian, Greek, and Roman sources. As Max Müller, the great Indologist, told a class of young probationers for the Indian Civil Service in 1882, it is a part of modern Western history, but it has a place in what is the very life of history, the history of the human mind. Its precise meaning in British usage in the nineteenth century was described in what is known as the Interpretation Act passed by the British Parliament in 1889. 'The expression "India",' the Act stated, 'shall mean British India, together with any territories of any native prince or chief under the suzerainty of her Majesty, exercised under the Governor General, or through any other officer subordinate to the Governor General of India.' The imperialism of this naming of their country understandably annoyed many Indian nationalists, and when the constitution of independent India was being written, some members of the Constituent Assembly argued for the use of the ancient and indigenous name, Bharat, which is in fact used in the Hindi translation. But the name 'India', as Prime Minister Jawaharlal Nehru and others argued, had become part of the vocabulary of world civilization.

The drawing of boundaries between that imperial construct and neighbouring political entities is a determining feature of the political development of all eight modern states of South Asia and is one of the most significant innovations introduced into the ancient polities of South Asia. The modern nation state is itself a modern innovation, for which fixed boundary lines acknowledged by all contiguous states are a primary characteristic, closely related to the concept of sovereignty as recognized in international law as well as to the growth of nationalism. And yet, as a writer noted in 1918, when the redrawing of boundary lines was an intense international preoccupation, 'the evolution of the conception of a boundary line, and the records of the attempts made to realise it and its influence on the development of states, are sections of political history which do not appear to have received much attention' (Fawcett 1918, 24).

In asserting that boundary lines are a modern device, a distinction is being made between a frontier and a boundary, not always recognized by writers. Sir Henry McMahon, who gave his name to one of the most famous and fateful boundaries between India and China, made the following differentiation between the two concepts:

> A frontier often has a wider and more general meaning than a boundary, and a frontier sometimes refers to a wide tract of border country, or to a hinterland or buffer states, undefined by any external boundary line. Such until recent times were the Northwest Frontier and the Northeast Frontier; the one comprising the wide and indefinite area of independent tribes on the Indian–Afghan border, and the other a wide tract of a similarly indefinite nature on the Indian borders of Tibet and China. (McMahon 1935, 4)

Frontiers were marks of an expanding power in the Indian subcontinent for the Mughal Empire throughout the sixteenth and seventieth centuries and for the British Indian Empire during the period with which this book is concerned. As a modern geographer puts it, a frontier is a manifestation of the spontaneous tendency for growth of the ecumene, the vanguard of a forward-moving political culture bent on occupying contiguous spaces. A boundary, on the other hand, is an enclosing, a shutting in, 'a term appropriate to the present concept of a state, that is, a state as sovereign (or autonomous spatial unit, one among many' (Kristoff 1959, 270). This concept of a boundary as a fixed line on the ground, accurately represented on a map, and described in a treaty by two impinging sovereignties, is a mark of the modern state system. McMahon insisted on clarity in understanding the two differences between two processes in South Asia as elsewhere in creating linear boundaries. One was delimitation, 'the determination of a boundary line by treaty or otherwise, and its definition in written, verbal terms'; the other is demarcation, 'the actual laying down of a boundary line on the ground, and its definition by boundary pillars or other similar physical means' (McMahon 1935).

That the creating of boundaries was a major preoccupation of the British in India is attested to by the enormous mass of documents on the issue in the archives of the Company and of the Government of India. It is one of the many attributes of the modern nation state that was transferred to the Indian subcontinent by the British as they transformed frontiers into boundaries, just as spatial relations were transformed by the steam engine, the telegraph, and the postal system. Indian nationalists such as Jawaharlal Nehru were correct when they insisted that these were not gifts of civilization by the British to India, but elements of world revolutions in transportation that were coincidental in time to the British commercial intrusion into India in the form of the Company, the first of the great multinationals (Nehru 1946, 294–306).

The Company had begun trading in India in 1600, but there are remarkably few references to this in contemporary Indian documents, public or private. That this is so was because the trade was small in terms of the Mughal Empire's total economy and the Company was operating on the coastal margins of the subcontinent, far from the great centres of Mughal political power in Agra and Delhi. The Company's trade was carried on at the sufferance of the Mughal authorities from the 'factories': fortified warehouses in various places located in the villages that eventually developed into the great metropolises of Calcutta, Madras, and Bombay, known as 'Presidencies' because of the title of president assumed by the Company's chief official in these regions. Calcutta in Bengal, the wealthiest of the Mughal provinces, was by far the most important of the three, and was the centre from which the Company began to establish political control of the subcontinent as the central control of the Mughal Empire weakened. This was a complex process, but the essential feature depended on the Company supporting one claimant over another in the struggle for the very lucrative office of nawab, the Mughal Emperor's governor of the province, or *suba*.

The first decisive step towards the Company's involvement in political control came in 1757 at the Battle of Plassey when its officials teamed up with influential members of the Hindu commercial classes to back the overthrow of Nawab Siraj ud-Daulah and to replace him with one his officers, Mir Jafar. The Company's contribution to this action, under the leadership of Robert Clive, was the provision of three thousand well-disciplined soldiers, two-thirds of whom were Indian mercenaries. The Company had made the discovery that Indian troops could be hired at far less expense than soldiers brought out from Britain and they survived better under Indian conditions. As General Sir Arthur Wellesley, later Duke of Wellington, put it, the Indians were sturdy sons of yeomen, while the British soldiers were the dregs of the slums of England and Ireland. This is a cruel observation, but not wholly untrue.

The next decisive step, fateful for the control of Bengal and the contiguous Mughal provinces of Bihar and Orissa and for British power in India, was the Treaty of Allahabad in 1765 by which the Mughal emperor made the Company the *diwan*, financial officer, of the three great provinces. Mughal provincial governments were divided between two offices: those of the the nawab and the governor of the suba in general charge. The office of the diwan, however, was directly under the emperor in Delhi and in charge of the collection of revenue. It was this office that was transferred to the Company in what its officials in Bengal reported to the directors in London as a 'great revolution'. Their possessions and influence were rendered permanent and secure, Clive told them, and no Indian power would be able to overthrow them. 'All revolutions,' he declared, 'must henceforward be at an end.' Clive summed up this belief in a classic formulation of the commercial basis of imperialism as stated in his report to the Company's directors in London:

> Every nation trading to the East Indies has usually imported silver for a return in commodities. The acquisition of the Dewani has rendered this mode of traffic no longer necessary for the English Company: our investment may be furnished, our expenses, civil and military paid, and a large quantity of bullion annually be sent to China [for importing Chinese goods into Europe], tho' we import not a single dollar. (British Library 1767, 27)

This appeared to be a fulfilment of this hope expressed as early as 1686 when the Company seemed to be getting a secure foothold in the subcontinent, and the directors wrote to their people 'to establish such a secure polity of civil and military power and create and secure such a large revenue ... as may be the foundation of a large, well-grounded sure dominion in India for all time to come' (British Library 1686).

This fantasy was never fulfilled in the way Clive expected due to his own corruption and rapacity and that of the Company's other officials as well as their ignorance of the revenue system. Nevertheless, P.J. Marshal, a careful historian of the period, sums up the real significance of what had happened when he writes that 'by 1765 an independent [Indian] government in Bengal had virtually no existence. ... For all practical purposes, power had been transferred to the British' (Marshall 1988).

Almost immediately, the Company's officials became aware that while they were on their way to becoming the heirs of a vast part of the Mughal Empire, they had very little knowledge of the actual outer boundaries of the territory they had acquired by the treaty of 1765 that had given them the shaky legitimacy within the Indian state system. When the news of the vast territorial acquisitions reached the directors in London—it took four months or so for the mail to reach from India—they were not pleased, as they recognized that new boundaries meant new expenses for defence and the likelihood of war with new neighbours. They reminded their servants in India that their concern should be with commercial profits, and that in the past they had expressly ordered the leaders of the Company to 'never extend [their] possessions beyond [their] present bounds' (Sinha 1955). What the directors in London did not do was to order their servants (this was the normal designation for their officials in India) to divest themselves of the territorial gains they had made; they only insisted on staying within what they referred to as the 'ancient boundaries' of the Company at Calcutta, Madras, and Bombay. The officials in India ('the men on the spot', as later generations liked to style themselves) discovered that to continue to trade in the condition of the Mughal Empire in the eighteenth century, they had to become the real power in Bengal, exercising administrative, legislative, and military functions as well as the right to collect the revenue which they had forced the Mughal emperor to assign to them. This marks the beginning of an expansionist movement that was to encompass first the boundaries of the Mughal inheritance of Bengal, Bihar, and Orissa; then towards the mountain ranges, separating this territory from the vaguely understood northeast areas of Tibet, Nepal, and Burma; then the movement up the Gangetic plains leading inevitably to the Indus valleys and the mountains beyond in search for a permanent and viable boundary.

In 1765, that some of the Company's servants in Bengal, and perhaps in London, were thinking of expansion to the heart of the empire is suggested in a letter from Clive to the directors in London. 'A march on Delhi,' he wrote in 1767, 'would be not only a vain and foolish project but attended with certain destruction to your army.' The directors responded that their servants in India should impress on the other Indian powers that 'we aim not at conquest and dominion, but security in carrying on a free trade equally beneficial to them and us'. Concurrent with these movements, right from the years after 1765, was the search for boundaries with the states that bordered on the 'ancient boundaries' of their important trading territories in Madras and Bombay. The preliminary and tentative attempts to rationalize the boundaries of Bengal, Orissa, and Bihar became the major concern of British rule in India. Almost always, the officials stated their mission as the establishment of 'law and order', which required the demarcation of linear boundaries and their defence, which in turn required the recognition of British sovereignty. This meant a clear notice that if the British recognized any intrusions— by either the neighbouring states or their subjects—beyond the lines, it would be met by force. The British reasoned that this was the only argument such states understood. Internal law and order, a profitable trade, and peace with neighbouring states were all dependent upon such defined, defensible boundaries. If all the immense number of documents on the subject of foreign relations were digitized and subject to a word search, there is no doubt that the results of a search for the subject 'defensible boundaries' would be overwhelming in its affirmation of this point.

The Company officials in Bengal were strengthened in their search for boundaries by the reports of James Rennell (1742–1830), who was appointed with the high-sounding title of Surveyor General of Bengal in 1764 at the age of 22. The reports were part of what has been called 'The Romance of the Indian Frontiers'. In the first important work on the geography and boundaries of the new possession, he summed up his views:

> On the north and east it has no warlike neighbors; and has, moreover, a formidable barrier of mountains, rivers, or extensive wastes. ... On the south is a seacoast, guarded by shallows and an impenetrable woods. ... It is on the west only that an enemy is to be apprehended, and even there the natural barrier is strong. (Rennell 2010)

This early understanding of the natural boundaries of Bengal—the mountain wall and the sea—conceals the fact that mountains provide a very vague and porous boundary.

The Company's officials soon learned that while there were careful internal boundaries of revenue districts, these did not apply to districts bordering on Rennell's 'formidable' mountain barriers. The Himalayas do not anywhere provide clear-cut lines of demarcation. Everywhere there are transitional zones with lower ranges of hills, with rivers and valleys leading from the plains to the mountains. The Himalayan region itself was made up of the areas now known as Tibet, Nepal, Sikkim, and Bhutan, which had not been added to the Mughal conquests. In the northwest, Afghanistan was a Mughal suba, and unsuccessful attempts were made to reclaim areas of Central Asia as parts of the Mughal dynastic inheritance. The Mughal Empire, without boundaries as understood in Western Europe, was self-consciously expansionist, predicated on the conquest of the whole subcontinent, and both expansion and contraction of its frontier claims could take place with little formal change in the conditions of sovereignty. The position of the Company was very different; while increasingly being controlled by the British Parliament, its existence depended upon profitable trade and, after the acquisition of the diwani (governing office), boundaries acknowledged by neighbouring polities on the threat of force.

The boundary issue was complicated by political ferment that was taking place all along the land borders of the territories that had come under British control in 1765. The main actors were to continue to be involved all through the next century as the British tried to define their territorial claims; these actors will be briefly introduced here. One group can be thought of as part of the Indian state system that developed as the central authority of the Mughal Empire, weakened in the first half of the eighteenth century. Regional and local entities with bases of economic and military power paid less and less attention to the imperial institution and its edicts emanating from Delhi. These Indian state system groups included the Mughal governors of different subas, the most important being Bengal and its related subas, a region that would become a dominant force in the shaping of modern India. It also included Awadh (the British officials transcribed this as Oudh) and Haiderabad (Habib 1982; Schwartzberg 1978).

Less directly related to the Mughal imperial institution, and with different cultural and political antecedents, were other internal powers that challenged British attempts to draw boundary lines that encroached on their territories and sovereignty. Reaction by these states to British intrusion is the major explanation to the wars and skirmishes after

1765, and while there were numerous of these internal challengers to the British, there were three that posed the most serious threats. One came from Mysore in the South, where Haider Ali (1721–1782), a Muslim general in the army of the old Wadiyar dynasty, overthrew the ruler and ruled the region with his son, Tipu Sultan (1750–1799). An even more serious and longer lasting challenge came from the armies of a number of able chieftains of the Marathas, a linguistic and ethnic grouping whose power was centred in Western India. A third challenge came from North India in the old Mughal suba of Lahore (in the Punjab region), where the Sikhs, defined by their history and religion, had begun to oust the Mughal authorities by the 1750s.

All these groups—the Mughal governors in Bengal, Awadh, and Haiderabad and the Mysore rulers, the Marathas, and the Sikhs—interacted with each other, sometimes as allies, sometimes as enemies. After 1765, they interacted in the same ways with the new British power.

These powers were all internal to the subcontinent, and the boundaries that were formed as the result of interacting with each other and with the British authorities became the boundaries of the great provinces of British India—Bengal, Madras, Bombay, United Provinces, Central Provinces, as well of the native and princely states. There were other boundaries, however, that were even more crucial to the development of a viable British state: those that bordered the volatile powers located along the perimeter of peninsular India.

In the eastern Himalayan ranges, the British in Bengal were vaguely aware of the activity of organized powers later identified as Tibet, Nepal, Bhutan, and Burma. The one that first captured the intention of the British in Bengal—and would keep it for the next century—were tribesmen in the northwest who are referred to in the correspondence of the time as 'Abdalis', Pakhtun clans from the area between Kandahar and Heart who formed the nucleus of an Afghan state in the period from 1747 to 1773. The Afghans invaded India a number of times, and, having established their power at Lahore in 1752, sacked Delhi in 1757. By 1767, the British in Calcutta were aware that there might be danger to their new possessions from this formidable power in North India. The Afghans, as some officials observed, were projecting some great enterprise which they feared would disturb the repose and deeply affect the political system of India. But the officials in London warned their servants in India not to exceed the boundaries of the Company's territories, as that meant added expense to defend them. The Company officials in Calcutta, however, argued that there was every likelihood that the Afghans would disregard the Company's territorial claims, especially if they found support in Awadh or other Indian powers. It must be apparent, they argued, that it was necessary to take a long view of the Indian political situation, and they summed up their position in 1767:

> It must be apparent that the future of our possessions depends in a great measure upon the divided state of Empire; whenever any one power arises superior to the rest we have everything to apprehend from that superiority, and therefore policy dictates that we ought to be on our guard against all attempts toward attaining supreme dominion in Indostan, whether from Abdalles, Marattas, or others. (Sinha 1955)

This is an early version of the policy of 'divide and conquer' that Indian nationalists in the twentieth century would accuse the British of using to maintain their rule by dividing Hindus and Muslims. They had reasons for fearing that the Afghans would invade Bengal: they seemed to have secure bases in the northwest hills, they controlled the Punjab, and had captured Delhi, the capital of the Mughal Empire.

The Company's officials in Eastern India saw a solution to the Afghan threat by seeking to have the suba of Awadh act as a buffer between them and the Afghans controlling Delhi and its environs. This they attempted to accomplish when, after the defeat of the feeble forces of the Mughal emperor and those of the nawab of Awadh at Buxar in 1764, they imposed the Treaty of Allahabad on the emperor, and reinstated the nawab of Awadh in power, although he had to pay heavy indemnities; thus the nawab becoming increasingly involved with the British. Awadh's role as a frontier buffer against the Afghans was not really needed because the Afghans apparently had no intention of invading the British possessions.

At about the same time, the Nepalese in the eastern ranges of the Himalayas caught the attention of the British, as did the vaguely known Assamese, Tibetans, and the Burmese. The Company became involved in the Nepal region when Jai Prakash, the ruler of the petty kingdom in the Kathmandu valley, appealed to its agent at Patna for help against his neighbour Prithvi Narayan, the Gurkha ruler who was engaged in the conquest of the little kingdoms in the region. The argument that the Patna agent used with Calcutta for helping Jai Prakash was that he had promised trading concessions, while Prithvi Narayan was not only disturbing the peace, but was also blocking trade routes that the Company used.

What Prithvi Narayan and his successors were unwilling to do was to meet with the Company's officials and agree on a boundary line between the two powers. When the British pressed the issue, they were met with silence or evasive answers. Possibly, the Nepalese saw this as an attempt by the British to gain territory, but they may also have seen it as an attempt to limit Prithvi Narayan's expansionist aims. Also, the treaties and boundary lines that the British wanted would have made them responsible for the actions of the hill rajas over which Narayan had little actual control. The development of workable relations with the fluid situation in India in the period from 1765 to 1798 was almost wholly the result of decisions made in Calcutta, not London. In the rapidly changing political world of India, it was not possible for the Company officials in London to have any real control over the responses of their servants in India, who had to act when they felt the Company's possessions threatened.

In 1770, a new direction would be given to the boundary question when the Company's agents in the northern districts of Bihar and Bengal argued that 'natural frontiers' of the British territory were not the vague regions known as the tarai (or terai), alluvial lowlands north of the Gangetic plain at the foothills of the Himalayas. This raised the larger question of what the 'natural frontiers' were, not only of the Indian state but of the mountain nations of Nepal, Tibet, and Bhutan. This notion would be behind many of the efforts to clarify not just frontiers but increasingly state boundaries. The issue of what was a 'natural' boundary was one that was significant for issues of trade and security as well as identity, and would be an obsession for the eighteenth and nineteenth centuries in South Asia, one that continues to this day.

In the modern state formation in the region that began in the eighteenth century, three fundamental aspects of that process that continue in the present day are the focus of this book: first, the definition of national borders; second, asserting sovereignty within these borders; and third, making treaties intended to guarantee stability in the region.

Many other factors are involved in the process, but these three are of particular interest because of the long historical development of a variety of political entities in the region. South Asia as the name for the region encompassing these states is a new term in the geographical lexicon, but it a useful one dictated by contemporary political changes, and their grouping reflects long historical cultural and political developments. All of the countries in the region have historical or semi-historical ancient lineages, but none of them really fit into generally accepted definitions of 'modern states' until the eighteenth and nineteenth centuries. This book's concern for the creation of the modern state is in the period from 1757 to 1857, dates not arbitrarily chosen, but marking defining events related to borders, sovereignty, and treaties.

Bibliography

British Library. 1767. 'Live to Select Committee, 16 January 1767'. *Select Committee Proceedings*. London: India Office Records (henceforth IOR).

———. 'Dispatch to Fort St. George', Letter Book 8. London: IOR.

Edney, Mathew. 1997. *Mapping an Empire: The Geographic Construction of British India, 1765–1843*. Chicago: University of Chicago Press.

Embree, Ainslie, T. 1989. 'Frontiers into Boundaries: The Evolution of the Modern State'. In *Imagining India, Essays on Indian History*, edited by Mark Juergensmeyer. Delhi: Oxford University Press.

———. 2010. 'Democratization as Scaffolding for Regional Integration'. In *Does South Asia Exist*, edited by Rafiq Dossani, Daniel C. Sneider, and Vikram Sood. Stanford: Walter Shorenstein Asia Scientific Research Institute.

Fawcett, G.B. 1918. *Frontiers: A Study in Political Geography*. Oxford: Clarendon Press.

Habib, Irfan. 1982. *An Atlas of the Mughal Empire: Political and Economic Maps with Detailed Notes*. Delhi: Oxford University Press.

Horstmann, Alexander, Martin Saxer, and Alessandro Rippa, eds. 2018. *Routledge Handbook of Asian Borderlands*. London: Routledge.

Kristoff, Ladis. 1959. 'The Nature of Frontiers and Boundaries'. In *Annals of the Association of American Geographers*. London: Taylor and Francis.

Lyall, Sir Alfred. 1891. 'Frontiers and Protectorates'. *The Nineteenth Century*.

Marshall, P.J. 1988. 'Bengal: The British Bridgehead in Eastern India 1740–1828'. In *The New Cambridge History of India*.

Max Muller. 1919. *India: What It Can Teach Us*. New York: Funk and Wagnalls.

McMahon, Sir Henry A. 1935. 'International Boundaries'. *Journal of the Royal Society of Arts*.

Moran, Arik. 2019. *Kingship and Polity on the Himalayan Borderland*. Amsterdam: University of Amsterdam Press.

Nehru, Jawaharlal. 1946. *The Discovery of India*. New York: John Day.

Rennell, James. 2010. *Memoir of a Map of Hindoostan; or the Mogul's Empire: With an Examination of Some Positions in the Former System of Indian Geography; and Some Illustrations of the Present One*. London: Gale ECCO.

Sahlins, Peter. 1989. *Boundaries: The Making of France and Spain in the Pyrenees*. Berkeley: University of California Press.

Schwartzberg, Joseph. 1978. *A Historical Atlas of South Asia*. Chicago: University of Chicago Press.

Sinha, N.K. 1955. *Fort William—India House Correspondence and Other Contemporary Papers Relating Thereto*. Delhi: National Archives of India.

1   Frontiers and Borders

t an early stage of the border dispute between China and India, the Chinese suggested that there should be no great difficulty in the two countries negotiating a mutually agreeable boundary since the current Indian claims were based on British imperialist activities, and 'the great Indian people, who treasure peace, can in no way be held responsible for all the acts of aggression committed by Britain with India as its base' (Ministry of External Affairs 1960). At the dawn of India's Independence, the then premier of China, Chou En-Lai, had told Indian Prime Minister Jawaharlal Nehru that he realized the boundary issue was a complicated question left over by history, but since India and China had both been long subjected to imperialist aggression, they might be expected to hold identical views on the subject.

The Chinese may not have intended this kind of argument to be provocative, for there could be no doubt that the disputed boundary lines had had their origin in the period of British rule. The historical assumptions and assertions that fill the Chinese and Indian letters and memoranda at the time, however, raise fundamental questions about the legitimacy of borders and the Indian government's attitudes about the actions of its predecessor.

The Chinese assertion that the borders of India had no more legitimacy than the power of the foreign ruler that had delimited them brought the rejoinder from India that the boundaries as defined by the former imperialist power were, in fact, integral to Indian nationhood. The northern frontier of India, it was argued in an official memorandum, 'has lain approximately where it now runs for nearly three thousand years', and the people enclosed by it had always regarded themselves 'as Indians and remained within the Indian fold' (Ministry of External Affairs 1959).

This insistence by the political heirs of the Indian National Congress on the inviolability of nineteenth-century frontiers has a note of peculiar irony because Indian nationalists from the 1880s up to the time of Independence had expressed frequent hostility to the colonial government's border policies (Prasad 1960, passim). The war with Afghanistan in 1878–9 evoked more criticism from Indians than any previous action of the government; it was denounced as an extravagance that India could not afford, especially at a time when the government was unable to relieve the victims of the famine that had recently desolated large areas of India (Goftar 1879). The annexation of Burma was condemned at the very first session of the Indian National Congress as 'unwise, unjust, and immoral', and it was argued that since the annexations of Sindh and Punjab were the outcome of the Afghanistan war, 'the aggression of Russia might be said to be traceable to these early aggressions of our own British government' (Indian National Congress 1885). The same sentiments were expressed twenty years later when Francis Younghusband's expedition to Tibet was denounced as 'foreign aggression' (Natesan 1909, 148).

But this attitude should not be taken as wholly representative of Indian opinion, for there are frequent expressions of an almost strident militarism to be found in some Indian language newspapers is the 1860s and 1870s. A Bengali newspaper chastised the government in 1864 for not having dealt severely enough with the Bhutanese who intruded into India, on the grounds that they were barbarous people understanding only force. In 1878, another paper called for a war to teach Russia not to interfere on the northern frontiers. It boasted that Maratha horsemen would soon ride about the streets of Moscow (Prakash 1864). This early territorial nationalism was echoed not only in the border dispute with China, but also, in some ways, more strikingly in the passionate claim that Goa was India *irredenta* (controlled by a foreign power). The argument that the Goan territory had not belonged to either the Mughal Empire or the British, and hence had not been under the control of an Indian government for four hundred years, was irrelevant to Indian nationalist sentiment. The existence of an enclave owing allegiance to a foreign power was untenable in the 1960s, although in the past it would have been a normal political arrangement in either India or Europe.

The northwest frontier was of overwhelming concern to the Government of India throughout the nineteenth century and became the major non-Indian boundary of Pakistan in 1947. It has not been the scene of such dramatic confrontations as the northeast frontier, partly because of the transformation of Afghanistan into a buffer state. It has not, however, been quiescent.

After 1947, groups of Pathan (Pushtu) tribesmen in the old Northwest Frontier Province demanded a separate state, Pushtoonistan. Their claims were encouraged by the creation of Afghanistan, whose leaders argued that the Durand Line boundary delimited by Afghanistan and Great Britain in 1893 was invalid, as it was an artificial demarcation that separated the tribal groups. This appeal to 'Pushtu' nationality was rejected by the Pakistan government with the simple declaration that 'the Durand Line has been, is and will continue to be the international boundary between Pakistan and Afghanistan' (Chowdhury 1956, 53). The Durand Line was specifically identified as demarcating Pakistani nationality by Liaquat Ali Khan, Pakistan's first prime minister, in 1950, three years after the creation of Pakistan: 'The people of the Northwest Frontier Province and of the tribal territory on the Pakistan side of the Durand Line are "good Pakistanis"' (Khan 1950).

Both India and Pakistan were undertaking one of the most difficult tasks successor states can be required to perform: 'the assumption of responsibility for a former imperial frontier' (Kirk 1962, 131). During the years of nationalist struggle, energies had been concentrated on relations with the administrative structures of the imperial power and, especially in the crucial years immediately before the transfer of power, on the tensions resulting from the competing nationalisms represented by the Indian National Congress on the one hand and the Muslim League on the other. Furthermore, the most urgent foreign policy issues in the last thirty years of imperial rule—the period of coming of political age of most of the nationalist leaders—were almost wholly centred far beyond the Indian periphery. The militarism of Japan in 1930, the Spanish Civil War (1936–9), and the rise of Hitler (in the 1930s) were of passionate intellectual concern to men such as Jawaharlal Nehru, but they did not impinge in any immediate geographical sense on India. Concern with external frontiers was, on the whole, a new and disquieting problem for Indian and Pakistani nationalism.

This identification of nationalism in both India and Pakistan with the boundaries created by the former imperial power to define the limits of its expansion is an indication of the importance in the nation-building process of many seemingly irrelevant factors. A recent study of the growth of Indian nationalism has pointed out that 'much attention has been paid to the apparent conflicts between imperialism and nationalism; it would be at least equally profitable to study their real partnership' (Seal 1968, 342). In the perspective of history, some of the most imperialistic of activities such as defining the boundaries of empire, though almost wholly ignored by analysts of nationalism, were crucial elements in the making of the nations of India and Pakistan. Such anomalies and ironies are part of what Ruth Benedict called 'one of the handicaps of the twentieth century', the fact that 'we still have the vaguest and most biased notions, not only of what makes Japan a nation of Japanese, but of what makes the United States a nation of Americans, France a nation of Frenchmen, and Russia of Russians' (Benedict 1989, 13).

India and Pakistan belong pre-eminently in this list. To say that India became a nation state in the nineteenth century is not to deny the astonishing continuity over nearly three millennia of Indian civilization through a clearly recognizable style in religion, social customs, art, and literature. But in India, as in Europe, the nation state is a modern phenomenon, and the delimitation of fixed and widely accepted boundaries is one of the most important characteristics of such states.

Yet, as a writer noted in 1918, when the redrawing of boundaries was an international preoccupation, 'the evolution of the conception of a boundary line, and the records of the attempts made to realize it and of its influence on the development of states, are sections of political history which do not appear to have received much attention' (Fawcett 1918, 24). Neither the ancient world nor feudal Europe, nor even the great powers represented at the Congress of Vienna in 1815 thought of nationality as coterminous with political frontiers. The intimate connection between nationalism and boundaries, as lines marked both on maps and on the ground as well as being described in documents, is suggested by their very late appearance in European history.

In asserting that boundary lines are a modern device, the distinction that political geographers insist on making between a frontier and a boundary, in contrast to their interchangeable use by many writers, is of great importance. The frontier is an area, often a zone of transition not only between ethnic groups, but also between geographic regions; a boundary is a line drawn on the ground and on a map (Gordon East 1967, 98; Prescott 1965). As was mentioned in the introduction to this book, Sir Henry McMahon, who gave his name to one of the most disputed of modern boundaries, made a clear distinction between frontiers and boundaries. 'A frontier often has a wider and more general meaning than a boundary,' McMahon stated, explaining that 'a frontier sometimes refers to a wide tract of border country, or to hinterlands or buffer states, undefined by any external boundary lines' (McMahon 1935, 4).

All the great empires and kingdoms of the past had frontiers which were of profound importance for their history, but these were essentially different from the boundaries of modern states. Paul de La Pradelle, in a well-known work on the relation of frontiers to international law, argues that the modern legal concept of a frontier was impossible in the great empires of the past because they thought of themselves as continually expanding to become universal empires (La Pradelle 1930 [1928]).

The boundary as a fixed line marked on the ground, accurately represented on a map, and described in a treaty by two impinging sovereignties recognizing each other's territory is, as I have mentioned earlier, a feature intimately associated with the rise of the modern nation state. The mutual acceptance of sovereignty is crucial for it differentiates modern boundary lines from such famous frontier constructions as Offa's Dyke, Hadrian's Wall, or the Great Wall of China. These were essentially defence works, implying neither contractual agreement with regard to territory nor recognition by the Chinese or the Romans that the barbarians beyond the wall possessed a sovereignty of the same order as that of their emperors (Lattimore 1940, 238).

A special relevance of the concern with frontiers for the state-making process has been suggested by S.N. Eisenstadt in *The Political Systems of Empire*. The 'historical bureaucratic empires', among which he includes the Indian Empire of the nineteenth century, differ from what he calls patrimonial and feudal states, in that they have 'autonomous political goals', differentiating the state from other spheres of society. A major corollary of such autonomous goals becomes an attempt 'to establish a unified, relatively homogenous rule over a given territory, and a more or less clear definition of the frontiers of this territory' (Eisenstadt 1963, 19–21). One need not follow all of Eisenstadt's analysis to see how suggestive it is for nineteenth-century developments in India. Concern for the frontier becomes, very soon after the establishment of the British regime, a primary focus of attention in India, helping to transform a trading company into a state. In sheer quantitative terms, it could probably be shown that no other subject occupied so much of the time of the higher echelons of the political bureaucracy, including the Governor General. Lord Curzon, for whom frontiers were almost an obsession, believed that one of the reasons why he was forced to resign, apart from his quarrel with Lord Kitchener, was his insistence on 'the payment of due [respect] … to Indian authority in determining India's needs'. An example was the British government's renunciation of his Tibetan policies, which had been necessary for the protection of India's frontier, but which had been sacrificed for British interests (Raleigh 1906, 587, 44–5).

According to Sir G.N. Clark, the earliest case of a frontier drawn with precision on a map was in 1718 (Clark 1947, 144). The growth of the power of the king and the emphasis on his unquestioned supremacy over all competing authorities is one part of the explanation for the growth of fixed linear borders; another was 'the growing size, cost, permanence and military value of fortifications' (Clark 1947, 143). The movement, then, from the zonal frontier to the linear boundary was an essential element in the growth of the modern state. The analogy to what happened in India in the nineteenth century is clear: frontiers as undefined, even if recognizable, areas that mark the early degree of development of the new state, but this finally gives way to the linear boundary. From frontier to boundary was thus one of the transitional stages of political life for India, as it was for Europe.

The ancient ritual of the horse sacrifice, an elaborate rite that had its origins in the most ancient levels of the Indian tradition, was an apt symbol for Indian sovereignty. As a mark of ambition worthy of a king and as a substantiation of legitimacy, a ruler would release a horse to wander for a year; wherever it could make its way to was claimed for royal patrimony. Related to this was the king's claim to be the universal ruler, a pretension not just confined to great kings but one also made by petty chiefs whose writ did not run much beyond their ancestral fields. It was the transitory nature of such claims that was derided in one of the great Hindu religious texts, the *Vishnu Purana*. Earth is pictured as saying that 'when I hear a king sending word to another by his ambassador, "this earth is mine", immediately resign your pretensions to it; I am moved to violent laughter at first, but it soon subsides in pity for the infatuated fool' (*The Vishnu Purana* 1840, 488).

Frontiers, in the sense of zonal regions, were of great importance for all the great emperors and kings of India, but there is little evidence that linear boundaries were known (Day 1944, 133–42). What is immediately apparent is the use of fortified outposts along the periphery of a state to defend it from enemies. These forts for defending passes and main routes are a dominant feature of the Indian landscape. Many of them, including such magnificent sites as Mandu and Daulatabad, had been strong points long before they were refortified by the Muslim rulers of the Delhi Sultanate. The importance of such forts throughout Indian history is shown in the *Arthashastra* of Kautilya. On all the four boundaries of a kingdom, Kautilya advises, forts should be erected against the enemy. The suitable areas for such frontier outposts are those that have been emphasized in all traditional political societies: deserts, mountains, forests, and the banks of great rivers. Such forts were meant for carrying the war into the enemy's lands: 'Having taken my stand in my impregnable fortress at the border of my country, I can harass the works of my enemy.' The identification of the enemy is made with brutal simplicity: 'The king who is situated anywhere immediately on the circumference of the conqueror's territory is termed the enemy' (*The Arthashastra* 1915, 56, 322, 329). For Asoka (c.269–232 BCE), the great emperor whose imperial ambitions are memorialized in edicts carved on rocks and pillars throughout India, the idea of linear boundaries defining equal sovereignties would have been an incongruity. He expanded the empire he inherited by force of arms and then guarded its frontiers against intrusion, but his dream was a kingdom of righteousness, a universal empire that would encompass the known world. It was this vision that led him to invite rulers beyond the frontiers of his empire to accept the principles of righteousness (Hultzsch 1925, 70).

The frontiers of the great medieval Hindu kingdom of Vijayanagar seem to have followed the classic pattern: strongly fortified outposts in open country, well-guarded passes, and some areas surrounded by inhospitable and uninhabited lands. On the extreme east, there was a dense jungle, which the Portuguese traveller Domingo Paes described as 'the densest possible to be seen, in which there are great beasts, and this forms so strong a fortress that it protects both sides' (Sewell 1900, 244). On the other frontiers were fortified cities, but the strongest fortifications with walls and towers were around the capital itself.

As with almost all of the great kingdoms of India, large areas of Vijayanagar remained in the hands of rulers who had been defeated but retained autonomy after acknowledging the suzerainty of the Vijayanagar king. The Wodeyar Dynasty of Mysore, which was founded in the early fifteenth century, became feudatories of Vijayanagar but carried on a virtually independent existence, including making war with the dynasty that survived the downfall of its overlord. In such a political situation, frontiers, much less boundaries, have little meaning. Dynastic cohesion and local bases of strongly guarded power are the political realities, not the formal claims or obligations of suzerainty (Rao 1943, 31–43). Whenever the Vijaynagar kings felt strong enough, they sought to expand beyond these outposts to their neighbours to the north, as did the Deccan Sultanates. One of these kingdoms, Golkunda, does seem to have had something approaching an agreed linear frontier with its northern neighbour, the Mughal Empire, during the seventeenth century (Sherwani 1964, 677–8). But it is significant that the information about boundaries comes from the European travellers Tavernier and De Thénenat, who may simply have been referring to octroi posts of the kind they were familiar with in France. De Thévenot speaks of 'les bornes du Mogolistan' (the boundaries of the Mughal Empire), and of the trees that make 'la dernière Terre du Mogol' (the end of the land of the Mughals), but he immediately refers to the payment of tolls. He also makes the point that in Golkunda the taxes were collected by great lords, not the king (Thévenot 1684, 276).

The nature of Maratha power precluded the development of even semi-permanent frontiers, much less anything approaching linear boundaries. Shivaji (1627–1680) established an independent kingdom with a well-articulated administrative structure, but to the Mughals, it was the rebel-held territory. In the eighteenth century, Maratha power was characterized by its rapid expansion, and its frontiers were flexible in the extreme. The great Maratha chieftains, such as Scindia and Hoekar, were essentially 'Wardens of Marches' (as some at the time described them), agents of the head of the Maratha Confederacy, but pushing forward into new areas and ruling it themselves.

Beyond India, the rulers of the borderlands were continually responding to pressures from India, but they also had frontiers with other rulers, including, in the case of Burma and Nepal, the Chinese emperor. Throughout this region, the limits of territorial claims were in constant movement, depending upon local situations. A typical, and understandable, attitude was shown by the Burmese in 1823 when the British met with their officials to discuss boundary problems. When the British asked the Burmese to show them where the boundary between Burma and Bengal was located, they were told, 'Our king knows the extent of his own dominion, and no one can set limits to it but himself' (Robertson 1853, 18).

Territorial sovereignty in India meant, in pragmatic terms, the ability to collect revenue and command the loyalty of local chieftains in time of war. The outer limits of such control would expand or contract, depending upon the abilities and resources of a ruler at a particular time, but in a well-established kingdom, there would be blocks of territory integrated into a permanent pattern of administrative control. The most detailed information on the working out of this pattern comes from the Mughal Empire, and it is reasonably clear that the frontier areas were excluded.

There were a number of practical reasons why this was so, all of which have analogies in the histories of other great empires. First of all, the frontier was never regarded as a fixed limit; at most, it marked a temporary halt. From the very beginning of Mughal power in India, under Babar in

1526 to its furthest extension under Aurangzeb (r. 1658–1707) at the end of the seventeenth century, it was always an empire of expansion. Within India itself, the Mughals sought, as had previous dynasties, to extend their power until it covered all of the subcontinent. They claimed suzerainty over all the kingdoms of India through the legal fiction that they were the successors of the Sultanate of Delhi, but in fact expansion eastward to Bengal and southward to the Deccan kingdoms was an almost irresistible challenge for an ambitious ruler. In the northwest, their frontier policy had a dual motivation: defense of the Indus plain from the tribal peoples of the mountains, and in a more attenuated form, the re-conquest of their ancient patrimony in Central Asia (Rahim 1937, 81–94, 188–99). They succeeded in maintaining control over the Afghanistan plateau centred on Kabul, but they made no progress beyond it, and the tribal areas between Kabul and the Indus plains were held only with unremitting care. Their ambitions within India were virtually achieved during Aurangzeb's reign, but within a generation, his successors began to lose effective control of the huge empire. The frontiers then defined contraction, not expansion.

Another historical characteristic the Mughals shared with other empires that made for indefinite frontiers rather than linear boundaries was the practice of leaving some border areas in the hands of tributary chieftains. What was demanded was an alliance for frontier defence, not for internal control. Such arrangements were made with local chieftains on both the northwest and northeast frontiers. In the long and indecisive struggle in the northeast for control of Assam, the Mughals maintained the ruler of Koch Bihar, a border state, as a tributary because of the help he could give them against mutual enemies (Bhattacharya 1929, 23–4). Related to this arrangement was the very prevalent practice of one chieftain having claims for tribute or revenue from another's territory. In India, as in medieval Europe, lordship and sovereignty were two quite different concepts (Petit-Dutaillis 1936, 12).

Overlapping jurisdictions were an obvious hindrance to the development of boundaries as a precise definition of sovereignty in territorial terms. A late, but not unusual example, is given in a treaty signed in 1751 between the nawab of Bengal and the raja of Nagpur. The Subarnarekha river provided a definite demarcation between the two jurisdictions, but the nawab was given tax rights over lands south of the river in the Raja's territory, while some of the Raja's tributary chieftains collected taxes from the nawab's side of the river. Adding to the complexity was the fact that the nawab was an official, at least in theory, of the Mughal emperor in Delhi, and the Raja was an officer of the Peshwa, the head or the Maratha confederacy, who was himself, again in theory, an appointee of the Mughals (Ray 1957, 285–90).

Finally, a simple technological fact has a direct bearing on the drawing of boundaries: the lack of accurate instruments for making land surveys. The process of marking a line on the ground on the basis of some kind of written description and then transferring it to a map with precision is an achievement associated with advances in surveying techniques in the eighteenth century (Ancel 1938, 1). Nor do the Mughals seem to have had much interest in cartography, judging from the almost complete absence of maps that originated in India. The contrast with China is striking, where detailed maps were being produced in the sixth century BCE, with Chinese maps remaining superior to European ones up to the Renaissance (Needham 1959, 500–23). James Rennell, who made the first accurate maps of India from 1767 to 1777, only mentions having made use of one map drawn by an Indian and acknowledges the help it gave him in identifying the courses of the rivers of Punjab (Rennell 1785). This map is apparently lost, but another late Mughal map recording the northwest frontier surveys is found in the records of the Survey of India (Phillimore 1952, 111–14). Ordinarily, instead of maps, the Mughals measured distances quite accurately between cities and set up mileposts along their roads.

The considerable precision of the boundaries of the internal divisions of the Mughal Empire provides an instructive contrast with the external frontiers. The basic source of information on these divisions came from the *Ain-i-Akbari*, the great descriptive work compiled by Akbar's minister Abu'l-Fażl (1551–1602). The empire was divided into twelve *subas*, or provinces, and these, in turn, were divided and subdivided into *sarkars* and *mohals* respectively. Abu'l-Fażl did not give the boundaries of the mohals, but his lists, in conjunction with surviving rent-rolls and the settlement reports made by the British early in the nineteenth century, make possible their reconstruction (Abu'l-Fażl 1891, 115–393). This work was mainly the result of careful studies of the vital subas of the Gangetic plains in Delhi, Agra, Oudh, Allahabad, Bihar, and Bengal by

Sir Henry Elliot, H. Blochman, and John Beames (Elliot 1869). What is at once apparent is that the sarkars and their subdivisions, the mohals, in the central areas of the subas were well defined, but on the peripheries, there was a great deal of vagueness.

Beames's analysis of the suba of Oudh, which stretched from the Ganges to the Nepal borders, is particularly important for the discussion of the external frontiers. The mohals were defined in terms of cultivated soil and taxable lands, not the actual area, and in Gorakhpur, one of the border sarkars, very little acreage was given, although it stretched for miles. In contrast to the internal districts, Beames concluded that 'the boundaries of the mohals in the north of this sarkar cannot be restored with any approach to accuracy', because they had not been defined by the Mughals (Beames 1884, 281, 44). In these areas in the terai, the dense jungle area that divides India from Nepal, local chieftains gave nominal allegiance to the Mughals, but there was nothing like a fixed boundary. Most of such areas were simply listed as '*ghair mumkin*', or uncultivated waste (Siddiqi 1964, 73–83).

The *Ain's* statement that the boundaries of the suba of Bihar were the high mountains of the north at first seems to indicate a definite boundary, but in fact, the border area, as described in the list of mohals, was obviously vague and unknown (Abu'l-Faẓl 1887, 139–46, 152). Mountains and hills, which in theory seem to be such clear-cut lines of demarcation, are, in practice, illusive boundaries, as the history of modern India was to show. In the south of Bihar, where the early Mughal administration ended with the hilly and irregular country south of the Ganges, the boundaries were equally vague (Beames 1884, 163–5). The administration was more tentative along the external borders, little influenced by the patterns of revenue collections that characterized the central areas. The division between the subas of Bengal and Bihar, for example, was marked by a stone wall running from the Ganges to the hills, but there is no mention of such walls on the external frontiers (Sarkar and Majumdar 1948, 1, 8).

The distinction in function between internal boundaries and external ones is of import. Interior boundaries are a function of the ruler's own power and depend upon what La Pradelle calls 'le droit public internal' (internal public law); external boundaries in the modern sense imply recognition of 'le droit public international' (international public law), which did not exist along the Indian borders (La Pradelle 1930 [1928], 25). The external frontier marks the limits of the exercise of sovereign power, while internal boundaries are for administrative convenience. The Mughals, like the Romans, marked the boundaries of their cantons and cities, but not their outer borders; the only marks there were fortifications to contain the Barbarians (Petit-Dutaillis 1936, 11).

In the eighteenth century, political conditions militated against either the possibility or desirability of fixed boundaries. As already noted, Maratha domination was associated with a constantly moving frontier. Their spectacular successes in advancing as far from their homelands as Punjab, the interior of Bengal, and Tanjore in the far south erased old frontiers and created new ones as the Maratha military leaders established themselves in outposts such as Gwalior. And all along the borders of India, a similar ferment of expansion was transforming political relations in the Indian borderlands.

The causes of this political ferment are obscure, and while it is tempting to link it with the decay of Mughal power, only in Afghanistan is the connection direct. Chinese expansion in Central Asia in the middle years of the century probably set some new currents in motion in contiguous states. In any case, new political dynamism manifested itself along the mountain perimeter and in Burma in the rise of able leaders who built up strong power bases that were used for expansion against their neighbours.

In the northwest, Kabul, the fortress that guarded access to the Indian plains while serving as the Mughals' link to Central Asia fell to the great Persian conqueror, Nadir Shah, in 1738. Nadir Shah invaded India and sacked Delhi in 1739, but he made no attempt to hold it as a permanent possession. After his death in 1747, the Afghan chieftain Ahmad Shah Abdali established his authority over the three strongholds of the Afghan plateau—Herat, Kabul, and Kandahar. This was a very unstable political structure, as the Afghan chieftains maintained their independence, but it marks the emergence of Afghanistan as a separate power among the Indian borderlands. For the next century and a half, internal political conditions in Afghanistan were of momentous consequence to India (Haig 1937, 357–72).

In the Nepal region, Prithvi Narayan Shah, the ruler of Gorkha, one of the small kingdoms that made up what is now Nepal, brought the whole area under his control in the 1760s through systematic wars of conquest against his neighbours (Levi 1905, 266–7; Regmi 1961, 68–9). In Burma, at about the same time, the very able and energetic young ruler, Alaungpaya (1752–1760), defeated his enemies, the Mons, and began a career of expansion that made Burma into a powerful kingdom (Harvey 1925, 219–43).

The expansionist policies of these rulers along the Indian borderlands meant that the British were not the only aggressive power in the area, and the frontier policy both in the early period and later in the nineteenth century must be seen in relation to strong, able rulers, not, as the story is so often told, in terms of the irresistible march of Western powers. All three states were able to contain British power and, at times, to defeat it. As will be seen further in the book, the search for frontiers with these states was at times a search for equilibrium, not for territorial conquest.

The Mughals reached their position of maximum control and almost immediately their empire began to disintegrate; the British achieved a comparable territorial hegemony in India in the 1850s and survived for almost a hundred years. Furthermore, the two successor states, India and Pakistan, seem likely to maintain in considerable measure the old boundaries of imperial control. There are, of course, many factors involved, but one important reason, as this study attempts to demonstrate, was that the imperialists of the nineteenth century in India, in contrast to those of the sixteenth and seventeenth centuries, were continually in search of defined frontiers and permanent linear boundaries. The British in India were as expansionist in practice as the Mughals, although they did not have expansionist aims of the precise kind that characterized the empire that preceded them.

The modern Indian state began, in terms of political, administrative, and constitutional development, with the establishment of British power in Bengal by the East India Company in the 1760s. This marked the beginning of an expansionist movement that has many analogies with the development of previous Indian empires, not least that of the Mughals. From the beginning, the problems of defining the boundaries of power were of primary political importance, and the movement up the Gangetic plains to Punjab and then to the mountain ranges beyond the Indus and in the northeast towards Tibet and Burma can be seen as a search for a permanent and viable frontier.

The preliminary and tentative attempt made to rationalize the Bengal–Orissa border in the early days of British rule became one of the major—and, in some ways, perhaps, the primary—concern of British rule in India. Defence required attention to frontiers, and beyond that, the introduction of the standards and practices of a government administered to the models of the contemporary Western world meant the delimitation and demarcation of linear boundaries to define sovereignty. These terms—delimitation and demarcation—were given a precise definition for boundary used by Sir Henry McMahon. Delimitation means 'the determination of a boundary line by treaty or otherwise, and its definition in written, verbal terms; demarcation is 'the actual laying down of a boundary line on the ground and its definition by boundary pillars or other similar physical means' (McMahon 1935, 4)

Uniformity in administrative methods, distinctions between citizen and non-citizen, and a clear notice to neighbouring sovereignties that beyond this line there could be no intrusions—all these commonplace features of the modern state were involved in border demarcation. As such, the concern with borders and frontiers was a vital element in the whole process of modernization of which the articulation of a nationalist ideology was an essential feature. This study, by examining how the boundaries of India—that is, the area that now includes both India and Pakistan—were created in the eighteenth and nineteenth centuries, will note the significance of the frontier in government policy, the reasons for some of the decisions that were made, and some of the consequences that followed from them. The geographic area of concern is the outward land frontier, the great arc stretching from the Gwadar Bay on the Persian border to a point on the Mekong river where Burma, China, and Indochina (primarily Thailand and Laos, in this case) met at approximately N 22° and E 101°. The frontier then followed a very irregular course southward to Victoria Point (as it is frequently called), the tip of Southern Myanmar or Burma. The most northerly point on this great arc was Povala Sehveikovski in the Taghdumbash Pamirs, at about N 37°40 and E 75°. There were a few places under the Government of India outside this arc—notably Aden on the southwestern tip of Arabia—but it was the land mass that constituted India. Throughout the centuries, 'India had been an ill-defined expression but was given precise official meaning in the Interpretation Act passed by the British Parliament in 1889'. The expression 'India', the Act stated, as was mentioned in the introduction to this book, 'shall mean British India' (Parliament of the United Kingdom 1889). This meant that such frontier states as Kashmir—the directly ruled territories—although not part of 'British India', were nevertheless part of India.

The contrast between this enormous expanse of territory and the original area controlled by the British East India Company in Bengal and enclaves at Bombay and Madras made it inevitable that frontiers and boundaries would play so crucial a role in the making of modern India. Like the Mughal Empire in the sixteenth and seventeenth centuries or the American and Russian in the nineteenth, this was the land of the moving frontier. But it differed from all of them, as they did from each other, both in its creation and function within the society itself. As noted earlier, the development from zonal frontiers to linear boundaries is part of the movement that differentiates the modern state from its predecessors. This process was complicated in India by the extraordinary diversity of terrain, ethnic groups, and levels of political development encountered along the borderlands that circumscribed the 'India' of the Act of 1889. The delimitation and demarcation of an actual boundary line were in themselves tasks of a magnitude not encountered along any other border, but prior to these technical stages being reached, and as the necessary prolegomena to the decisions on which they were based, was a century of intense political activity.

The period between the last decade of the nineteenth and the first of the twentieth century has been rightly called 'the most intensive period of boundary instruction in the Earth's history' (Prescott 1965). The last undemarcated frontiers were being replaced everywhere by linear boundaries, marked with precision both on the ground and on maps. The demarcation of boundaries was both a cause and a result of the intense international tensions that characterized the period, and all the great alliances and counter-alliances from the Three Emperors' League of 1873 to Entente Cordiale of 1904 reflected the concern of the great powers to preserve the existing frontier.

In Europe itself, the last twenty-five years of the nineteenth century saw an astonishing number of territorial changes. Most of these were on the European borders of the Ottoman Empire, the product both of the desire of nationalities to have state boundaries to conform with linguistic, ethnic, and religious affiliations, as well as the pressures of Russia and Austria on the Turks. The Treaty of Berlin in 1878 attempted to mediate claims and rationalize boundaries, but changes continued to be made for the rest of the century (Prescott 1965). In Africa, the tensions of European international politics found a focus at the end of the century in competition for territory which resulted in the drawing of numerous new boundaries. The result was the creation of political units that often bore little relation to tribal or linguistic groupings or even existing political entities. Most of the European claims were for territory that had been scarcely explored, let alone surveyed, and the boundaries that were actually delimited and demarcated were only a small proportion of the total. Of the 161,000 miles of boundaries claimed by Britain in 1909, only 21,150 miles had been marked and ratified by treaties with the other powers and tribal chieftains (Ireland 1938, 17–26, 230–42). In South America, by the 1890s, most of the major countries completed the transition from undefined frontiers to fixed boundaries.

Argentina and Chile almost found themselves at war as they tried to give actual geographic designation to the phrase that had long served to mark the frontier: 'the loftiest peaks of the Andes which divide the water.' The distinction between 'highest peaks' and 'watershed' was one which was to cause trouble in a number of areas, but it was finally settled in 1896. Another famous quarrel occurred when Venezuela disputed the claims that Great Britain made for the border with British Guiana (Whittington 2016). An analogy to some aspects of the post-1947 situation in India is that both were continuing an argument that had been carried on by the former rulers, the Spaniards, and the Dutch. The United States supported Venezuela's cause with the interesting argument that the Monroe Doctrine meant the United States would guarantee, against European interference, the boundaries of a former colony as they existed before the colony became independent (Ireland 1941, 272). Even the boundary between Canada and the United States came to attention in the 1890s, and in 1908, a treaty was signed for the complete demarcation of the border from the Atlantic to the Pacific (Fairbank 1973, 481–2). And in the Far East, the Russo-Japanese war in 1905 resulted in the drawing of new, and clearly demarcated, frontiers that altered the power relationships in the area (Rawlinson and Curzon 1907, 22).

All these political and diplomatic activities throughout the world emphasize the importance to modern states of defined boundaries. They had their counterparts along the frontiers of India, with the definition of the borders between Afghanistan and Russia in 1884, the Afghan–Indian border in 1893, and the McMahon Line between India and Tibet in 1914. This was the final stage of the search for the frontiers of India under the last power to control the whole land mass of the Indian subcontinent. It was marked by a discussion—partly theoretical, partly practical—by a group of talented and knowledgeable men on the significance of the frontiers for India's future that perhaps was not equalled in relation to any of the other boundary decisions made during this period. Of the many who wrote and spoke on the subject, the views of three are of special interest because of the influential positions they occupied, the wide circulation that their views received at the time, and their intellectual grasp of the political and social significance of frontiers in the life of a nation. Their Indian careers taken together span nearly eighty years, from 1827 to 1905, but all three were dealing with the same problems around the 1880s and were familiar with each other's views.

Sir Henry Rawlinson (1810–1895) went to India in 1827, and after a career as a soldier, including service in the First Afghan War (1841–2), was appointed the British Consul in Baghdad. He was an amateur scholar of great renown, as the first successful decipherer of Persian cuneiform, and had conducted wide-ranging and important excavations. This scholar was relevant for his attitude towards the Indian frontiers, for though his attainments were quite extraordinary, he was only one of the numerous nineteenth-century British officials whose knowledge of the past gave them a proprietary sense towards the area's cultural achievements. As a member of Parliament and the India Council and as president of the Royal Asiatic and the Royal Geographical societies, he had influential forums for his views on the future of India's northern frontiers (Boggs 1940, 22).

Sir Alfred Lyall (1835–1911) arrived in India as a member of the civil service in 1856; he became foreign secretary of the Government of India and Lieutenant-Governor of the Northwest Provinces. After his retirement, he wrote a number of books on Indian history and religion, which have an intellectual clarity and precision that have seldom been equalled in writings on India.

The third member of the group was Lord Curzon (1859–1925), who used his wide knowledge of Central Asian and the Indian borderlands as parliamentary undersecretary for foreign affairs and as Governor General of India (1898–1905). He was the author of important studies on Persia and Central Asia, and he summed up his views on boundary questions in a small book that has been widely quoted for its concise statements on the Indian frontier (Spykman 1942, 437).

Their particular contributions to actual decisions were tied to the vagaries of specific political situations, but their ideas provide a useful perspective for the long history of the search for frontiers and the transition from undefined zones to boundary lines. They were writing at the end of the period and interpreting, and in some cases justifying, not only the actions of the past, but also to a remarkable degree their understanding of what frontiers and boundaries meant to India, justifications that had informed their search almost from the beginning.

All the writers on Indian frontiers would have given their consent to the comment that 'a good boundary is one which functions well and a bad boundary is one which functions poorly' (Curzon 1907, 26). And in elaborating the meaning of function, they would have accepted the distinction made by a modern writer between the definition of a boundary in providing a clear differentiation between two legal systems and its function in separating two conflicting sovereignties (Rawlinson 1875, 141). The frontiers were understood in terms of defence: not as the furthermost limits to which sovereignty could be extended but as the area that should be held to protect the subcontinent. For this purpose, what was needed was a boundary within or along what Curzon called a 'Frontier of Separation', in contrast to a 'Frontier of Contact' (Curzon 1889, 384). The powerful attraction of classical allusions for nineteenth-century Englishmen meant that they saw the origins of such 'Frontiers of Separation' in the practices of the Roman Empire, either to keep back barbarians, as in the West, or, as in the East, to prevent collision with the powerful Parthian Empire. In India, the same frontier served both functions, with the tribal people as the barbarians and the Russians the powerful state with whom there should be no direct contact.

For Rawlinson, the simultaneous expansion of the Indian and Russian empires was remarkable, so that, as he wrote in 1865, 'instead of two empires being divided by half the continent of Asia, as of old, there is now intervening between their political frontiers a mere narrow strip of territory, a few hundred miles across' (Lyall 1891). Rawlinson, like Curzon and the others, saw nothing to be condemned in Russian expansion any more than British expansion in India; Russia was a civilized power pursuing her manifest destiny. As Curzon travelled through Central Asia and saw what Russia had accomplished, he 'could not repress a feeling of gratitude to those who had substituted peace for chronic warfare and order for barbaric anarchy' (Lyall 1891, 319). The issue was the course of action that the Government of India should take regarding the frontier. Contact between India and Russia was to be avoided for many reasons, but not least because the discontent that inevitably smouldered in India, as in any conquered country, might be fanned into flame by the continuity of another European power. This was a point to which Rawlinson often returned, emphasizing that the Muslims of North India especially had an undying hatred of the British. If the Russians were able to make use of this, he warned, it would probably mean the end of British power in India.

The maintenance of frontiers of separation in the face of the simultaneous advance of the two great powers seemed possible only through the creation of some form of protectorates to act as buffers. The most cogent statement on the idea of protectorates was made by Lyall in 1891. The true frontier of India, he argued, did not tally with the border of administrative jurisdiction, but was 'the utmost political boundary projected, as one might say, beyond the administrative border' (Curzon 1889, 4). This distinction between boundaries of jurisdiction and boundaries of influence had marked the whole growth of modern India: protectorates had been established over the kingdoms contiguous with Bengal until the Bengal government could absorb them. Then the mountain rim was reached, and instead of this ending the need of protectorates, it increased them. In confrontation with another major power, 'the moving and fluctuating borderlines begin at once to fix and harden; disputes fall under the cognizance of regular diplomacy, and questions of war and peace become the concern of civilized governments' (Curzon 1894, 417). The affairs of the client states, notably Afghanistan, became part of the life of the protecting power.

Since the creation and support of a client state such as Afghanistan meant the exclusion of the competing great power with attendant tensions and opportunities for a crisis, it might have seemed sensible to think instead of neutralized states, along the pattern of Belgium and Switzerland, rather than protectorates. But to Lyall, this was an impractical dream in Asia because Oriental rulers would too easily fall prey to the intrigue, disorder, and jealousy that characterized their kingdoms. This kind of reasoning that oriental states by nature lacked the capacity for political order, whether justified or not, was a potent factor in much thinking about India and its problems.

Lyall's idea of frontiers beyond the political boundary was given the name 'Three-fold Frontier' by Curzon, with his flair for coining a phrase (Lyall 1899, 368–73). This summarized very well the concept of the Indian frontier that Lyall and others had striven to elaborate. One frontier was the administrative boundary up to which the Government of India exercised its full authority enforcing its own legal and political systems as the standard for society. Beyond this was a zone claimed as Indian territory, in which the government made no attempt to impose its laws or political jurisdiction but permitted tribal chieftains to order their own affairs. The outer edge of this zone was then demarcated by a fixed boundary. Beyond the tribal zone was the third area, the protectorate, an independent kingdom, but tied by special treaties of friendship and obligation to the Government of India. The classic example of such a border area was, of course, in the northwest. There was a defined administrative line in the Northwest Frontier Province, beyond which was the tribal zone, its boundary with Afghanistan defined by the Durand Line. And Afghanistan, the protectorate, in turn, had its outer edge delimited by the boundary agreements of 1885. On the northeastern frontier, concern with the demarcation of the three-fold frontier was less urgent because of the weakness of China. Curzon's bold attempt to extend, in a tentative form at least, the protectorate system over Tibet, was aimed at Russia, not China. He was convinced that China was a spent force, unlikely to be of any political consequence. How bad a prophet he was is suggested by his summary of the Far Eastern situation in 1894: 'That China would ever seriously clutch at the keys of empire, or challenge the racial domination of the West, I am quite unable to believe' (Jones 1959, 250). Lyall, more substantive to historical reality, was less certain that China need not be taken into account; commenting on Curzon's views in 1899, he wondered if there were no dynamic forces in China that might be awakened, as in Japan, that might fundamentally alter the situation along the northeastern boundary (Lattimore 1962, 1170).

Two important aspects of the search for frontiers tend to be obscured by the attention given to defensive potential. The tone of much of the writing on the Indian frontier sometimes suggested that the location of the boundary was a matter to be decided unilaterally by one power, without taking into account the interests of the other parties (Jones 1959, 250). Yet, even Rawlinson—vigorous in his warnings against Russian expansionism and a fervent exponent of the argument that frontiers that would be of maximum benefit to India's security should be created— always recognized that the active consent of the border states concerned was necessary, and, when Russia was involved, prolonged and careful diplomatic negotiations would be the normal course to allow in defining frontiers.

The other point is somewhat more theoretical but of greater importance. Owen Lattimore in his studies of China's frontier history has insisted that to see the frontiers of the great empires only in terms of defence against intruders is to miss much of their significance. The frontier, whether a zone or a linear boundary, is intended to set the limits for expansion from within. Efficient administration, taking into account economic resources and military requirements, has to decide how large a territory can be controlled and to reach out too far beyond the periphery of this manageable whole is wasteful (Lattimore 1962, 1170). This is quite a precise way of rephrasing one of the great central arguments of modern Indian history. One of the charges made against Warren Hastings was that he had wasted the resources of Bengal on wars of expansion, and Wellesley was recalled after bringing vast new territories under British control for the same reason (Embree 1962). Then in the 1860s and 1870s came the great debate between the advocates of 'Masterful Inactivity', and those of a 'Forward Policy'. One side, for which Sir John Lawrence was the spokesman, argued that India's resources did not justify expansion beyond the Indus; the other side, of which Sir Henry Rawlinson was a representative, insisted that the correct boundary of India's resources required such a precautionary move (Pounds 1951, 146–57). Lyall was against making claims for territory without realizing that whatever line was drawn to define the extent of political influence required some expression of actual authority. For this reason, he argued, 'the political and financial condition of India renders it imperatively necessary to circumscribe as closely as may be possible the extension of our dominion over the Afghan highlands, and this can only be done by settling authoritatively a consistent policy, based upon a plain recognition of definite objects, and a careful, proportionate comparison of their value with the cost of obtaining them' (Durand 1913, 218).

The concern with strategy and defence necessarily involved an emphasis on 'natural frontiers', a phrase and concept that had become part of the vocabulary of politics in the nineteenth century. But the term was seldom used in writings on India with the meaning that 'natural frontiers' were those that were designed by nature to coincide with the limits of nationality. This idea received its first strong impulse during the French Revolution when, abandoning the old arguments for territory based on historical claims, the revolutionaries spoke of France's destiny on the Rhine (Curzon 1889, 54). Sorel, the great historian of the revolution, summed up the end product of this belief in natural frontiers to which a country expounded by right in his remark, 'La politique française avait 'été' destinée par la géographie' (French politics had been 'destined' by geography) (Fawcett 1918, 86–7). Curzon dismissed this understanding of natural frontiers based on 'ambition, or expediency, or more often sentiment' (Holdich 1916). For Curzon, natural frontiers meant those great obstacles of nature—deserts, rivers, marshes, and, above all, mountains—which could be used as frontiers of separation and defence. The search for such frontiers was a dominant feature of territorial expansion. Such natural defensive features did not exist anywhere in Bengal 'from the Sunderbunds northwestward along the plains of India, and so [the British] were urged only the needs of attaining such a frontier till their power reached the foot of the northwest passes' (Curzon 1889, 19).

What was to be sought—according to Sir Thomas Holdich, the surveyor and explorer who translated into actual territorial demarcations the political arguments of Rawlinson, Lyall, and Curzon—was always a line of defence. Those who argued that racial, cultural, and linguistic needs were of primary importance in defining frontiers knew nothing, he insisted, of the actualities of political geography. The creation of natural frontiers required taking advantage, through political power and geographical knowledge, of a terrain that would 'ensure peace and goodwill between contiguous people by putting a definite edge to the national political horizon, so as to limit unauthorized expansion and trespass' (Curzon 1889, 20, 53). This meant, according to Curzon, India's securing of not just the crest of the mountains, but the vital areas around it, including valleys and canyons and other strategic approaches.

Lines drawn for the purpose of defence had more than military significance, however. To a large extent, they made possible the assertions of territoriality and sovereignty that make possible the modern notion of a nation, or a cluster of nations. Holdich had made this point about Afghanistan when he remarked that it had become a national entity only when the Russians and British had drawn a boundary around it (Davis 1927, 4).

Partly as a way of legitimizing British rule, but largely as a conviction arrived at from their understanding of Indian political and social structures, the best-informed among the British officials in India had always insisted that the subcontinent comprised of not one but many nationalities, sharply distinguished from each other by religion, language, race, and regional customs. 'The first and most essential thing to learn about India,' according to John Strachey, one of the ablest of the late nineteenth-century administrators, was 'that there is not and never was an India; that men of Bombay, the Punjab, Bengal, and Madras should ever feel that they belong to one great Indian race, is impossible' (Curzon 1889, 5).

When the interpreters of the frontier argued for the primacy of strategic considerations in deciding their location they were not arguing for an aggressive militarism or that frontier strategy was an end in itself. The memorable phrase that was applied to the concern with Russian and British activities in the northern areas, 'the Great Game', is misleading. It was not, as H.W.C. Davis who popularized the phrase suggested, 'a grandiose policy, framed with a superb indifference to the obvious risks and the obvious difficulties of ways and means' (Davis 1927, 4). There was no 'policy' as such, and as this study will show, there was always a very careful counting of the cost, even when errors were made. The frontiers and frontier policies were of enormous importance because of what they defended: imperial India.

This is what Curzon had in mind when he wrote, 'I would invite you to consider what Frontiers mean ... and what part they play in the life of nations' (Ratzel 1897, 279–313). The new frontiers made possible the development of an ordered and stable political society in India, with all the promise for economic and social progress which would replace the stagnation of the past. England would benefit from the wide opportunities for trade and capital investment.

In international politics, the new frontiers gave India a position in the world she had never enjoyed before. The others would have agreed with Curzon that because of the frontiers, 'on the west, India must exercise a predominant influence over the destinies of Persia and Afghanistan; on the north, it can veto any rival in Tibet; on the North-East and East it can exert greater pressure upon China, and it is one of the guardians of the autonomous existence of Siam' (Jones 1959, 249). Few Indian or Pakistani patriots in the first flush of post-Independence dreams of their countries' place in the world would have gone much beyond these claims.

Yet, all these possibilities did not exhaust the meaning of the Indian frontiers as seen by those involved in their creation. Beyond the material advantages were the spiritual ones, the influence the frontiers exercised on the spirit of man and the life of society. A belief in the special virtues of frontier life and the peculiar significance of frontiers for a nation's history was part of the intellectual climate of the time. In Germany, Friedrich Ratzel developed in the 1890s what he called 'political geography', a semi-mystical concept of 'space'. Only those states have lasting vitality, he argued, which can grow from the continental periphery of their 'space' into the interior (Ancel 1938). This movement towards the frontier becomes the movement towards national growth, as the spirit of the expanding frontier vitalizes society. This was summed up in the law that 'the frontier is a peripheral organ of the state, the bearer of its growth and its security, conforming to all changes of the state organism' (Ratzel 1897, 301–3). In its ability to expand and to maintain its vitality, the frontier becomes not just an index to the power of the state but the source of that power (Curzon 1889, 55). And India was destined for greatness on this account because its organizing power, based on the periphery, had succeeded in controlling the wedge of land that sank into Asia (Turner 1920, 1–380).

This sense of the destiny of India because of her frontiers was an important aspect of the thought of Lyall and Curzon, who was especially impressed with Friedrick Jackson Turner's thesis of the importance of the frontier in American' history (Turner 1920, 1–380). Turner had summed up his analysis of the meaning of the frontier in words that Curzon later paraphrased to apply to India:

> That coarseness and strength combined with acuteness and inquisitive-ness; that practical, inventive turn of mind, quick to find expedients; that masterful grasp of material things, lacking in the artistic but powerful to effect great ends; that restless, nervous energy; these are the traits of the frontier, or traits called out elsewhere because of the existence of the frontier. (Turner 1920, 37)

The frontiers of India, Curzon believed, could provide the same qualities and serve the same function. Their men would be saved from 'the corroding ease and morbid excitements of western civilization'. The frontiers provided scope for courage, for 'without a world to conquer or a duty to perform', men 'would rot of atrophy and inanition' (Curzon 1907, 55–8).

This vision of the function of the frontier as a place for testing and renewal, which in one form or another dominates so much of the nineteenth-century writing about India, found its laureate in Rudyard Kipling. In 'Ganga Din'—perhaps his most famous, and most misun-derstood, poem—Kipling celebrated the paradox of the frontier: while its creation and defence made for enmities, it imparted a spiritual and physical vitality that united the strong. Kipling's preoccupation with the frontier as a symbol of life-giving conflict was an immediate reflection of social Darwinism, but its deeper roots were in that historical experi-ence of the making of modern India, which was the basis for policies elaborated by Rawlinson, Lyall, and Curzon. From the very beginning of the British intrusion as a political force in Bengal in the middle of the eighteenth century, problems relating to the frontiers had absorbed the interests and the energies of the new administrators. Many of these problems were inherent in the geography of the regions they controlled; many were the product of the fact that the East India Company, in a formal sense the legatees of Mughal authority in Bengal, derived its real legitimacy from the position of Great Britain as a world power; oth-ers grew out of the understanding of sovereignty, especially in relation to neighbouring powers, that was integral to the Western state system but was a new factor in the political life of the whole Indian region.

The search for solutions to frontier problems thus marched with the establishment and spread of British power in India.

Bibliography

Abu'l-Fażl, 'Allāmī. 1887. *The Ain I Akbari*, translated by Colonel H.S. Jarrett. Calcutta: Baptist Mission Press.

———. 1891[1877]. *The Ain I Akbari*, translated by Colonel H.S. Jarrett, vol. II. Calcutta: Baptist Mission Press.

Ancel, Jacques. 1938. *Geographie des Frontières*. Paris: Librairie Gallimard.

Arthashastra, The. 1915. Translated by R. Shamasastry. Bangalore: The Government Press, 1915.

Beames, John. 1884. 'On Geography of India in the Reign of Akbar'. *Journal of the Asiatic Society of Bengal*, 53: 215–32.

———. 1885. 'On Geography of India in the Reign of Akbar'. *Journal of the Asiatic Society*, 54: 162–82.

Benedict, Ruth. 1989. *The Chrysanthemum and the Sword*. Boston: Houghton Mifflin.

Bhattacharya, Suvendra Nath. 1929. *A History of Mughal North-East Frontier Policy*. Calcutta: Chuckerverty, Chatterjee and Co.

Blochmann, H. 1873. 'Contributions to the Geography and History of Bengal'. *Journal of the Asiatic Society of Bengal*, 42: 209–310.

———. 1874. 'Contributions to the Geography and History of Bengal'. *Journal of the Asiatic Society of Bengal*, 43: 280–309

———. 1875. 'Contributions to the Geography and History of Bengal'. *Journal of the Asiatic Society of Bengal*, 44: 275–306.

Boggs, S. Whittemore. 1940. *International Boundaries*. New York: Columbia University Press.

Chowdhury, Hamidul Huq. 1956. Speech Given by Minister of Foreign Affairs in Pakistan National Assembly, March 25, 1956'. Karachi: Archives of the Ministy of Foreign Affairs, Government of Pakistan.

Clark, Sir George Norman. 1947. *The Seventeenth Century*. Oxford: Clarendon Press.

Curzon, Lord George Nathaniel. 1889. *Russia in Central Asia in 1889*. London: Longmans, Green, and Company.

———. 1894. *Problems of the Far East*. London: Longmans, Green, and Company.

———. 1907. *Frontiers*. Oxford: Clarendon Press.

———. 1909a. *The Place of India in the Empire*. London: John Murray.

————. 1909b. 'The True Imperialism'. In *The Place of India in the Empire*. London: John Murray.

Davis, Henry William Carless. 1927. *The Great Game in Asia 1800–1844*. London: Oxford University Press.

Day, Winifred M. 1944. 'The Relative Permanence of Former Boundaries in India'. *Scottish Geographical Magazine* 65: 133–42.

Durand, Henry Mortimer. 1913. *Life of the Right and Hon. Sir. Alfred Comyn Lyall, P.C., K.C.B., G.C.I.E., D.C.L., LL.D.* Edinburgh, London: W. Blackwood and Sons.

Edney, Mathew. 1997. *Mapping an Empire: The Geographic Construction of British India, 1765–1843*. Chicago: University of Chicago Press.

Eisenstadt, Shmuel N. 1963. *The Political Systems of Empire*. New York: Free Press of Glencoe.

Elliott, Sir Henry M. 1869. 'Memoirs of the History'. In *Folklore and Distribution of the Places of the North Western Provinces of India*, edited by John Beames. London: Trubner and Co.

Embree, Ainslie T. 1962. *Charles Grant and British Rule in India*. New York: Columbia University Press.

Fairbank, John. 1973. *East Asia: Tradition and Transformation*. London: Allen & Unwin Ltd.

Fawcett, Charles Bungay. 1918. *Frontiers: A Study in Political Geography*. Oxford: Clarendon Press.

Goftar, Rast. 1879. '29 December 1878'. In *Report on Native Newspapers*. Bombay: Jame-Jamshed.

Gordon East, William. 1967. *The Geography behind History*. New York: W.W. Norton & Company.

Haig, Sir Wolseley. 1937. *Cambridge History of India*, edited by Sir Richard Burn. Cambridge: Cambridge University Press.

Harvey, E. Godfrey. 1925. *History of Burma*. London: Longmans.

Hertslet, Sir Edward. 1875. *The Map of Europe by Treaty: Political and Territorial Changes*. London: Butterworth and Harrison.

Hertslet, Sir Edward, R.W. Brant, H.L. Sherwood, and E. Russell. 1909. *The Map of Africa by Treaty*. London: H.M. Stationery Office.

Holdich, Sir Thomas Hungerford. 1909. *The Indian Borderlands 1880–1890*. London: Methuen.

————. 1916. *Political Frontiers and Boundary Making*. London: Macmillan and Co. Ltd.

Hultzsch, Eugen (ed.). 1925. 'Inscriptions of Ashoka: Thirteenth Pock Edict'. In *Corpus Inscriptionum Indicarum*. Oxford: Clarendon Press.

Indian National Congress. 1885. *Proceedings of the First Indian National Congress Held at Bombay, on the 28th, 29th and 30th of December 1885.* Bombay: All Indian Congress Committee.

Ireland, Gordon. 1938. *Boundaries Possessions and Conflicts in South America.* Cambridge: Harvard University Press.

———. 1941. *Boundaries Possessions and Conflicts in Central and North America and the Caribbean.* Cambridge: Harvard University Press.

Jones, Stephen B. 1959. 'Boundary Concepts in the Setting of Place and Time'. In *Annals of the Association of American Geographers.* Washington: Association of American Geographers.

Khan, Liaquat Ali. 1950. *Pushtoonistan: A Myth.* Karachi: Government of Pakistan.

Kirk, William. 1962. 'The Inner Asian Frontiers of India'. In *Transactions and Papers of the Institute of British Geographers*, no. 31. Lattimore, USA: Beacon Press.

Kristoff, Ladis K.D. 1959. 'The Nature of Frontiers and Boundaries'. In *Annals of the Association of American Geographers*, vol. 49. Chicago: Taylor and Francis Ltd.

La Pradelle, Paul de. 1930 [1928]. 'La Frontière: Études Droit Internationale'. *Journal of the Royal Institute of International Affairs* 8 (368): 90.

Lattimore, Owen. 1940. *Inner Asian Frontiers of China.* London: Oxford University Press.

———. 1962. *Studies in Frontier History.* London: Oxford University Press.

Levi, Sylvain. 1905. *Le Nepal.* Paris: Musee Guimet.

Lyall, Sir Alfred. 1879. 'On Afghan Affairs', 9 January 1879, and 'Minute', 8 October 1897. In *Lyall Papers*, Mss. Eur.F.132137. Delhi: India Office Library.

———. 1891. 'Frontiers and Protectorates'. *The Nineteenth Century*, vol. 30, p. 318. London: Kegan Paul & Co.

———. 1899. *Asiatic Studies.* London: John Murray.

McMahon, Vincent Arthur Henry. 1935. 'International Boundaries'. *Journal of the Royal Society of Art* 84: 4.

Ministry of External Affairs. 1959. 'Memorandum Given by the Embassy of India to the Ministry of Affairs of China, 30 October 1959'. *Memoranda and Letters Exchanged between the Governments of India and China*, September–November 1959, White Paper No. II. New Delhi: Government of India.

———. 1960. 'Ministry of Foreign Affairs of China to the Embassy of India on China, 26 December 1959'. *Memoranda and Letters Exchanged between the Governments of India and China*, November 1959, White Paper No. III. New Delhi: Government of India.

Natesan, Ganapathi Agraharam Annadhurai Ayyar. 1909. *The Indian National Congress*. Madras: Natesan.

Needham, Joseph. 1959. *Science and Civilization in China*. Cambridge: Cambridge University Press.

Parliament of the United Kingdom. 1889. *The Interpretation Act 1889* (52 & 53 Vict c 63), Section 18.

Petit-Dutaillis, C. 1936. *The Feudal Monarchy in France and England from the Tenth to the Thirteenth Century*. London: Kegan Paul.

Phillimore, R.H. 1952. 'Three Indian Maps'. *International Journal for the History of Cartography* 91195 (2): 111–14. Imago Mundi Ltd.

Prakash, Som. 1864. '28 December 1864'. In *Report on Native Newspapers, Bengal: 1863–64*.

Prasad, Bimla. 1960. *The Origins of Indian Foreign Policy, the Indian National Congress and World Affairs 1885–1947*. Calcutta: Bookland.

Prescott, John Robert Victor. 1965. *The Geography of Frontiers and Boundaries*. London: Hutchinson University Library.

Pounds, Norman J.G. 1951. 'The Origin of the Idea of Natural Frontiers in France'. *Annals of the Association of American Geographers*. Washington: Association of American Geographers.

Rahim, Abdur. 1937. 'Mughal Relations with Central Asia'. *Islamic Culture*, vol. 11. Hyderabad, Deccan: Islamic Culture Board, 1937.

Raleigh, Sir Thomas, ed. 1906. *Lord Curzon in India*. London: Macmillan.

Ratzel, Friedrich. 1897. 'Studies in Political Areas'. *American Journal of Sociology*, 3: 279–313, 449–63.

———. 1898. 'Studies in Political Areas'. *American Journal of Sociology* 4: 366–79.

Rao, C. Hayavadana. 1943. *History of Mysore 1399–1799 A.D.* Bangalore: The Government Press.

Rawlinson, Sir Henry. 1875. *England and Russia in the East*. London: John Murray.

———. 1878a. 'The Afghan Crisis'. *The Nineteenth Century*, vol. 3. London: Kegan Paul & Co.

———. 1878b. 'The Results of the Afghan War'. *The Nineteenth Century*, vol. 6. London: Kegan Paul & Co.

Rawlinson, Lyall, and Lord George Nathaniel Curzon. 1907. *Frontiers*. Oxford: Clarendon Press.

Ray, Bhabani Charan. 1957. 'British Attempts to Settle the Boundary Line between Bengal and Orissa'. *Journal of the Bihar Research Society* 43: 285.

Regmi, D.R. 1961. *Modern Nepal*. Calcutta: Tirma Mukhopadhyay.

Rennell, James. 1785. *Memoirs of a Map of Hindoostan*. London: Rennell.

Robertson, Thomas Campbell. 1853. *Political Incidents of the First Burmese War.* London: Richard Bentley.

Sarkar, Sir Jadunath, and Ramesh Chandra Majumdar. 1948. *History of Bengal, Muslim Period 1200–1757* AD. Ramna, Dacca: University of Dacca.

Seal, Anil. 1968. *The Emergence of Indian Nationalism.* Cambridge: Cambridge University Press.

Sewell, Robert. 1900. 'Narrative of Domingo Paes'. In *A Forgotten Empire.* London: Swan Sonnenschien.

Sherwani, Haroon Khan. 1964. 'The Reign of Abdullah Qutb Shah: Economic Aspects'. *Journal of Indian History* 43: 677–8.

Siddiqi, Noman Ahmad. 1964. 'The Classification of Villages under the Mughals, in Indian Economic and Social History'. *The Indian Economic & Social History Review,* 1(3): 73–83.

Spykman, Nicholas John. 1942. 'Frontiers, Security, and International Organisation'. *The Geographical Review* 32.

Strachey, John. 1903. *India: Its Administration and Progress.* London: MacMillan's.

Thévenot, Jacques de. 1684. *Voyages de Mr de Thevenot Contenant La Relation de l'Indostan.* Paris.

Turner, Frederick Jackson. 1920. 'The Significance of the Frontier: An Address to the American Historical Association in 1893'. *The Frontier in American History.* New York: Henry Holt.

The Vishnu Purana. 1840. Translated by R.H. Wilson. London: John Murray.

Whittington, Keith E. (ed.). 2016. 'Richard Olney, Letter to Thomas Bayard (1895)'. In *American Political Thought.*

2   Defining the Mughal Inheritance, 1757–98

When it became apparent in the early 1750s that a struggle for succession was certain to take place in eastern India on the death of Alivardi Khan, the energetic governor ruler of the three Mughal provinces of Bengal, Bihar, and Orissa, the directors of the East India Company (hereafter Company) in London warned their servants in Calcutta not to get involved. 'Take all prudent measures to preserve our possessions,' they wrote, but 'observe the strictest neutrality between the competitors' (Gupta 1962, 37). Fifteen years later, after the outright disregard by the Company's officials of this guideline of action had ended in the transfer of effective power from the Mughal governors to the Company, the directors grudgingly accepted what had been done, but warned them: 'Never extend your possessions beyond your present bounds,' reminding them that their aim was not conquest of the other Indian states, but 'security in carrying on a free trade equally beneficial to them and to us' (*The Journal of the Bihar Research Society 1951*, 1981, 181). The London directive, insisting that no changes in frontiers should take place, and the actions in India that made changes inevitable form the paradigm of India's frontier history for the next 150 years: the contradiction between policy and decision being rooted in the nature of the Indian political system into which the Company entered. The essential fact in explaining the divergence is itself embodied in the contradiction, in that the transfer of power in Bengal in the 1760s was not the product of invasion by a foreign power but of shifts within the Indian political system itself.

The explication of this claim that this transfer of power was indigenous to Indian political life is found in the context of the pluralistic, very loosely integrated, Indian political system of the time, rather than in the more familiar historiographical pattern that sees it as part of European expansion. The primary political fact involved in what contemporaries called 'the revolution in Bengal' was that the Company had become an Indian power. While profound cultural implications followed from its origins in the Western world, it was its location in the interstices of Indian politics that assured its relevance to the developments that were transforming state relations in the whole South Asian area. By the middle of the eighteenth century, the salient feature of the Indian political life was that control of the vast Mughal patrimony, which at the death of Aurangzeb in 1707 had included almost all of the subcontinent in addition to the Afghan plateau, had passed into the hands of regional powers.

These various territorial powers can be closed under the general headings, indicating both their origins and the nature of their authority. In Oudh, Bengal, and Hyderabad, the rulers were the direct inheritors of the Mughal provincial administrative structures. As Muslims, they had a religious and cultural affinity with the Mughal court, although this did not count for very much when the lines were drawn in struggles for power, for they were as likely to ally with Hindus as with Muslims. The definition of their territories as the subas, or provinces, of the Empire did, however, give them a different character from the second category of powers—those that represented the resurgence of Hindu political life. Of these, the Marathas were by far the most important, with their almost complete control of western and central India and with foothold as far south as Tanjore. In the Punjab, the main contenders for power were the Sikhs, whose militant religious ideology gave cohesion to local chieftains in a two-way struggle with the Afghans on the west and the Mughals to the south. In Rajputana, the Rajput chieftains who had provided the Mughals with some of their ablest generals and were still available for administrative posts in the imperial structure moved towards autonomy by adding to their ancient territorial holdings at the expense of the Mughals and of each other. All of these indigenous Indian powers made use of existing Mughal administrative structures, but their dynamism and vitality were rooted in the complex amalgam of Hindu religion and culture. This was as true of the Sikhs, who in modern terms are thought of as a separate religious entity, as of the Marathas and Rajputs.

This resurgence of Hindu political leadership is probably the most significant aspect of the turbulent political history of India in the eighteenth century. In political terms, it was made possible by the practice both of the Delhi sultans (1206–1526) and the Mughal emperors of leaving power at the local level in the hands of existing authorities who were willing to collaborate with them in the collection of revenue and the maintenance of order. With the weakening of the central administration of the empire, these local powers, many of whom had ancient dynastic links with their regions, were able to consolidate their positions, and, as in the case of the Marathas, to build up new kingdoms by attacking the Mughal authorities. Only incidental reference is made in this study to these Hindu states that emerged in the eighteenth century; instead, attention is being given to the relationships between the power that emerged as the Government of India and those areas that constituted its external boundaries. But in the early period, the frontiers between the Maratha territories and Bengal were, of course, a factor of major political importance. These internal frontier relationships were different, however, from the external ones, both in their origins and in their results. They were internally grounded in the immediate historical experience of all of the subcontinent having been part of the Mughal imperial system, whereas the external relations concerned territories that had not been part of the Mughal Empire, or, as in the case of Afghanistan, were outside the geographic limits of the subcontinent. The territorial powers that represented the reassertion of the indigenous cultures—the Marathas, the Sikhs, the Rajputs—were, moreover, the ultimate inheritors of the nation state these external policies defined.

The direct incorporation of the Company into the political system of mid-eighteenth-century India can be located between two symbolic dates, the Battle of Plassey on 23 June 1757 and the *farmans* (royal edicts) issued by Emperor Shah Alam on 12 August 1765 after the Battle of Buxar, appointing his 'faithful servants and sincere well-wishers ... the high and mighty, the noblest of exalted nobles, the chief of illustrious warriors, the English Company, as *diwan* of the three *subas* of Bihar, Orissa, and Bengal' (italics in original). The three provinces had been under the Governor of Bengal since early in the century when Murshid Quli Khan had been appointed diwan of all of them by Aurangzeb. The inclusion of Orissa was, however, something of an empty gesture in 1765, since most of it had passed into the hands of the Marathas between 1751 and 1760.

The first decisive step was taken in 1757 when, in the characteristic fashion of the contemporary political system, the East India Company officials, under the leadership of Robert Clive, had combined with influential members of the Hindu commercial classes to back a coup d'etat that overthrew Nawab Shujah-ud-daulah, replacing him with one of his generals, Mir Jafar.

The Company's contribution to the coup was a small but fairly well-disciplined body of troops, consisting of about three thousand men, of whom two-thirds were Indian mercenaries. However, Clive and his successors soon found that while possession of this compact mobile fighting force could be used to transfer power from one ruler to another, it could not ensure that their client would remain subservient to their interests. After Mir Jafar made desperate efforts to assert his independence, he was replaced in 1760 by his son-in-law, Mir Qasim, but he too almost immediately set out to regain the actual power of his office. When the Company officials deposed him in 1763, he turned for help to Emperor Shah Alam and his wazir, Shujah-ud-daulah, the Governor of Oudh. Shah Alam was a fugitive, having been driven from Delhi by enemies in the royal court, but his title still carried the memory of Mughal greatness. The alliance between the three has sometimes been pictured rather romantically as an attempt to defend the Mughal Empire from the foreign intruder, but it was simply a move in the complex jockeying for advantage among the regional powers. Shah Alam hoped to extract a high price for restoring Mir Qasim to power, but he had no intention of getting rid of the English; he concluded a minatory letter by bidding them to stop interfering in the Emperor's government, yet carry on the Company's trade as formerly and confine themselves to commercial affairs. He tried to make peace with the English even after fighting had started, but his terms were not acceptable, and he was defeated at the Battle of Buxar on 23 October 1764.

Modern historians have been fairly unanimous in regarding Buxar, not Plassey, as the battle that established British power in India. In fact, however, very little was changed by Buxar: the fundamental factor, the intrusion of the British through the Company into the Indian political system had already been accomplished. Shah Shuja's kingdom was left intact except for the districts of Allahabad and Kora, which were given to the emperor, because the Bengal officials wanted Oudh as a buffer along their northwest frontiers. For the officials in Calcutta, their success in the battle was an opportunity to reinforce their position as it had existed before the alliance, with themselves as a territorial power, little different in status from Oudh.

Concern with frontier security was from the very beginning an impelling motive in that transformation, which—as Shuja-ud-daulah had complained—had made it possible for the British to turn out and establish nawabs as per their preferences. Nor was the granting of the farman appointing the Company as diwan wholly a consequential result of Buxar, for while in one sense it was a concession forced out of the defeated emperor, in fact, as early as 1760 Shah Alam had seen the possibilities of an alliance with the British based on appointing them as both diwan and nawab of Bengal. But unsure of the implications of such a move for relations with Oudh and the other Indian power, the Company officials had temporized. They recognized him as Emperor but refused to use their army to help him regain Delhi.

Under the Mughal system of provincial administration, power was divided between the nawab, who had overall responsibility, including the maintenance of law and order, and the diwan who was in charge of the assessment and collection of the imperial revenues, but who also had judicial jurisdiction in cases relating to land and revenue. How deeply the revenue and judicial functions of the *diwani* (chief administrative office) affected the lives of the people is suggested by the similar aspirations enunciated for the office in statements very different in origin in time and place. One was the farman sent by Aurangzeb to the diwan of Gujarat in 1668, ordering him to protect the peasants from all those who oppressed them in any way. The other was at the directive of the Company's Bengal Council to its revenue officials in 1769, reminding them that their commission included 'exploring and eradicating numberless oppressions, which are as grievous to the poor as injurious to the government', and urging them to deal with the lowliest individual so that his heart might be raised 'from oppression and despondency to security and joy' (Field 1885, 467). The translation of these pious hopes into action was undoubtedly as faulty in 1668 as it was in 1769. Nearer to reality in both periods was the grim reminder in the Emperor's farman that if the peasants tried to avoid cultivating then they should be beaten. Even this, however, testifies to the diwan's wide powers.

During the period of imperial power, the nawab and the diwan, both of whom were imperial appointees, kept watch on each other, but as the governors become independent, the diwan naturally became subservient to him. The appointment of the Company as diwan implied, then, in a formal sense, a return to the normative pattern of provincial government, with the two aspects of imperial power differentiated and reinforcing the central authority. This was only fiction, however, even though the Emperor's dream of the British using their power to take him back to Delhi was hated by some of the Company officials because of the prospect it opened up of expanded influence through undercutting their Indian rivals. The office of nawab remained in 1765, but the occupant was compelled to delegate his power to a deputy chosen by the British who worked with their own deputies who administered the functions of the diwani. The pretense of the nawab's rule continued for a few more years. Eventually, however, the accumulation of knowledge about the administrative system and a growing self-confidence in their own power to withstand any acts of resistance to the old ruling group prompted the Company officials during Warren Hastings' administration to take direct control of the government. By the coup d'etat of 1757, the Company had become part of the Indian state system through intervention in a succession struggle.

The emperor's farman was a characteristic instrument of the Indian state system for the legitimization of the facts of power. One of the basic elements of the eighteenth-century political system was the refusal of the regional powers as they moved towards independence, including the regulation of their own dynastic successions, to use titles that would have implied sovereignty. The only sovereign in India was the emperor of Delhi, as insisted by the rulers of Oudh and Hyderabad at a later time when the English suggested that they should take a royal title. Even more striking was the insistence by the Hindu powers on receiving farmans from the emperor stating they were his loyal servants, acting as his agents in governing their territories. The farman of 1765 gave the Company the same basis of legitimacy as the other Indian powers. That this relationship was intelligible in Asia outside of India is suggested by the report a Chinese agent made to Peking later in the century that Bengal was ruled by a foreigner who was a vassal to the Delhi emperor.

The significance of the legitimization of the Company into the Indian state system by the imperial farman was underlined by the other consequences that were believed to follow from it. One was economic, which was given its classic formulation by Clive in 1767.

> Every nation trading to the East India has usually imported silver for a return in commodities. The acquisition of the Dewanny has rendered this mode of traffic no longer necessary for the English Company: our investment may be furnished, our expenses civil and military paid, and a large quantity of bullion annually be sent to China, tho' we import not a single dollar. (Aitchinson 1864, 391)

The reasons for the failure of this entrancing vision to materialize were not understood at the time, being generally attributed to the greed and rapacity of either of the Company's officials or of the Indians who operated the mechanisms of government for them. But this is a simplification. The economic troubles of the Company were actually integral to the process of the Company ceasing to be a trading company and becoming an Indian power. The political implications of the transfer for the future were stated with equal prescience by Clive in his initial report to London: 'By the acquisition of the Dewanny, your possessions are and influence are rendered permanent and secure since no future Nabob will have power or riches sufficient to attempt your overthrow by either force or corruption. All revolutions must henceforward be at an end' (*Parliamentary Debates* 1808, 1009). This proved true, for almost two hundred years there were no significant revolutions, with

the complicated exception at the end of 1857 in the territories controlled by the British. By becoming a part of the eighteenth-century
Indian states system, the British transformed it. They controlled one
of the state's essential elements, the possibility through 'force or corruption', of effecting the transfer of power within the region from one
group to another.

In the transformation of Indian political life from the pluralistic
system of 1757 into the integrated nation state that emerged in the nineteenth century, one of the vital causal factors was the concern with the
frontiers of the territories they had acquired and the relationship with
the territories beyond them. At times almost an obsession, this concern
was in part a product of insecurity, but it was rooted in political fact—
the absence in India of frontiers that defined boundaries accepted by two
adjoining sovereign states. Boundaries clearly demarcated on the ground
and drawn on maps implied a corollary; a system of relationships based
on them were formalized in treaties with neighbouring states. While this
was an innovation in Europe in the eighteenth century, it had already
been part of accepted political thinking in India by the time the British
were establishing themselves in Bengal.

For this reason, the officials of the new Bengal government were told
that one of their most urgent tasks, after getting a summary of the history of the provinces, would be to fix the ancient boundaries. The general
position was summed up a few years later by the first great geographer
of India, James Rennell.

> The natural situation of Bengal is singularly happy with respect to secu-
> rity from attacks of foreign enemies. On the north and east it has no
> warlike neighbors; and, has, moreover a formidable barrier of mountains,
> rivers, or extensive wastes, towards those quarters should such an enemy
> start up. On the fourth (south) is a seacoast, guarded by sallows and
> impenetrable woods, and with only one port (and even that difficult of
> access) in an extent of three hundred miles. It is on the west only that an
> enemy is to be apprehended, and even there the natural barrier is strong.
> (Rennell 1788, 115)

This understanding of the nature of the frontiers of Bengal is similar to the one that became common for all of India, and the emphasis
on the impregnable mountain barriers providing natural frontiers is a

cliché in most texts on India. It conceals the basic geographic fact that the mountains provide a very vague and ambiguous frontier in almost all areas.'Warlike enemies' are not so much the problem in border areas as the definition of boundary lines up to which political control can be extended without infringing on counter claims of other territorial powers.

The farmans transferring power to the Company made no mention of the boundaries of the provinces, and the officials soon discovered that the rent rolls, with their careful statements of revenue districts, were reliable only for the internal settled districts, which were bounded by other Mughal areas, with the boundaries of the external districts having little precision.

The western boundary of the Bengal acquisition was fairly well known, as much of it had marked the division between the Mughal provinces of Oudh and Bihar. South of the Ganges, the Karamnasa river provided a fairly definite boundary, but this appears to have been partly accidental, not the deliberate design of the Mughal officials, since at some points both banks of the river were in Oudh, at others in Bihar. In the 1760s, however, the Bengal officials regarded the Karamnasa as their defensible frontier. North of the Ganges, the border with Oudh was Saran, the westernmost of the Bihar sarkars. Towards the north, in what later became Champaran district, the Gandak river was the frontier, but like the other Himalayan rivers flowing across the Gangetic plain, it frequently shifted its course, making it unreliable over a long period as a permanent landmark. The northern limits, as of the rest of the northern districts of Bihar and Bengal, was the characteristic zonal area of the Mughals described in Chapter 1.

The Himalayas on small-scale maps look like unmistakable frontiers, but in fact they did not anywhere provide clear cut lines of territorial demarcation. Everywhere there are transitional zones, with lower ranges of hills, and rivers and valleys leading from the plains to the mountains, with the whole mountain range faced by the terai, the lowland hills adjacent to it. The Himalayan region—made up of Nepal, Sikkim, and Bhutan—was also a transitional area in political and cultural terms, having been influenced by both the Indic and Sinic civilizations, although never integrated into the great imperial political structures of either region. Sikkim and Bhutan were not kingdoms in the European or even the contemporary Indian sense, but congeries of complicated spiritual and temporal jurisdictions. Nepal was different with patterns of kingship related to the Indian model. The borders with the political powers of the plains were, however, ill-defined.

The hills and adjacent areas of the Terai were held by chieftains who had never been conquered by the Mughals. The neighbouring areas on the plains were held by chieftains who had submitted to the Mughals, but had been allowed to remain practically independent. The two groups of chieftains fought for control of the intervening Terai, which remained, in effect, an unadministered zonal area.

In the northwest corner of Bengal, the frontier district was bounded not by Sikkim or Bhutan but by the intervening kingdom of Koch Bihar, whose rulers had regained their independence after a brief occupation by the Mughals in the 1660s. Koch Bihar is of special interest in providing an exception to the general rule that the empire's outer frontiers are not sharply defined. According to the English traveller Ralph Fitch, in the 1580s it was surrounded by sharp pointed cones. These were probably intended for defence, not just to serve as boundary markers, and were, of course, put up by the Koch Bihar rulers, not the Mughal. Beyond Koch Bihar, the Mughals had also in the same period defeated the Ahom kings of Assam, but they had soon lost control of most of the area, retaining in 1765 only a narrow strip of land on the northern bank of the Brahmputra. The Manas river was the boundary with the Ahom kingdom. The eastern frontier crossed the Brahmaputra where it turns southward, following the Garo, Khasi, and Jaintia Hills until they joined the north–south ranges of the Tripura and Lushai Hills. These hill frontiers in the east, like the ones formed by the mountains in the north, were marked by many transitional features as they approached the plains, but they stood in contrast to the great lowland valleys of the Maghna and Surma rivers which they enclosed. South of this, across the Fenny river, was the thin coastal strip of Chittagong, which the Mughals had captured from Arakan, the kingdom that at this time separated Bengal from Burma. The territory of Bengal was separated from Burma's elsewhere by Assam, the tribal peoples of the Naga Hills, and the hill states of Cachar, Jaintia, Manipur, and Tripura. This eastern border marked both the limits of successful Mughal military conquest and of Islamic missionary work. Neither Hinduism nor Islam had penetrated into the tribal areas thus leaving them outside the main cultural and political forces of Indian life.

The southern, or internal, boundaries were of the same character. The Mughals had not extended administrative control over the hilly areas of Bihar south of the Gangetic plains, but, as in the north, had made use of semi-independent chieftains to provide transitional frontiers. In the 1740s, the Marathas under the Bhonsle rule centred in Nagpur had extended their influence over most of the Mughal province of Orissa, and these conquests had been formally recognized in a treaty with the nawab of Bengal in 1751. The Subarnarekha river then became the boundary between the possessions of the nawab, of which the Company was the legatee, and those of the Bhonsles. Changes in this southern frontier took place during the next fifty years, but as a by-product of internal expansion, rather than as a motivating factor. The search for frontiers that would define the limits of the Government of Bengal was principally related to the areas that looked outward—to the northwest, the north, and the east. The powers concerned, in corresponding geographic order, and to use modern national designations, are the Afghans, the Nepalese, the Bhutanese, the Tibetans, the Assamese, and the Burmese, with the Chinese involved because of their claims in the Himalayan kingdoms.

The Mughal frontier pattern had served an imperial structure that was self-consciously expansionist, with a foreign policy predicated on the conquest of the whole Indian land mass as well as an assertion of dynastic claims far into Central Asia. The loose relationship of the frontier chieftains to the imperial authority and the vagueness of the external boundaries were integral to this policy, providing a measure of frontier defence at a small expense to the central treasury, and making possible both expansion and contraction of the imperial authority with little formal change in the conditions of sovereignty. The execution of this expansionist foreign policy depended ultimately upon the land revenue collection system, which was the heart of the Mughal administration, but it was not organically related to it. The Company's position was very different: from the 1760s until the end of the century almost all responsible opinion rejected the expansion of British control beyond the boundaries of Bengal and its associated territories. Clive himself was the most persuasive spokesman for this point of view, always insisting that the boundaries of the provinces received under the diwani must not be exceeded. While weakness and disunity of the other Indian powers prevented them from mounting a concerted attack, expansion beyond the provinces would mean an involvement beyond the resources of the Bengal government. 'A march on Delhi,' he warned those who in 1767 wanted to gain control of the imperial capital, 'would be not only a vain and fruitless project but attended with certain destruction to your army' (Malleson 1893). The new government was concerned with the land revenue, as were all Indian governments, but their primary interest, reiterated in a multitude of letters and memoranda, was external security and internal stability that would make possible a prosperous trade. London authorities had replied to the news of the acquisition of the diwani with the warning that their officials should impress upon the other Indian powers that 'we aim not at conquest and dominion, but security in carrying on a free trade equally beneficial to them and to us' (Beveridge 1867, 694). The rapid expansion of British power in the next fifty years makes these protestations sound hypocritical, but they were rooted in both the desire for profit from trade and the growing strength of the contemporary ideological commitment to free trade.

While strict neutrality and non-alignment were the watchwords of policy both in Calcutta and London in the 1760s, the very nature of the Mughal frontiers militated against the fulfilment of the simplistic vision of Bengal as a self-contained unit, free from entanglements with either Indian or foreign powers. The new government's task was to relate the policy to the realities imposed by the political system in India. The development of a workable foreign policy, it must be emphasized, during the period from 1757 to 1798 was almost wholly the function of the local officials in Bengal. 'British' is used as a shorthand to indicate the orientation of the new power, not to imply that the responsibility for either policy decisions or their execution was located in London. In the swiftly changing world of eighteenth-century Indian politics, it was possible to have only the most nominal control from London: it was a year after the diwani had been acquired that the officials in Calcutta received letters giving the reaction of their employers in London. The dominant position of the officials in India in making the actual decisions affecting foreign relations was to continue throughout the nineteenth century, constituting one of the essential factors for an understanding of India's foreign relations.

Relations with four powers—the Afghans, the Nepalese, the Tibetans, and the Burmese—are of particular interest; and of great importance for the development of these relations in the second half of the eighteenth century was the political ferment taking place along the whole Indian perimeter, as was discussed in the previous chapter. In general terms, this ferment was characterized by the emergence of leaders who, from power bases within the different regions, moved against weaker chieftains to establish kingdoms that were aggressively expansionist. On the Afghan plateau, including the old Mughal sarkar of Kabul, Ahmad Shah Duranni (ruled from 1747–72) welded the tribal chieftains into a confederacy that became a major force in the politics of the region. At the time of his death, he controlled territory from the Indus to within two hundred miles of the Caspian Sea, and from the Oxus in the north to the Arabian Sea. Although these conquests did not remain intact for many years after his death, the central core remained to become modern Afghanistan. At about the same time, Prithvi Narayan Shah (ruled from 1742–75), the ruler of the little kingdom of Gorkha in the Nepalese hills, conquered the other rulers of the Kathmandu valley, creating the modern kingdom of Nepal. In Burma, the Mons kingdom was defeated by the young Burmese leader Alaungpaya (ruled from 1752–60), who expanded his power in a series of rapid movements against the old dynasties of the area. There is no obvious causal link between the contemporary emergence of these three expansionists powers on the borders of India in the middle of the seventeenth century, but their internal developments as well as those of India were all affected by the emergence at the same time of the British as a territorial power in India.

In the context of the later growth of the Indian empire, the three seem relatively negligible, but in the latter half of the eighteenth century they were all serious threats to the new Indian power. All along the border of the subcontinent, from the Afghan hills through to Burma, a ferment of internal political change and expansionism was transforming the traditional political groupings. The whole area had acquired what a French geographer called 'frontieres plastiques' (Ancel 1938, 52).

Even before the formal recognition of their status in 1765, the Company officials had been impelled towards active political movement by Ahmad Shah Durrani's invasions. The series of raids that had established Afghan power at Lahore by 1752, with Delhi being looted in 1757, had alarmed the whole political world of North India, but the British saw a particular threat from the Afghans for their position in Bengal. This was succinctly summed up by a Bengal official in 1767.

> I think it must be apparent that the future tranquility of our possessions depends in a great measure upon the divided state of Empire; whenever any one power rises superior to the rest we have everything to apprehend from that superiority, and therefore policy dictates that we ought to be on our guard against all attempts toward attaining supreme dominion in Indostan, whether from Abdalles, Marattas, or other.

Apparently, Ahmad Shah never intended to extend his territory outside western Punjab, but the British could not be sure that, as a contemporary put it, he was not 'projecting some great enterprise which may disturb the repose and deeply affect the political system of India'. In addition to this general threat to the Company's political position, there was a special cause for worry since Shah Alam, whom the Afghans supported as emperor, had been driven from Delhi by court factions and had taken refuge in Bengal. Unless the Company supported him, Ahmad Shah might invade Bengal to press his case. Both threats were met by diplomatic manoeuvres intended to convince the Afghans of their neutrality, at the same preventing the other North Indian powers, principally the Marathas and the ruler of Oudh, from forming an alliance with the Afghans either out of fear or the hope of expanding their own power.

To summarize a complicated and not very interesting episode, the way the Company's government met the threat of the Afghan invasion was by making Oudh a buffer state. The wazir of Oudh could sensibly have rejected this role and formed an alliance with the Afghans against the British. That he did not do so seems largely because of internal dissensions.

The Bengal official had handled the question of recognizing Shah Alam as emperor with considerable finesse. When Shah Abdali corresponded directly with the Company officials in 1761, indicating that he regarded them as the real power and not the nawab, and demanding that they treat Shah Alam with the respect that was due to the throne of Delhi, they had assured him of their loyalty both to the Shah and the

Emperor. But when the Emperor had asked them to issue coins in his name and to have him mentioned in the *khutba* (the Friday sermon) as a mark of his sovereignty, they pledged they would be glad to do so if he could give them an indication that the nobles at the Delhi court gave their approval. Nor would they involve themselves by agreeing to the emperor's pleas for military assistance to return to Delhi, as this would have angered the Marathas. Instead, they encouraged the Marathas to help the Sikhs, who bore the main brunt of the opposition to the Afghans, while making clear that they themselves would not move across their frontier, the Karamnasa river, unless Oudh was threatened.

They had no great desire to get involved in a war on behalf of the wazir of Oudh, especially as the treaty with the wazir, promising help to him if his territories were invaded, included the saving phrase, 'consistent with our own safety'. But they recognized that if they took refuge in this, they would lose the confidence not only of Oudh but of other Indian rulers in British premises. They were thus confronted with the dilemma that was to reappear many times in dealing with buffer states, whose existence tended to lead to the very involvement which they were supposed to obviate. The solution that the Company officials reluctantly reached in 1767, with full awareness of where it might lead, was that they could not let their reputation suffer through not protecting their ally, even though this might mean they would have, as one of them put it, 'exceeded those boundaries which we regard as the proper line of defence, were our views absolutely confined to the immediate security of the Company's possessions'. The dependence on Oudh in the 1760s was the beginning of the long search for a northwestern frontier with a buffer state beyond it, and on the whole, it was successful. The danger that the ruler of Oudh, fearing for his own position, would form an alliance with the Shah against the Sikhs, Marathas, and the English was lessened both by his fear of the Company's army and by the promises of support to maintain his independence.

Another component in the diplomatic duel between Ahmad Shah and the Company's officials in Bengal was the activity of Mir Qasim, the nawab they had deposed and defeated. Although he had been deserted by his former ally, the ruler of Oudh, his claims to Bengal made him a potential threat to their security when he allied himself with the Afghans in 1767. The existence of powerful groups within Oudh and the Bengal territories that were still not certain of the final outcome of the Bengal revolution came to light when the British discovered that the Banaras bankers were using letters of credit to convey to Mir Qasim part of the vast wealth he had left behind with them when he fled. This incident indicates how superficial the penetration of the new government was into the economic structure of the region.

The invasion of 1767 was the last major threat by the Afghans to Bengal. Mir Qasim and the Ruhelas, the Afghan chieftains who had established themselves in the Gangetic plain north of Oudh, urged him to make one final attempt to settle the affairs of the empire in his favour and thereby re-establishing Mughal authority in Delhi; but the Sikhs by now had become masters of the Punjab and barred his way. The stabilization of the northwestern frontier through the interposition of the buffer state of Oudh was only a temporary expedient, with continual adjustment being required by the changing conditions of the Indian political system, but it was successful, for the time being, in its aim of protecting Bengal without the Company's armies becoming involved beyond its borders.

The president of the council was able to report with satisfaction at the end of 1769 that because of the internal troubles of three of the major powers—the Sikhs, the Marathas, and the Afghans—peace seemed assured. 'Personal weakness, civil dissensions and political precautions,' he wrote, 'all conspire to establish our security on a broad and durable basis.'

The avoidance of a confrontation in the 1760s with the Afghans was thus attained by the method that, with various modifications, was to be used many times by the Government of India: dependence on a buffer state to which pressures could be applied to insure its dependability without commitments towards internal control. But it was on the whole a source of frontier instability. Within two decades, Oudh was replaced as the northwest buffer by the Sikhs, who in turn gave way to the Afghans, with each time relationships leading to internal breakdowns in the buffer state and war between it and the Indian government.

With powers that did not pose the same potential challenge to security as the Afghans did in the eighteenth century or the Russians in the nineteenth century, it was possible to envisage another set of relationships based on treaties and the definition of frontiers. The tentative exploration of such forms of interstate policies was demonstrated in this period along the northern and eastern frontiers. On the northwestern frontier, the Bengal officials had been forced into diplomatic involvement by the need of securing their territories from the effects of the Afghan intrusion, but their first involvement on the northern frontier was more voluntary. Early in 1767, Jai Prakash, the ruler of the little state of Kathmandu, appealed to the Company's agent at Patna for assistance against Prithvi Narayan, the Gurkha ruler who at this time was completing his conquest of the little Nepalese kingdoms. Since Prithvi Narayan had imposed a complete blockade on the old trade route that ran from Patna through Kathmandu to Tibet, there was a sound argument for helping the Kathmandu ruler, especially as he promised new concessions if he were restored to power.

Any prospects of improving trade were alluring, for already the euphoric hopes engendered by the acquisition of the diwani were proving false. 'In the present declining state of commerce and scarcity of current specie, we more readily embrace a measure,' the Calcutta Council decided, 'which promises to open new sources of trade and stores of money to replace those annual drains of Treasury we are directed to make for supplying the China investment' (Long 1869, 530). The land revenues which had been meant to pay for goods to be sent to Europe and China were hard to collect. Furthermore, even when the Company's agents had money, they found that an increased demand led to poorer quality goods being supplied. There was also the chance that trade with Nepal might open up a market for the woollen cloth, which political pressures in England forced the Company to buy for export. This was the beginning of a dream, which was to persist for many years, that, as it was put later, English goods 'might be disposed of in the immense territories in the north and northeast of India, where there is a great variety of climate and which are inhabited by millions of people in almost every stage of civilization'. Also, while there is no mention of this in the contemporary correspondence, a possible parallel with the situation in Bengal itself must have occurred to some of the officials, with support to Jai Prakash leading to the establishment of British political influence at Kathmandu.

The result of these expectations was that a small detachment under Captain Kinloch was sent to Nepal in 1767. He had been assured that there were no hills or rivers to be crossed, and that there would be plentiful food supply; instead he found torrential rains, no roads or bridges, and a hostile population that attacked his columns as they struggled through the mountains. The reports on Prithvi Narayan's army were also equally misleading. It was armed, they were told, with bows and arrows, swords, and matchlocks, but in fact his success in building up his kingdom was based on his introduction of European methods of military discipline as well as of arms. Knowing virtually nothing of Nepal, the Calcutta officials had acted on the advice of the Company's agent at Patna, who, in turn, had been influenced by the reports sent to him from his assistant at Bettiah, the frontier town in northern Bihar. When he was censured for his misleading advice, the Patna agent defended the action, despite its failure to fulfil any of the original expectations it had aroused, by arguing that despite its inability to assist Kathmandu, the expedition had been justified in terms of frontier policy. All the country north of Bettiah to the hills, including the districts of Bara, Parsa, and Rautahat, had been seized, depriving the Gurkha ruler of revenues and food supplies, and giving protection to the people of Bihar who had been plundered by the hill chieftains operating from the area. Frontier protection and definition thus became the primary issue, with the original emphasis on trade moving to the background. The Calcutta officials grudgingly accepted the explanation, unwilling to forgo the advantages accruing from the acquisition of the new territory, and in any case uncertain of the facts. In one form or another, the action of local officials in actually initiating frontier policy that had to be accepted by the central government was a pattern to be repeated throughout the nineteenth century.

The abortive attempt to support the Kathmandu ruler against Prithvi Narayan, along with the seizure of the terai lands north of Bettiah, was the beginning of the breakdown of the frontier system that, with all its ambiguities, had served the purposes of Mughal polity reasonably well. Along both sides of the frontier region, movements for the clarification of old claims and definition of revenue districts marked the change. A beginning was made on the Nepal side with Prithvi Narayan's decision to close his borders to all foreigners, including Indian traders. The Italian Capuchins who had been established in Kathmandu since 1715 had already been expelled.

This policy of exclusion was no doubt in considerable measure a reflection of Prithvi Narayan's conviction that, as he told the Tibetans in 1774, Europeans could not be trusted within one's border. The experience of the nawabs of Bengal, with which he was familiar, might have suggested exclusion as a common sense measure, but one suspects there is something more to it than this, that it was a product also of forces within the Nepalese context itself. There are a number of suggestive clues. One is the title he took for himself, *Parbat-ki-Padshah* (King of the Mountains), indicating both his achievements and his ambitions. Another is the support given to him by the Brahmans against Jai Prakash, the ruler of Kathmandu. The Malla dynasty, to which Jai Prakash belonged, was also Hindu, but less orthodox than the Gurkha rulers, who maintained the Rajput tradition of being the guardians of Brahmanical Hinduism. What seems to have been formed was an alliance, however vaguely articulated, between Brahmanical orthodoxy and a ruler who had a vision of an integrated Himalayan kingdom. In such a situation, exclusion was more than a protection against foreign intrusion—it was also an assertion of self-identity in political and cultural terms. When modern Nepali writers depict Prithivi Narayan as 'father of the nation', seeing in his conquest of the Mallas and other rulers a movement towards national integration, their use of history is not wholly anachronistic, however unaware he may have been of nationalism as an ideology. Like the British in India, his creation of new frontiers made nationalism possible by giving its base a physical definition.

Events in Nepal would have forced attention to the border regions, even without the provocation of the Kinloch expedition. Prithvi Narayan was as anxious to assert his authority over the hill rajas on his side of the border as the Bengal government was over the frontier zamindars on its northern borders. As he extended his control, some of the hill rajas sought the help of the Bengal government, just as the ruler of Kathmandu had sought, and the temptation to contain the expansion of Gurkha power by giving them support was strong. By 1770, the Company's agents in the northern districts were arguing the case for 'natural frontiers', that is, the foothills of the Himalayas, rather than the vague regions in the terai where the claims of the hill rajas met those of the Bengal and Bihar zamindars.

The problems of Morang, a hill state that controlled part of the terai north of the district of Purnea, provide an illustrative model for this aspect of frontier politics. The ruler was threatened not only by Prithvi Narayan but also by internal factional struggles. A former diwan of the kingdom organized an uprising against him, and the zamindars of Bhatgaon transferred their allegiance from him to the raja of Sikkim, who in turn, according to the Morang ruler, held his territory from Bhutan. The fragility and complexity of such relationships precludes the assumption that entities such as Morang can be thought of as a 'state' in modern terms with known territorial limits. Its existence as an independent entity was almost wholly a function of the ruler's ability to command, on the one hand, allegiance from his own chieftains, for which the payment of revenue by them was the major symbol, and, on the other, to maintain good relations with his most powerful neighbour, in this case, the Gurkha ruler. His appeal to the Bengal government for help was thus a desperate attempt to shore up his own position while maintaining his state's integrity against the expansionist drive of the Gurkhas. The advantages that would accrue to Bengal from an alliance with the Morang chieftain were persuasively argued by the Company's agent at Purnea: access to valuable timber resources; opportunities to send goods into the Nepal hills; and, above all, control of the terai, giving the frontier districts a fixed and secure boundary. Possession of the terai up to the foothills, with the Morang raja as a client in the hills themselves, would have given surer protection to Bengal from incursions from the east. The failure of the Kinloch expedition having made the Bengal officials cautious, they were now anxious to come to terms with the Gurkhas than to attempt to check their power, and they decided not to seek the extension of their frontier. In 1776 they formally stated their lack of interest in taking over Morang.

Questions of legitimacy based on the actual extent of the Mughal inheritance were also still of same importance, as when the Bengal government in 1751 during Hastings' regime relinquished its control over the two districts of Rautahat and Pachrauta on the grounds that these were not included in the original diwani grant. Acquisition of these districts, along with Morang, would have given Bengal a frontier with immediate access to the hill country, including the Kathmandu valley, but the Bengal officials were not ready for such a move in the 1770s.

Their concern was with trade, not with further territorial expansion. The understanding of imperialism that sees expansion as a function of trade finds no support in the discussions and decisions taken in Calcutta in the 1770s; what the Company officials wanted was an accommodation with Prithvi Narayan permitting the development of trade. They were quite content in having him control the Himalayan region, as they had come to the conclusion that his rule could offer better guarantees for commercial security than that of the petty kings he had overthrown. Many of the hill rajas continued through the 1780s to seek British support for an attack on the Gurkha rulers, which would have given ample opportunity for an adjustment in their favour of the frontiers of the terai. The Calcutta government maintained its policy of neutrality in these internal quarrels.

The probing operations along the Nepalese foothills that had begun with Kinloch's expedition came to an end for some years after the decision was made not to make alliances with the hill rajas. But while there were no further clashes with Prithvi Narayan, who before his death in 1775 had succeeded in bringing all the vast stretches of mountain territory from the Sutlej river to Sikkim under his control, the undefined border was unsatisfactory. Given the nature of the terrain, the actual political control exercised over most of this area was necessarily minimal, but the mere assertion of a claim along the mountain range meant that the Bengal officials had to act as if the Nepalese were assuming the same sort of political responsibility as they were. Thus, when raids were made on the northern Bihar and Bengal districts from the Nepalese hills, the British were first inclined to regard these as deliberate acts of aggression committed by the Gurkha rulers, who for their part considered the prevention of such raids the concern of the Bengal authorities or of the Nepal government. They soon realized, however, that the Nepalese ruler quite genuinely did not regard such activity as, in any sense, aggression. Furthermore, he was often unaware that it had taken place. His control was over the chieftains in their relationships to him, not over their internal authority in their districts, and only minimally ever their actions along their external frontiers. A somewhat similar situation developed in the next decade along the Burmese frontier. The situation was complicated in some of the terai by the Nepalese ruler having claims on the lands of the hill rajas. Thus, after he had conquered the hill kingdom of Makwanpur, Prithvi Narayan took over the former ruler's leases on terai lands from the Bengal government, apparently without either party noting the ambiguous legal position created.

What Prithvi Narayan and his successors were unwilling to do was to define the border where the two sovereignties met, even though the Bengal officials at this time were more interested in prevention of disputes, which hindered the development of trade and the orderly collection of land revenue, than in further territorial acquisition in the terai. When the British pressed the Nepalese officials for an agreement on a fixed boundary, they were usually met by silence or an evasive reply, as when Prithvi Narayan's representative refused to discuss the ownership of Bajitpur and Amirpur on the grounds that he did not have authority to do so. A modern Nepalese history ascribes this attitude to Prithvi Narayan's understanding of British intentions to extend their control, but it probably can be more accurately seen as a product of his unwillingness to make commitments that would limit his expansionist aims, while at the same time forcing him to take responsibility for the chieftains from whom he had forced allegiance. For the same reason, he refused all formal treaties with the British, as these too would not have permitted the flexibility his system of government demanded.

The emphasis on frontier relationships for the encouragement of trade rather than for the creation of 'natural' frontiers that characterized the Bengal government's policy in the 1770s led in the 1750s to a shift in interest from Nepal to the Bengal–Bhutan border. Quite fortuitously, as far as one can tell from the records, troubles in the little border state of Koch Bihar provided the actual occasion for the first involvement of the Bengal government in Bhutanese and Tibetan politics.

Koch Bihar in 1770, like the hill territories, defied conventional political classification. To speak of it as either a kingdom or a state is to ascribe to it an exactness of political definition it did not possess, and yet it was something more than a revenue district held by a zamindar, even allowing for the variegated usage by the Mughals of this term. Because it had been conquered and held by the Mughals for a short time in the seventeenth century, it was nominally part of the Bengal suba, but its independence from Bengal was so complete that no claim was asserted on it after the transfer of the diwani to the Company. A claim of suzerainty was made, however, by the rulers of Assam on the grounds that they had established their dynasty early in the sixteenth century. Then, sometime around 1770, a strong ruler in Bhutan duplicated the experience of the countries of the rest of the mountain perimeter by conquering territory from his neighbours, moving first against Sikkim and then against Koch Bihar. The sanction for the Bhutanese invasion of Koch Bihar was an appeal from one of the claimants in a succession struggle, but after he was placed in control by the Bhutanese, his rival Dharendra Narayan asked for help in 1772 from the Company's agent in Rangpur.

The agent's reading of the situation as favourable for intervention was accepted by Calcutta. Dhirendra Narayan was in no position to bargain over the terms proposed by the Company: he acknowledged his subjection to the Company and made over half of his annual revenues. The first of those subsidiary alliances—which under Wellesley and Lord Hastings were to become the preferred pattern for dealing with the internal Indian powers—the settlement with Koch Bihar, was of special concern to Warren Hastings, the then governor of Bengal. While he was opposed to further territorial conquests, he would always favour, he argued, undertakings which can 'complete the line of our possessions or add to its security' (Gleig 1841, 278). He was not envisaging Koch Bihar as a buffer, in the way that Oudh was, since it was obviously too weak to oppose an invasion from the north, nor in any case was Bhutan a threat or in the same order as the Afghans; what he had in mind was a modification of the Mughal frontier system. Koch Bihar would be a client of Bengal, with the ruler paying for being placed in power and being kept there, while providing internal boundaries to the northwest revenue districts. The northern frontier remained in the lowlands, at a more or less uniform distance from the foothills of the mountains.

An opportunity to revise this lowland frontier came as an aftermath of the intervention in Koch Bihar when the Company's troops, having driven the Bhutanese out of Koch Bihar, penetrated beyond its northern frontiers into the Bhutanese territory known as the Duars, the area of passes and valleys leading from the lowlands into the mountains. At a later period, this was regarded as the 'natural' frontier of Bengal, but in 1773 there was no disposition to hold it. Security was only one aspect of frontier relationships; more fundamental for the Bengal officials was the forging of satisfactory political and commercial links with the border states in the hills. Purling, the Company's agent at Rangpur, who had originally urged intervention in Koch Bihar, now advised the return of their lands to the Bhutanese as a necessary step towards a peaceful settlement since the lowlands were their major source of food supply, and if it were taken from them, they would be compelled to make war again.

Hastings and the Calcutta Council had already acted on this advice to not make territorial demands on the Bhutanese when a letter arrived from the Panchen Lama of Tibet, pleading for leniency towards the Bhutanese, even though they had been at fault in causing trouble on the Bengal frontiers. This approach from the Lama brought the Company for the first time into direct contact with the ambiguous and complicated political system of the Himalayan region. The letter referred to Bhutan as a dependency of Tibet and the writer, the Panchen Lama—or as he was known to the British at the time, the Tashi Lama—from his residence at Tashilhunpo, as the regent for the Dalai Lama, the ruler of Tibet.

If not deliberately misleading, both statements oversimplified the political situation in Bhutan and Tibet as well as concealed the most important factor in contemporary Himalayan polity, the position of China in the area. Bhutan's relationship to Tibet was defined in terms of spiritual allegiance, not political control, although Tibet—after numerous attempts to subdue the area—had forced the chieftains to acknowledge its authority in 1731. This did not imply actual political control, which the Tibetans were unable to assert, but it explains the Bhutanese request for assistance in 1773 and the Tibetan anxiety to play a mediating role as an expression of their authority.

The Bhutanese internal government was, by Western standards, anarchic and unstructured. Special religious sanctity resided in the Dharma Raja, whose position corresponded roughly to that of the Dalai Lama in Tibet; but his chief minister, the Deb Raja, was the visible centre of political power. He was regarded by both the Panchen Lama and the Bengal authorities as the responsible political authority. Actual territorial control, however, seems to have been in the hands of two chieftains known as the Jongpens or Penlops. What the Bengal officials were to discover later, although they had some inkling of it in the 1770s, was that this web of spiritual and political allegiances had a geographic location but no political centre. The structure the British were articulating on the basis of the Mughal inheritance and contemporary European administrative models was in every way the reverse of this, and the intrusion of the Bengal government, with its demands for the observation of treaties, the prevention of frontier raids, and freedom of trade, imposed strains that the Bhutan political arrangements could not bear.

There is some confusion about nomenclature in the region since the people in contemporary accounts of the whole area, including Tibet, were often referred to as 'Bhutanese', but the Bengal officials were aware that there was a political distinction between Bhutan and Tibet. Information had come from two principal sources: the Roman Catholic missionaries who had entered Tibet in the early seventeenth century and the Indian trader–pilgrims referred to in the records as 'gosains'. Although the most detailed account of the missionaries had not yet been published, some of the information they had collected and sent back to Europe had found its way into general circulation. Little is known of the gosains, although there are frequent references to them in the contemporary records. Described as men of 'humble deportment and holy character', who, 'although clad in the garb of poverty', were 'possessed of considerable wealth', they moved from Bengal through the Himalayan region, visiting the great pilgrim centres and carrying on trade (Markham 1876, 125). They were obvious sources of information, and they acted as go-betweens and agents for the British as they had done for previous Indian rulers. One of them, Puran Gir Gosain, who was employed for nearly twenty years, had an influential role in the negotiations with Bhutan and Tibet; however, the diary he wrote of his travels has not been preserved.

From such sources, Hastings concluded that the Tibetans were a quiet, industrious people, living under a well-regulated government, with a religion 'something similar to that of the Hindus'. It was also, according to these reports, a vast country, extending in the north to the country of the Kalmuks, in the west to Kashmir, in the east to China, and bounded in the south by the Buxedwar river. They also maintained the two persistent rumours about Tibet—that it had abundant supplies of gold and silver and that it carried on a considerable trade with China and Central Asia. The unsuccessful attempt to penetrate Nepal in 1767 had been spurred by the hope of linking the Indian trade of the Company with this trade, while at the same time meeting the chronic Indian demand for specie. The Panchen Lama's letter suggested the possibility of a new initiative, and Hastings, careful to give the impression that the Company's generous treatment of Bhutan was the result of the Lama's intervention on their behalf, sent a mission to Tibet under George Bogle in 1774, followed by one to Bhutan in 1776, and again to Tibet in 1783. None of them succeeded in establishing satisfactory relations with Tibet, but their appointment, and the discussions that followed, are important elements for the development of the frontier concept and its role in the transformation of the Company into a modern territorial power.

Neither the quest for natural frontiers nor security from a powerful neighbour was involved in the frontier relationships in the eastern Himalayas in the period; far more important were two peculiarly late eighteenth-century, or at least contemporary British, assumptions. One was that trade in itself was beneficial to society, with its encouragement being both the duty of the state and the justification of its existence. The other was that war was the inevitable enemy of trade. The directors of the Company underlined these assumptions when responding to the initiatives of their officials in Bengal in exploring trade possibilities in the Himalayas. Their intention, they insisted, 'in forming connections with any new states or powers [were] purely commercial'. Aware of how often in India the flag had followed trade, they were concerned that the new commercial thrust into the Himalayas would not be followed by territorial expansion, which in their reading of recent events in Indian history, had been so disastrous to their main concerns.

These assumptions were eloquently stated by Hastings in a memorandum in 1779 explaining and defending the Himalayan expeditions. He saw the movement beyond the Bengal plains as part of the transformation that had taken place in the political structure, an expression of the self-awareness of the Bengal officials for creating a new political order. To cross the mountains into Tibet was to place India in the intellectual climate of the time:

> Like the navigation of unknown seas, which are explored not for the attainment of any certain and prescribed object but for the discovery of what they may contain; in so new and remote a search, we can only propose to adventure for possibilities. The attempt may be crowned with the most splendid and substantial success, or it may terminate in the mere satisfaction of worthless curiosity. But the hazard is small, and the design is worthy of a rising state. (Bogle 1907)

The search for boundaries, the opening up of new trade routes, and the widening of geographical knowledge, all were part of the vitality of 'a rising state'.

The deprecating suggestion that the expedition might do little more than satisfy curiosity conceals one of the fundamental motivations of frontier exploration in this period. The possibility of trade was the justification of their expense, but the excitement they generated came from the possibility of the new knowledge that would accrue from them and, quite as important, the fascination of transferring Western science into virgin soil. In the next generation, the emphasis was to be on the introduction of Western ideas and values, symbolized by the enormous interest in the missionary movement; but in the 1750s, Hastings envisaged a relationship based on a mutual sharing of knowledge and information. This was ultimately a more simplistic, and probably more unrealistic, understanding of the nature of cultural contacts than that which informed the nineteenth-century reformers, but it colours the early frontier contacts, explaining both their appeal as humanistic gestures and their failures as political strategies.

The list of articles taken by Bogle's expedition in 1774 summarizes its hopeful purposes. In addition to the usual trading items such as samples of cloth and guns, there were barometers, thermometers, microscopes, watches, and quadrants in the supposition that the Tibetans would be as interested in the achievements of Western science as Hastings was in Tibet. Hastings also emphasized the importance of collecting botanical information and the bringing back to India of seeds and plants not known in India. This interest in natural history, which is so prominent a feature of the eighteenth-century intellectual life in Europe, was often misunderstood by the rulers of the Indian borderlands, who regarded it simply as a ruse for getting information about the country. As an English agent a few years later remarked about the refusal of one of the hill rajas to let him explore, it was 'difficult to persuade these savages that a European gentleman enters his country solely for the purpose of examining its vegetable products'. This was not intended to be ironical, since for Hastings and his generation the hunger for knowledge was as genuine as their hunger for wealth, with the one being as respectable a motivation as the other.

It was too much to expect that the political authorities in Tibet would reciprocate Hastings' enthusiasm for intellectual adventures. They were shrewd enough to know that even if the expeditions from Bengal were as innocent in their purpose as was claimed, the intrusion of the English as traders had the same implication for them as it had had for the rulers of Bengal. But in any case, the expectations of the Bengal government had in fact been based on a faulty understanding of the Tibetan situation. From the letter he had received, Hastings thought the Panchen Lama was the regent during the minority reign of the Dalai Lama, and that he was not in Lhasa because, as a holy man not wishing to get involved in worldly things, he had disputed his authority to laymen and retired to Tashilhunpo Monastery. Although the Panchen Lama ranked next to the Dalai Lama in spiritual authority in the dominant Yellow Hat sect of Tibetan Buddhism, his political influence depended upon his control of three districts. He may have been acting disingenuously in giving the Bengal authorities the impression that he was virtually the ruler of Tibet, but it is more likely that this was part of an attempt to build up his own position against that of the Dalai Lama. If so, he was checkmated by the Chinese, whose position in the Himalayan area at the time, while somewhat difficult to define with precision, was very real.

In 1774, when they began their exploratory movements towards Tibet, the Bengal authorities were unaware that the Chinese asserted general claims of suzerainty over much of the Himalayan region, including Bhutan and Nepal, and had actual control over the central Tibetan authority, of which the Dalai Lama was the head. Involved in this complex political situation were the two kinds of relationships that in Chinese political theory existed between the Chinese imperial institution and neighbouring countries. One was the so-called tributary system developed by the Ching dynasty; the other was the political control over areas outside the traditional Chinese boundaries. Here, 'tributary' has misleading connotations, especially in the Indian context of the tributary alliance system devised by the British for their relation with the Indian states in the nineteenth century, which essentially was intended to produce stability by isolating the Indian states from all external contacts except the British. The Chinese system was a formal device for fitting the non-Chinese peoples into the Chinese conception of the political and ethical centrality of China. Embassies brought goods as 'tributes' to the imperial court, which was regarded as an acknowledgement of Chinese suzerainty, with the acceptance of the gifts being equally important as a mark of imperial favour. The Chinese inclusion in their list of tributary states of such diverse areas as Burma, the Papacy, Nepal, and Holland indicates that the system was the expression of a stylized diplomacy more than a political reality.

The Chinese relationship with Tibet belonged to the other category, with actual control being exercised outside the boundaries of China proper. Although some historians argue that Tibet became a vassal state of China at the end of the thirteenth century, significant administrative authority was not exerted until the intervention of Emperor K'ang Hsi in Tibetan affairs in 1720. The Chinese during this period had embarked on a phase of territorial expansion, parallel in many ways to that of Britain in India at a later period. Thus, the intervention in Tibet in 1720 had been at least ostensibly on the invitation of the Tibetans during a succession dispute, just as intrusion by the Company in the affairs of their neighbours had often been through the negotiations of at least one party in a similar situation. Since the succession dispute in Tibet involved the Dalai Lama, the Chinese intervention had complicated religious as well as political implications, and no attempt was made at a direct takeover of the administration. Instead, they expressed their influence through a mechanism analogous to the British Residency in the Indian states in the nineteenth century. Two Chinese officials, known as Ambans, were established in Lhasa with a garrison of about two thousand men. This was not an army of occupation, but a reminder of the ultimate sanction on which the Amban's authority rested.

In the 1770s, Tibet was more than a sphere of influence for China and less than an integral part of the imperial territory; until its place in their hegemony was threatened, there was no need for the Chinese to be concerned with its frontiers or its external relations. There was no question that the Chinese were the controlling authorities, as the Government of India was at a later period in such great Indian states as Hyderabad, with the comparison qualified, of course, by Tibet's remoteness and inaccessibility from the Chinese heartlands. And with this assertion of control over Tibet went an equal or greater political domination, in which Bhutan had a special place. Bhutan is specifically mentioned in a rescript of 1731 as having come under Chinese suzerainty. Although the overtures made by the Bogle mission towards opening up trade between Tibet and India were at first welcomed by the Panchen Lama, nothing came of them or of the subsequent attempt under Samuel Turner in 1783. Expectations had been based on the two false premises that Tibet was rich in gold and that an easy trade route could be opened up with China, but the Chinese were not disposed to consider British presence for either diplomacy or trade. This attitude must be seen in the context of the contemporary dilemma created for the Chinese government by the aggressive British presence at Canton. The Chinese regarded the trading concessions made there as more than adequate and they viewed the attempt to open up new channels of trade through Tibet with suspicion. In effect, two mutually incomprehensible systems were meeting in Tibet: the late eighteenth-century British conviction that unfettered trade was the backbone of the state, and the Chinese assumption that trade must be closely supervised in order to render it subservient to the interests of the state. The contrast was sharpened by the Bengal government being composed of traders, for whom trade was part of their everyday life, with the benefit that followed from its expansion needing no proof. The Chinese suspicion of traders was especially disappointing as Bogle had been convinced that the Tibetans were favourable to trade. 'The genius of this government,' he had written in 1775, 'like that of most kingdoms of Hindustan, is favorable to commerce; no duties are levied, on goods, and trade is protected from all exactions' (Markham 1876).

Later historiography of British rule in India, whether of the variety that glorified in its expansion as the just deserts of superior virtue or of the school that saw it as the archetype of imperialist aggression, attributed far more power to it to control events than it actually possessed. Its influence in the borderlands was always tenuous depending very largely upon political conditions within the area itself, not upon the policy of the Government of India. This was particularly true in the late eighteenth century, with frontier relationships in the northeast being determined only minimally by the Bengal government. Events in Tibet and Nepal in which it had little influence, along with the Chinese presence, were the decisive factors.

A crisis for all four countries—Nepal, China, Tibet, and Bengal—developed in 1774 when the Nepalese government, still in the expansionist mood imparted to it by Prithvi Narayan, invaded Sikkim. The political status of Sikkim was as ambiguous as that of Bhutan, with its dominant ruling group being of Tibetan origin, and having political and religious ties with the Dalai Lama. George Bogle was in Tibet when news arrived of the invasion, and he tried without success to convince the Panchen Lama that an alliance with the British would be the best way to meet this threat to a Tibetan vassal; especially as the Nepalese would turn their attention northwards after overrunning Sikkim. The Lama knew that the Nepalese had adopted Western military discipline and weapons, but he was contemptuous of their skill in using them, and, furthermore, he was aware, as Bogle was not, that such an attack would immediately bring the Chinese into action. This was what happened when the Nepalese finally did invade Tibet in 1788.

At first the Nepalese were met with little resistance, and the Tibetans ceded to them a number of border districts and agreed to pay an annual tribute. At the same time, in a seeming reversal of roles, the Nepalese agreed to pay a tribute to China. The apparent explanation of this curious action is that the Chinese commanders in Lhasa had been forced to cede the districts; but according to a Chinese source, wanting to conceal their weakness from the imperial court had persuaded the Nepalese, in return for concessions, to go along with the symbolic act of paying tribute. The Panchen Lama and the Nepalese ruler both approached the British for help, but the Governor General refused to get involved. The Nepalese invaded Tibet again in 1791 when one of the claimants in a succession dispute for the office of Panchen Lama appealed to them for help. This time they were not content with conquests along the border, but marched into the interior, sacking the great monastery at Tashilhumpo, the headquarters of the Panchen Lama.

The sack of Tashilhumpo was too dramatic to be concealed from the imperial authorities in Peking, as the previous attack had been, and a Chinese army was dispatched to Tibet in 1792. The Nepalese fled before it, and tried to make peace, but the Chinese used the occasion to assert their paramount status in the Himalayan region. As tributaries of Tibet—and hence of China—Sikkim and Bhutan were ordered to send troops, and a request was also made to the Bengal government for assistance. According to a later Chinese account, the Chinese commander offered to partition Nepal if the British would help in the war. There is no verification of this extraordinary offer in the Bengal records, but the Governor General had received one letter from the Chinese, which he was unable to get translated in Calcutta, and conceivably the partition suggestion was made in it. The Nepalese countered the Chinese over-tures to the Bengal government, hinting at new concessions that might be made, but Lord Cornwallis once more emphasized Bengal's neutral-ity in the dispute between its neighbours. Both Tibet and Nepal were informed that

> the English Company have nothing more at heart than to maintain the most cordial and friendly terms with all the powers in India and particu-larly with those whose countries be contiguous to their own, and—they are careful not to impinge the rule of friendship by interference in a hos-tile manner in the disputes of others except when self-defence or wanton attacks compel them.

This high-minded statement was to be duplicated many times in similar situations by the Government of India during the next century. That events matched policy in 1792, which they often did not later, was an indication not so much of Cornwallis's greater sincerity as of the ability of China to dominate the Himalayan borderlands. Cornwallis's advice to the Nepal ruler not to quarrel with Tibet, which, since it was a dependency of China would lead to troubles throughout the area, was an accurate summary of the contemporary situation. After the Chinese sent an army against them, the Nepalese government agreed to make the symbolic gesture of allegiance by sending presents to their emperor.

The general direction of these events in the Himalayas is clear: a reassertion of Chinese hegemony and a rejection of contacts with the British in Bengal. The Chinese were successful not so much because of their ability to apply military pressure, but because on the whole this policy of exclusion suited the Himalayan rulers, the symbolism of formal allegiance to China had fewer dangerous implications than had relations with Bengal. The distrust of such relationships was shown in the failure of the two missions that were sent to Nepal in the 1790s in the hope of profiting by Nepalese anxiety in regard to Chinese intentions. One mission in 1792 was led by William Kirkpatrick, a Company servant whose perceptive account was the first reliable one of Nepalese social and political conditions since the Roman Catholic missionaries had been expelled nearly thirty years before. The second was led by Maulvi Abdul Qadir, one of the many Indians whose abilities played a crucial role in the establishment of British power in the late eighteenth century.

These missions had essentially the same motivations as those Hastings had sent to Tibet: the establishment of trade and the gathering of information. Curiously, the interest in frontier definition at this time came from the Nepalese side, with the Raja anxious to use the British interest in trade for a favourable settlement of the border districts between Morang and Purnea. The Bengal government's willingness to make the adjustments, which meant the extension of Nepalese control into a section of the terai well beyond the foothills, is an indication that at this period a desire to stabilize interstate relationships, not natural frontiers, was dominant.

Trade, not security, was also a decisive factor in relations with the countries along the eastern frontiers of Bengal, including Assam, the eastern hill states, and Burma during the period from 1757 to 1798. This meant that in general the Bengal government was not inclined to stress its territorial claims, preferring vaguely defined borders to quarrels with the neighbouring states. This policy was followed even when, as during the Cornwallis administration, it ran counter to the main thrust of the government towards an administration patterned on Western models. Clearly defined boundaries were essential for the smooth working of Cornwallis's most famous innovation, the Permanent Settlement of the land revenue between the zamindars and the government. But he found that his orders for a survey of the boundaries between Oudh and Bihar had increased, not diminished, the points of friction. He concluded that 'there are so many obstacles continually occurring in the progress of such a demarcation that ... we have found by experience that it is better to suffer the occasional evils arising from disputed limits, than to incur the risk of the still greater, that arise out of the endeavour finally to decide them'.

The results of the pressures of the new kind of state that was being created in Bengal were demonstrated strikingly in Assam. In common with the rest of the border countries, Assam experienced political upheavals in the middle of the eighteenth century, but these were not followed, as in Burma, Nepal, and Afghanistan, by the establishment of a strong new dynasty able to provide political stability. The explanation for Assam's failure to survive as an independent entity, despite its ancient status, is probably to be found to a considerable extent in the intervention of the Bengal government in its affairs in 1792 following a request for help from the Raja of Assam.

Cornwallis had listed Assam in 1788 among the border states with which new channels of trade could have been opened up, but its policy of excluding foreigners had prevented any worthwhile commercial contacts from developing. Acceding to the Raja's request was one way of showing the Company's good faith, especially since the Raja blamed his troubles on an influx of mercenaries from Bengal in the service of one of his rebellious chieftains. Cornwallis was cautious in his commitment, knowing that sources of information were scanty and contradictory, and that he would have to depend upon the Company's agents in the frontier districts, whose personal involvement in the troubles was suspected, and, above all, upon the judgement of Captain Welsh, the army officer who was sent with 360 soldiers to the Assam border. Welsh's orders had the open-ended ambiguity of those given later in dozens of similar situations. While Cornwallis was emphatic that the Bengal government had no wish to 'acquire an influence in the internal management of the affairs of Assam', Welsh was to drive out the Bengal mercenaries and help the Raja establish his rightful authority. In doing this, he was to avoid bloodshed, using force only when necessary, and withdrawing as soon as possible.

Welsh soon discovered that the Company had been called in not to help the Raja rid his country of troublesome intruders from Bengal, but to support one of the sides in a civil war, and it was the side that by no means had the monopoly of either legitimacy or popular support. According to his own report, the first important account made by a European, Assam had 'monarchical and aristocratical' constitutions, buttressed by a system of checks and balances on royal authority. The eighteenth-century British model that coloured Welsh's perceptions had little relevance, however, for the realities of contemporary Assamese political life. The Ahom ruling class, the Shah tribesmen who had conquered the area in the fourteenth century, were torn by internal factional feuds, with Gaurinath, the raja who had appealed to the Company for help, being opposed by many of the territorial chieftains who controlled the country. In addition, there was an uprising at this time by the Moamarias, a group of low-caste, non-Ahom peoples unified by allegiance to an anti-Brahmanical religious sect founded in the early seventeenth century. It was this dual threat to his authority that had made the Raja appeal for help. Welsh's little contingent was successful in re-establishing his authority, as his opponents were not able to use even the few modern weapons they had, but neither the king nor his ministers had enough backing from any important element of the population to maintain themselves without the Company's military support. This, too, was a situation to be duplicated many times in the history of intervention by the Government of India in the affairs of neighbouring states.

At first, Welsh had written with enthusiasm of his task of assisting a rightful ruler. But his correspondence with Cornwallis soon assumed the censorious tone of the isolated Westerner out of his depth in Indian politics as he realized that his efforts at creating a stable government were being undermined by the Raja himself and his ministers. The king did not attend to business; he spent his time 'either washing or praying, and when he is to be seen, he is intoxicated with eating opium. ... The ignorance, caprice, execrable cruelty and oppression' of the debauched young king were matched by his ministers and low favourites, who were 'the dread, detestation, and shame of the great, the courage and execration of the people' (Kar 2002, 358). Only the Company's contingent kept them in power, but if it had withdrawn, worse confusion would follow, with everyone who had been involved with the British being marked for destruction. Welsh, caught up in the emotions and passions of the situation, saw the evils of the situation, but urged that he be left in control until, as he put it, the ancient constitution was restored and a revolution had taken place in the attitudes of the principal chiefs. Cornwallis unwillingly acquiesced, but his successor, Sir John Shore, with his long experience of India, was less dependent upon the advice of local officials and ordered the end of the Company's involvement. He was not reversing Cornwallis's frontier policy—only admitting its failure. While he thought it reasonable to have sought the raja's friendship through lending him support, there was no reason for continuing to help him if his own people had turned against him.

Not only contemporaries but later historians, both British and Assamese, have blamed Shore for the anarchy that followed the withdrawal of the Bengal forces. But it is probably a truer reading of the pattern of events to see the British intervention as having worked to maintain a weak ruler, who, without outside support, would have been replaced by a stronger claimant. Assam might then conceivably have remained independent, although the uprisings of the Moamarias led to internal confusion that probably would have sooner or later resulted in its absorption by India. The minimum price of survival for a weak state bordering a powerful one is internal stability, which Assam could not achieve, given both its political inheritance and its open frontiers with Bengal.

Along the rest of the eastern frontier, events were less dramatic, although Burmese expansionism combined with the uncertain relationships between Bengal and the hill states to make for generally unstable frontiers. Here, as along the Nepal borders, the Bengal inheritance consisted of claims of sovereignty that the Mughals had kept deliberately vague. The Tripura area provides a good, although perhaps not quite typical, example of the problems involved. The ruler of what was known in the nineteenth century as the state of Hill Tripura, or Tippera, as well as the adjacent district of Tripura in the plains, had become a tributary chieftain of the Mughals in the early seventeenth century, when their power reached its easternmost extension. The Mughals had never actually penetrated the hill area to any depth, but they made no distinction between the raja's position there and in his lands in the plains, where their power to exert control was much greater. When the Company as the Mughal successor took over the area in 1761, the Raja was treated as an independent ruler of the hill areas, while being recognized as the zamindar of the plains area. Having the same person as an independent ruler on one side of the border and as a subject of the Bengal government on the other side inevitably made for difficulties. Like many eighteenth-century territorial arrangements, it was arrived at somewhat casually, but was not easily undone.

Even more casual was the way in which the hill state of Manipur had been brought at a very early point into the orbit of the Bengal government, extending in at least a tentative way its territorial interests much beyond those it had inherited from the Mughals. Even before the status of the Company had been formalized by the grant of the diwani, the Bengal officials had signed a treaty with the ruler of Manipur that, without too much exaggeration, can be called the first international agreement entered into by the government of modern India. The pattern of events leading to this foreshadowed later ones: during a succession dispute, one of the claimants had appealed for help, and the officials had agreed, hoping, with an optimism based on a faulty knowledge of geography, that this might be a step towards development of trade with China through an inland route across the hills. Another argument for the alliance was that it would help contain the aggressive movements of the Burmese in the area.

Burmese expansionism, along with that of the Nepalese and the Afghans, is one of the facts of eighteenth-century political life that has always to be balanced against British expansionism in India. That one failed more quickly than the other is a measure of the importance of such long range imponderables as the superiority of western technology, not of the immediate significance in the political developments of the last half of the century.

One of the arguments used against Shore's decision to withdraw the Bengal contingent from what had in effect become a temporary occupation of the country was that a power vacuum would result, leading to a Burmese intrusion either through deliberate aggression or on the invitation of one of the factions. That this happened within a few years is not evidence, as has been sometimes suggested, of Shore's failure to understand border problems. Since Walsh's experience had shown the incapacity of the Assam ruler and his ministers to establish a government that could exist without the support of the Bengal troops, it offered, therefore, no protection as a buffer state to Bengal.

To have forestalled the attacks by Burma on Assam that began in 1816 would have required effective occupation of Assam by the Bengal government in 1792, an action which would have been contrary to the whole contemporary policy of conciliating the border states. If necessary to defend Bengal from the Burmese, this could be better done on the existing frontier, the Manas river, rather than in the hostile and unstable political atmosphere of Assam.

The Company's first acquaintance with the energetic expansionism of the new Burmese dynasty came when the very able young ruler Alaungpaya (1752–60) destroyed its settlement on Negrais island in the Irrawaddy delta in 1759. Along with the contemporary preoccupation with Bengal, which absorbed the energies of the Company's officials, this setback deflected interest in Burma itself to India. But in any case, Burma followed the example of the other countries in the area by moving towards a policy of exclusion. For thirty years, there was little contact, but the conquest of Arakan by the Burmese in 1785 altered the

picture, giving Bengal and Burma for the first time a common frontier in
Chittagong district, the most easterly region of the Mughal inheritance.
The Bengal authorities now had to come to terms with an aggressive
ruler who apparently had dreams of extending his power into Bengal.
This danger was not taken very seriously in Calcutta, but Shore's government was anxious to avoid any incidents that might lead to war. Since
most of the frontier areas were a tangle of hills and jungles, the crucial
area was along the coast. Here, apparently, a well-defined border existed,
the Naf river, which might have been expected to prevent the kind of
territorial disputes that developed elsewhere as the Bengal government
assessed the limits of its revenue administration. But the value of the
Naf as a frontier was, as in many cases of 'natural' frontiers, almost
wholly illusory, with neither the geographical nor the political realities
corresponding to the neat definition of the maps.

Although Chittagong had been one of the earliest areas to come
under the Company's control, having been ceded by Mir Kasim in 1760,
virtually nothing was known in 1794 of its frontier region. When the
first military expedition entered the area, the commander concluded
that the Naf seemed to be 'the just boundary' with Arakan, and that it
was apparently the river shown on Rennell's great map of Bengal as the
'Dumbuck'. A little later he reported that far from being a high, wooded
area suitable for a frontier post, as he had been told, the surrounding
area was virtually a salt marsh, submerged during the monsoon season,
and the rest of the year it was cut up by streams and gullies which made
the movement of men and equipment difficult. Even more important,
while the Bengal authorities spoke of the Naf as the boundary line with
Burma, the Burmese were apparently unaware not only of this claim but
also of the political significance of boundaries as the British understood
them. The correspondence of the period makes clear that the idea of a
line defining absolute territorial rights in the sense understood by the
British was quite unfamiliar to them. It was not that they rejected the
British claim, but until they came in conflict with the local authorities
in 1794, they were not aware that the claim had been made or what its
implications were. For them, as for the rulers of the countries along the
rest of the periphery of India, a neutral zone or no-man's-land existed
between them and the Mughal possessions; they made no absolute
claims over it, nor did the Mughals.

The conflicting ideas of sovereign rights in a frontier area became of immediate political significance in 1794 when a large number of refugees fled from Arakan across the Naf into Chittagong district, and the local Burmese governor sent an army across the river to bring them back. Once there, he built stockades to house his troops as he prepared a campaign to capture the leaders of the refugees.

The giving of shelter to fugitives was always a sensitive issue in Indian politics, with rulers regarding it as an overt display of hostility when a neighbouring country permitted them to enter and then refused to give them up. This had been a major factor in the invasion by Nadir Shah of India in 1739 and of the tension between the nawabs of Bengal and the Calcutta authorities that led to the Company's coup d'etat in 1757. The Burmese argued, as had Nadir Shah and the nawabs, that refugees were either criminals who had fled to escape justice or, quite as important, useful citizens whose flight deprived the ruler of taxes and rents. Also an important factor in the attitude of the Bengal government in 1794 was the reputation that the Burmese had, in the words of a later report, of being 'the most barbarous and sanguinary of all Eastern Nations'. Since this reputation was based on the stories of the ferocious cruelty with which they treated prisoners as well as their own soldiers and the peoples of the countries they conquered, the local authorities in Chittagong were reluctant to take responsibility for driving the refugees back across the border.

In the crisis caused by the Burmese intrusion beyond what the Bengal authorities had come to regard as the boundary of their territories, the role of the district authorities was, as in almost all such cases, decisive. Their actions, not the policy of the central government, set the pattern for later developments. The civilian official in charge of the Chittagong district was Edward Colebrooke, a member of a family famous for its contribution to the knowledge of Indian history and culture as well as for its large share in the early administration of the Company's possessions. The commanding officer of the little army brigade was Lieutenant Colonel James Erskine, whose field reports are detailed and perceptive. While they differed sharply over specific matters, in general they agreed that the Burmese intrusion should not become the occasion for even an attack on the Burmese forces in Chittagong, much less a war with Burma.

In normal political circumstances the Burmese actions would have called for swift retaliatory action, for in addition to crossing the Naf in pursuit of the fugitives, they had built a road within Chittagong district to facilitate their movements. But according to the company officials in the area, this had been done in ignorance of the customs and laws of the British in regard to boundaries, and they were convinced that the Burmese commander's bewilderment at the strong reaction of the Bengal government was quite genuine. Not only had he not known that the British regarded the Naf as their frontier, but he saw no reason why they should object to his crossing it to recover his own subjects, since he had done no harm to British property, and was willing to pay the peasants for any harm his troops had done to their crops. The Burmese commander's action, the Company's agent wrote to the Council in Calcutta, 'tho inexcusable under the admitted rules of conduct between polished nations may be explained without attaching any idea of premeditated invasion to the authority which deputed him'. The British were concerned with concepts of territorial integrity that meant little to the Burmese, who thought of sovereignty largely in terms of rights over subjects; such rights could not be abrogated by a boundary line.

In sending this analysis of the Burmese attitudes to the frontier, the Company's agent apologized for 'substituting reasoning when it was called upon for facts', but he argued that this was necessary since 'the motives and views of remote governments can be judged only by analogy between their professions and their actions'. That the attempt to work out a settlement of the boundary and refugee problem with the Burmese commander failed was not the fault of either the Chittagong officials or the Burmese authorities in Arakan, but rather that Colebrooke's insistence on taking into account the Burmese conceptions of sovereignty could not be translated into actual negotiations. They discovered, for example, that the Burmese commander, by agreeing to withdraw across the Naf as a preliminary step towards settling the issues, had put his life in jeopardy; this is because according to Burmese custom, an unsuccessful military leader paid for his failure not only with his own life but also that of his whole family. Nor was the central Burmese government able to conceive what was commonplace to the British; for them, this seemed an admission of the British claims both to the frontiers and to their subjects who fled from their territories.

The result was that no real contacts were made with the central Burmese government at Ava during the year even though Shore sent two missions, one under Captain Michael Symes in 1795 and the other under Captain Michael Cox in 1796. Symes's instructions were to convince the Burmese that the Bengal government was interested in the politics of trade, not of war, and that frontier issues could be settled through negotiations. Cox had the additional task, reflecting the European situation, of persuading the Burmese to exclude the French from Burmese ports. Like so much else in this period, the reports of the two men are paradigms of many similar future missions to border areas. Symes found the Burmese to be open and friendly, ready to make arrangements for trade and commerce. Cox, a year or so later, reported a hostile reception at the royal court, which he characterized as 'an assembly of clowns', marked by cruelty, bad faith, and dishonesty. Part of the explanation for the very different interpretations of the Burmese situation is to be found simply in the temperament and style of the two envoys. Having established contacts with the Burmese, Symes was content with being treated as a private visitor, while Cox was insistent on his role as a diplomatic emissary. The Burmese apparently had no objection to personal relations with foreigners, but formalized diplomatic and commercial relations with Bengal could not be fitted into their state system. The frontier episode in Chittagong had exposed the contradictory principles on which the two governments operated, and this, combined with a growing fear of British intentions, produced what seemed to the Bengal government, an irrational xenophobia. Interstate trade, which meant so much to Bengal, was of little interest to the Burmese king and his court. The only area in which they were interested with any kind of reciprocal agreements was in relation to the frontier, but their understanding of significance of a frontier was so different from that of the Bengal officials that there was little possibility of any kind of negotiated settlement. Cox's perception of the intransigence of the Burmese was essentially correct, even though he could explain it only in terms of ill will and stupidity. The normalization of relations between Bengal and Burma, or as Cox termed it, the assertion and protection of British honour, would have led to war in the 1790s; and so it eventually did in the 1820s.

The arrival of Lord Wellesley in 1798 marks the end of the first phase of frontier relationships between the Government of Bengal and the countries along its external borders. The Company had become a part of the Indian state system in the early 1760s, and in 1798 was still outwardly one Indian regional power among many. But in fact, the Bengal administration, with its understanding of the functions and purposes of government derived from eighteenth-century European models, had already assumed many of the characteristics of a Western government rather than an Indian one. Administrative efficiency and modern technological skills combined to make it the most powerful of Indian states. It is missing the essential feature of the transformation that had taken place in the interstate relations to stress that through modern military technology, Bengal had become the most powerful of Indian states. The really significant change was that the Western idea of a state had been incorporated, however imperfectly, into its administrative structure.

On the whole, however, considering the widespread political changes at work along the Indian perimeter from Afghanistan through to Burma, there had been remarkably few major changes in the actual borders since the Company had emerged in the 1760s as one of the important regional powers in India. But this apparent stability of the geographical frontier marks vital changes in frontier relationships. While the Mughal geographic inheritance of Bengal and Bihar was not radically altered in its main external outlines, it received a definiteness it had never had before. The insistence by the British on defined limits of sovereignty had created problems for the border states that their political and administrative structures could not be far. This was particularly true of Bhutan, Tibet, Assam, Burma, and eventually of Afghanistan, though less so of Nepal, where, without too much straining of terminology, it may be argued that something like a process of political modernization had been begun in a tentative way by Prithvi Narayan Shah in Nepal.

Another generalization that can be made from a survey of frontier relationships during this period is that, perhaps more than any other single factor, the concern with borders and frontiers, gave the Company in Bengal what Hastings had called a polity 'worthy of a rising state'. When the officials in London were still fretfully reminding their servants in Calcutta that 'you should never appear as principals yourselves in any matter relative to the administration of the government', concern with borders, especially in the northwest, compelled the Company to assume the functions of actual political power. Elsewhere along the Bengal frontier, China was the dominating power throughout this period, a fact that is often forgotten because it fades from the political consciousness of the Indian government in the nineteenth century. China was never a military threat in the sense that Afghanistan was in the 1760s, but its power, or at least what the Bengal officials assumed was power, throughout the Himalayan area was to a large extent the determinant factor in dealing with the hill states, particularly Tibet. By 1798, the continuous pressures for definition of borders and the opening up of trade with China through the countries to the north had also given the officials in Calcutta both experience in diplomatic negotiations and an apparatus, however tentative, for their conduct. Almost without exception, the impetus for the actual negotiations had come from Bengal, not from London, with the Company's agents in such frontier districts as Purnea, Rangpur, and Chittagong making the decisive decisions. The new phase of frontier activity that opened with Wellesley's administration was largely based on these developments.

Bibliography

Aitchinson, C.U. 1864. 'A Collection of Treaties, Engagements, and Sunnuds Relating to India and Neighbouring Countries'. *Calcutta Review* 40: 391.

Ancel, Jacques. 1938. *Géographie des frontières*. Paris: Gallimard.

Aspinall, Arthur. 1931. *Cornwallis in Bengal*. Manchester, UK: Manchester University Press.

Bence-Jones, Mark. 1974. *Clive of India*. London: Constable & Robinson Limited.

Beveridge, Henry. 1867. *A Comprehensive History of India, Civil, Military, and Social, from the First Landing of the English, to the Suppression of the Sepoy Revolt*. London: Blackie and Son.

British Library. 'George Bogle to Miss Brown', 8 January 1775. MSS EUR E226/80, Asia Pacific and Africa Collections.

The Clive Collection, Comprising the Papers of Robert Clive, 1st Baron Clive of Plassey (1725-1774), Governor of Bengal 1757-1760 and 1765-1767; Edward Clive, 1st Earl of Powis (1754-1839), Governor of Madras 1798-1804 and other family members. 1728–1832. British Library, Asia, Pacific and Africa Collections, GB 59 MSS EUR G37.

East India Company. 1897. *List of Factory Records of the Late East India Company: Preserved in the Record Department of the India Office*. London: India Office.

Field, Charles Dickenson. 1885. *Landholding, and the Relation of Landlord and Tenant: In Various Countries*. Calcutta: Thacker, Spink and Company.

Forrest, George. 1892. *The Administration of Warren Hastings, 1772–1785*. Calcutta: Office of the Superintendent of Government Printing.

Forrest, G.W. (ed.). 1910. *Selections from the State Papers of the Governors-General of India: Warren Hastings*, 2 vols. Oxford: Blackwell's.

Gleig, George Robert. 1841. *Memoirs of the Life of the Right Hon. Warren Hastings, First Governor-General of Bengal*. London: Bentley.

Gupta, Brijen Kishore. 1962. *Sirajuddaullah and the East India Company, 1756–1757: Background to the Foundation of British Power in India*. Bangladesh: Brill Archive.

The Journal of the Bihar Research Society 1951, vol. xxxvii. 1981. Patna: The Bihar Research Society.

Kar, Bodhisattva. 2002. 'Energizing Tea, Enervating Opium: Culture of Commodities in Colonial Assam'. In *Space, Sexuality and Postcolonial Cultures*, edited by Manas Ray, ENRECA Papers Series. Calcutta: Centre for Studies in Social Sciences.

Keay, John. 1991. *The Honourable Company: A History of the English East India Company*. New York: Macmillan Publishing Company.

Long, James (ed.). 1869. 'Expedition to Nipal: Select Committee'. In *Selections from Unpublished Records of Government for the Years 1748–67*. Bengal: N. Trübner & Company.

Malleson, G.B. 1893. *The Political and Foreign Policy of Lord Clive: His Army-Administration and Its Consequences*. Oxford: The Clarendon Press.

Markham, Clements Robert. 1876. *Narratives of the Mission of George Bogle to Tibet, and of the Journey of Thomas Manning to Lhasa*. London: Trubner and Co.

Moon, Penderel. 1949. *Warren Hastings and British India*. London: Macmillan.

Parliamentary Debates: Official Report, Session of the Parliament of the United Kingdom of Great Britain and Ireland, 9 March 1808, vol. 10. London: Cox & Baylis.

Rennell, James. 1788. *Memoir of a Map of Hindoostan*. London, M. Brown.

———. 1910. *The Journals of Major James Rennell*. Calcutta: Baptist Mission Press and Asiatic Society.

Turnbull, Patrick. 1975. *Warren Hastings*. New English Library.

Wilbur, Marguerite Eyer. 1945. *The East India Company and the British Empire in the Far East*. Stanford, California: Stanford University Press.

Younghusband, Francis. 1910. *India and Tibet: A History of the Relations Which Have Subsisted between the Two Countries from the Time of Warren Hastings to 1910; With a Particular Account of the Mission to Lhasa of 1904*. London: John Murray.

3 The End of the Multi-State System, 1798–1833

During the first stage of its existence as a territorial power in India, from 1757 to 1798, the Company had been part of the multi-state system which developed in the early eighteenth century. This system, as it was argued in the previous chapter, was deeply rooted in the Indian historical experience, and the regional powers that emerged as independent entities with the decay of the central authority of the Mughal Empire corresponded in a considerable degree to previous political structures. But while the multi-state system was the characteristic political organization of the subcontinent in historic times, it was essentially unstable. An equally characteristic feature of Indian history was for one strong kingdom, particularly one based in the Gangetic plains, to move towards hegemony over the other powers. Even before 1798, the movement in Bengal towards an assumption of this historic role is observable, even though, almost without exception, responsible officials both in Bengal and Great Britain had denounced it—in the words of Charles Grant, one of the most vehement critics of territorial expansion—as 'the splendid road to ruin', which was pursued with brilliant success by Aurangzeb and had ended in the destruction of the Mughal Empire (quoted in Embree 1960).

After 1798, the process of expansion, based on Bengal and largely financed by its resources, proceed swiftly, most dramatically during the Wellesley administration (1798–1805), but not less significantly under Lord Hastings (1813–23) and Lord Amherst (1823–8). As a result of this expansion, the frontiers that had been tentatively defined during the early period were altered, partly through inclusion of territory that had been part of the Mughal Empire, but also through the annexation of new areas, notably in Assam and Burma. With these additions to the external frontiers, further imbalances and stresses were created in the border lands as well as within India itself.

Although during the Wellesley administration the Bengal government became not only the greatest power in India—both in extent of territory under its actual control and in terms of its military and political organization—the external frontiers were not greatly changed. The glamour of Wellesley's achievements has led to an over-emphasis of their actual territorial extent. In 1805, when Ranjit Singh was just beginning his undisputed control of the Punjab, the lower Sind valley was completely untouched by British expansion, and the Maratha chieftains, especially Holkar and Scindia, were still important powers. The expansion associated with Wellesley was largely internal, ensuring the dominance of the British throughout the Gangetic plain up to Delhi, along the coasts, and in the south. Relations with the Himalayan states and with Assam and Burma, which had been of such interest in the previous period, were of secondary importance now. The issue that had led to friction had not been solved, nor had the expectations of trade with the countries themselves—and through them, with China—been fulfilled. The energies of the Bengal government were now concentrated on the problem of internal consolidation. The one major addition to the external frontiers took place in the northwest, with the annexation of part of the lands of the wazir of Oudh and of the last surviving remnant of the territory of the Mughal emperor, the district around Delhi. These acquisitions were an expression of the changed status of the government of Bengal from being one of the powers of India to a position of paramountcy, but they were also intimately related to the beginning of that insistence on the crucial importance of the northwest frontier which dominates so much of the thinking of the Government of India throughout the nineteenth century.

The emergence of Afghanistan as a factor of political importance in northern India was partly a result of the ferment caused by the wars of the Wellesley administration, but, as in the 1760s, internal conditions in Afghanistan were at least equally important. For the new ruler, Zaman Shah, who had come to power in 1793, an expedition to India provided a common cause to unite the chieftains who were in effective control of most of the vast area conquered by his grandfather, Shah Abdali. Such an expedition was not, however, as it had been for many of his predecessors from the Afghan plateau, a raid for plunder, but an attempt to regain the areas of the Punjab taken from the Afghans by the Sikhs and, at the same time, to establish Afghan influence in the Mughal court (Varma 1968, 63–141). Since the aims were quite compatible with the Indian multi-state system, Zaman Shah's activities were of great interest to many of the Indian rulers, who saw in the reassertion of Afghan influence in North India an opportunity for a shift in the balance of power, and not a threat to their own independence, or to India as a cultural and political unit.

Information about Zaman Shah's plans to move into India had begun to reach Calcutta by 1795. The main channels of intelligence were the Company's residents at the courts of the Indian rulers, particularly William Palmer, who was with Daulat Rao Sindhia, the Maratha chieftain, and H.B. Lumsden, who was with the wazir of Oudh. Much of their information came from the *vakils*, or letter writers, that the various rulers maintained at the courts; but in addition they employed their own agents in Tibet, as traders or holy men. This incipient intelligence system was neither very large nor very reliable, with much of the information passed from the agents to the resident, who in turn passed it on with comments to Calcutta, being gossip or rumour. Very frequently, it was obviously meant to mislead the British or to persuade them to act in the interests of the agents themselves (*A Descriptive List of Vakil Reports*, 1967; *Foreign Political Consultations* 1967). Some of the most important information about Zaman Shah's movements and intentions in 1800 came from a merchant in Herat, who urged the British to take a strong position against him (*Foreign Secretary Correspondence*, no. 38). Since there was no practical way of checking their accuracy, the weight to be given to such reports depended largely upon the agent's reputation for trustworthiness. All of this had to be taken into account in assessing the significance of the reports on the Afghans that were supplied to Calcutta by the residents. While there was little doubt of Zaman Shah's intention to enter India, what was not clear was whether or not it posed a threat to the Company's territories. This was particularly difficult to decide because much of the information was filtered through the court of Daulat Rao Sindhia, who had an urgent personal interest in committing the Bengal government to a policy of opposition to the Afghans.

The Scindia chieftains, the Marathas rulers of Gwalior, had been the dominant political power in North India since Mahadji Scindia had seized Delhi and forced the Mughal emperor to recognize him as his protector (Sardesai 1935). As such, they were the prime target for the Afghans, who, according to the reports that reached the British agents, intended to drive them out of Delhi and restore the power of the emperor (*Foreign Political Proceedings*, 1796, 19 August, no. 14). This threat to the Marathas brought all their enemies and those who had suffered from their power into action against them, including not only the emperor himself, but also the Rajput rulers of Jodhpur and Jaipur (*Foreign Political Proceedings*, 1796, 28 October, no. 19). That these Hindu rulers, the guardians of the religious and cultural traditions of India, were ready to make common cause with the Muslim invader suggests how little applicability the slogans of modern nationalism have for the period; their interest was almost precisely the same as that of the Afghans—restoring the balance of power that had been destroyed by the dominance of Scindia. A few years earlier, the great Maratha leader Mahaki Scindia had himself proposed to Zaman Shah that they should jointly attack the Sikhs and divide the Punjab between them. However, at that time, the Maratha power had been at its zenith. Now with the death of Mahadji and the accession of a young ruler, other powers saw an opportunity to weaken the Marathas. In this situation, the Marathas sought an alliance with Bengal, arguing that the conquest of Delhi by the Afghans would imperil the power of the British equally with theirs.

The rejection by Sir John Shore, the Governor General of this proposal for an alliance, despite strong support for it from the Delhi Resident, was based on his conviction that even if Zaman Shah invaded the Punjab, the essential interest of the Bengal government would not be affected. The northwest frontier of Bengal remained protected by Oudh, and only a threat to it, not to the Marathas, would bring the Company's armies into action (*Foreign Political Proceedings*, 1796, 28 October, no. 19). Shore's analysis was firmly rooted in an acceptance of the multi-state system, and, like the other Indian rulers, he saw the impact of the Afghans in terms of the individual states, not of India as a whole. The weakening, or even the destruction, of Maratha power in North India might, he pointed out, have definite advantages for Bengal (Martin 1837, 'Shore to Wellesley Correspondence, March 7, 1798'). But in any case, self-interest would dictate resistance by both the Sikhs and the Marathas to an Afghan advance, giving the Company time to organize the defence of Oudh.

Thus, Shore's position in the instance, as in others of a similar kind, was not dictated, as often said, by a policy of neutrality, but by a shrewd assessment of the situation in terms of the protection of Bengal's frontiers. The changes initiated by Wellesley reflect both the emergence of what may be thought of as the Government of India, rather than just of Bengal, as well as, in quite specific terms, of the creation of new frontiers that called for new policies. The war in Europe also became an important factor at this juncture, with the possibility of an attempt by France to undermine the British position in India, either through actual invasion or through support to Indian rulers hostile to the British, being one of Wellesley's constant preoccupation.

But while these changes in the political situation account to a considerable degree for Wellesley's policies, another element was involved in a new evaluation of the status of the Indian states. According to his first biographer, the basis of Wellesley's great achievements was his perception based upon both morality and political wisdom that the Indian states could not be regarded as possessing the same intrinsic rights as did the British possessions. Only the grossest hypocrisy could suggest that 'we were bound to deal with the sovereigns of India on the same terms of equality as we should with any of the established monarchs of Europe' (Pearce 1846, 131–2). Robert Pearce was writing nearly 40 years after the events he was describing, but on the whole, this is a fair summary of Wellesley's justification of his conquests. While he often emphasized the oppressive corruption of the Indian rulers, it was primarily because of their political incapacity that they had forfeited their rights to be treated as sovereign states. Because, in his biographer's words, British power in India was 'invested with supremacy in virtue of European civilization and Anglo-Saxon energy', the adjustment off the northwest frontiers ultimately came to be concerned only with the protection of Bengal (Pearce 1846, 131–2).

Yet, despite the wide-ranging implications of this position, neither the extent of the changes in relation to the northwest frontier nor their direction were as great as was suggested by Wellesley's own colourful rhetoric or the accounts of historians. The contrast between his policies and those of his predecessors are often more in style than in content, with the actual working out of events being controlled by forces on the frontier itself as much as by new policies of the Bengal government. (For a different interpretation, see Varma 1968, 99).

In 1798, the rumours of an Afghan invasion raised the same question the Bengal government had faced in its infancy when Zaman Shah's grandfather, Ahmad Shah, had made his appearance in the Punjab. Beyond the northwest frontier of Bengal was the buffer state of Oudh. The Company's self-interest as well as treaty obligations required them to protect it in case of attack. But what were the arguments for forestalling an attack by moving beyond the boundaries of Oudh? This was the point of the query Wellesley addressed to Sir James Craig, the commander of the Company's armies on the western frontier shortly after his arrival: 'What is the extreme limit beyond the frontier of the Vizier to which the operations of the British could be advanced, without danger, to that frontier, and to the force to be so advanced' (Martin 1837, 'Wellesley to Craig, September 16, 1798', no. 262). Craig had already given his attention to this problem in what is perhaps the first extended discussion of defence requirements as the determining factor in deciding the location of the northwest frontier (Martin 1837, 278–82 'Note on Zaman Shah by Major General Sir James Craig' and 'Letter to Wellesley, October 6, 1798', Appendix E). His position is based on a foreshadowing of the later distinction between frontiers of administration, marking the limits of actual political control and frontiers of influence, where military power was either actually present or would be sent at any threat of the intrusion of another power. Such 'frontiers of influence' could include either a quasi-independent buffer state or an administered zone.

Craig's fundamental postulate was that a defensive war would be ruinous to the British positions in India, since there were no natural defence positions anywhere along the existing northwest borders; in India, even the Ganges and Jamuna rivers were not really defendable since they, for much of the year, were so easily fordable (Martin 1837, Appendix E). The need then was for positions beyond the actual frontiers—not just of Bengal itself, but of the buffer state of Oudh. The troops of the Oudh ruler were useless: insolent, licentious, undisciplined, and disaffected, 'they would embarrass their friends more than they would injure their enemies' (Martin 1837, Appendix E). An alliance with the Marathas, who held the territory around Delhi, was far more useful than dependence on Oudh. The implications of such an alliance were plain: 'Their frontier becomes, in fact, ours' (Martin 1836a, 297). Karnal, about a hundred miles north of Delhi, was, he thought, the reasonable limit for such a frontier. This is just beyond the historic battleground of Panipat, although he does not mention it; its significance was that it provided room for manoeuvre and retreat without drawing an enemy into one's own lands. Craig had no doubt about the danger of a retreat there or anywhere else in India at the time, since, as he put it, 'our enemies are as numerous as the inhabitants of the country', and would naturally use any reverse to their own advantage (Martin 1836b, 280).

The frontiers were as important for internal security as for defence from invasion, for in the early 1800s the British had no 'illusion of permanence' (Hutchins 1967). Any foreign intrusion into the Indian borderlands, much less into India proper, would lead, most of them were convinced, to simultaneous attacks from the Indian rulers. This fear that any attempted invasion would lead to uprisings within India remained a factor in frontier policy through the period of British rule, although for political reasons, it was not much stressed in later periods. In the early years of the nineteenth century, for example, there was the expectation both in the Government of India and in the Indian states that Nepal, as a Hindu kingdom, might provide leadership for an alliance of Hindu rulers, and that later in the century an invasion by Afghanistan might lead to an uprising by Indian Muslims. During the first war with Burma, one of the government's main consensus was 'the spirit of insurrection' that manifested itself in many parts of India.

Despite Wellesley's initial enthusiasm for a Maratha alliance, noth-ing came of it. He soon discovered that the Indian rulers outside the circle of British influence, especially the northern Maratha chieftains and the Sikhs, would not agree to the terms that he proposed, such as putting their troops under a British commander and posting their French officers away from the front (*Secret Correspondence*, 14 December 1798, no. 20). Much of the pressure for an alliance had come from the Company's resident with Scindia, who based his arguments on the expectation that a natural *solidarity* would lead the Hindu rulers to com-bine against the Muslim invader. Despite the antipathy of the Rajputs towards the Marathas because of their frequent inroads into their ter-ritories, 'their religious prejudices [should be] considered', he wrote to Wellesley. 'It is reasonable to suppose they would rather submit to pay the tribute now imposed upon them than commit their families to the mercy of a Mahommedan conqueror' (*Foreign Secretary Correspondence*, 23 November 1798). This is one of the earliest examples of the British conviction that general religious affinities were decisive in Indian poli-tics, and it was as erroneous then as in later periods. As early as 1788, the ruler of Jodhpur had urged the Afghans to invade India and other Rajputs continued through the years to maintain channels of communi-cation (*Poona Residency Correspondence*, 1936, 238).

The Rajputs had a double interest in the weakening of Maratha power: freeing themselves from the burden of paying tribute, and if the emperor were no longer under Maratha control, the possibility of restoration of the position they had so long held in the Mughal court and army. Wellesley also misread the loyalties of the French officers commanding many of the Scindia troops. When it was suggested to him that General Perron, the most powerful of the French command-ers, could be induced to make an alliance with the British, Wellesley answered that this was impossible: 'He must never forget that he is a Frenchmen' (*Foreign Secretary Correspondence*, 'Wellesley to J. Collins, November 23, 1798', no. 12). But nationality was no more decisive for the Europeans than religion had been for the Rajputs. Perron, having made an agreement with the British, soon after this took his fortune and returned to Europe (*Foreign Secretary Correspondence*, 24 April 1800, nos 6–42). Nor was Wellesley as certain as he had been on his arrival that Sir John Shore was wrong in tending to discount the genuineness of the threat of an invasion; he was finding that the report of the agents and residents exaggerated the danger (Martin 1837, 342, 'Wellesley to Dundas, November 12, 1798').

On the initiative of Jonathan Duncan, the governor of Bombay, Wellesley adopted a new strategy: an alliance with Persia to weaken Zaman Shah on his western frontiers. Neither Wellesley nor Duncan could have known that they were fulfilling a precept of classic Indian statecraft, that the king who is the enemy of your enemy is your friend (Kautilya 1960, 290). First through an Indian agent, Mehdi Ali, and then more formally through John Malcolm, the Persians were instigated to apply pressure on Zaman Shah's borders and to create disturbances within his territory so that he would have to turn his attention away from India. This was to be achieved by such familiar methods as the payments to officials, the promise of military assistance, and an appeal for the protection of a persecuted minority, for the Persian ruler was a Shia Muslim, and Zaman Shah, who was a Sunni, was alleged to have committed atrocities against the Shia population of Lahore (Kaye 1856, 513). These adventures in diplomacy worked, or at least so it seemed at the time, for Zaman Shah made no serious move towards India. But his hold over his chieftains was so precarious that he probably would have not been able to muster the resources in either men or material for an attack on India, even without the internal disturbances stirred up by what Wellesley called the 'judicious application of moderate sums of money' to his enemies (Varma 1968, 126).

Another dimension of the concern with the northwest frontier at this time was the fear of a combined French and Russian invasion through Persia and Afghanistan. That such an undertaking was probably almost impossible is irrelevant in the context of the time: what mattered was that Wellesley and many of those around him thought it was both possible and likely. The northwest frontier, therefore, became the focal point for security in a way that had never been true of the other frontiers, where the emphasis had been on establishing agreed boundaries to facilitate trade and revenue collection. Various features of the contemporary Indian situation tended to deepen the fear of an invasion from the northwest. Unlikely as it may seem in retrospect, given the character of early nineteenth-century Indian society, men like Wellesley took seriously the possibility of the spread of French revolutionary doctrines in India.

A more probable source of danger came from army officers who held important posts in the armies of many of the Indian states. The most powerful of these was General Perron, Scindia's officer, who had an army of forty thousand men with three hundred European officers. After 1797, as Scindia's deputy, he controlled Delhi and the surrounding areas. Then, before his defeat in 1799, there was the possibility of military assistance being given by the French to Tipu Sultan of Mysore, the ablest of Indian rulers and one most implacably opposed to the growth of the British power. Napolean's famous letter from Egypt, assuring Tipu that an 'innumerable and invincible army, full of desire of releasing and relieving you from the iron yoke of England', may have been little more than bombast, but it fed his hopes (Malcolm 1826, 310). Both religious affinities and political considerations made an alliance between Zaman Shah and Tipu Sultan seem a real possibility to Wellesley and his advisers, and the British agents reported a steady flow of communications between the two (*Foreign Political Proceedings*, 19 August 1796, no. 14). There were obviously formidable practical difficulties in forging any significant alliance between Afghanistan and Mysore, but the threat of concerted attacks from the north and south, especially with even minimal French assistance, had to be taken into account in determining the Bengal government's frontier policies. The war against Tipu Sultan as well as that against the Marathas from 1803 to 1805 was thus in a very real sense the expression of a government that recognized the whole of the subcontinent as integral to its existence (Brittlebank 1999).

As has already been emphasized, an awareness of India as a natural political unit was a common feature of Indian political life, but no previous Indian ruler, not even Aurangzeb at the moment of his greatest territorial expansion, had had either the military power or the administrative mechanisms to realize it in terms of actual political organization. Sir Thomas Holdich, the geographer and historian of borderlands, defined the function of a frontier as putting 'a definite edge to the national political horizon, so as to limit unauthorized expansion or trespass' (Holdich 1916, x). The search for such a political horizon on the northwest had begun in earnest with Malcolm's mission to Persia.

It is quite probable that the Indian agent Mehdi Ali Khan was as successful as Malcolm and his British successors in asserting the interests of the Indian government in the northwest area, but as with other

Indian agents, his effectiveness was confined to the events of a particular mission. An ironic omen on the anonymity of the Indian agents is that although Varma makes considerable use of Mehdi Ali Khan's reports, his name is not found in the index, although Malcom's is (Varma 1968, 122–8). The Indians remained shadowy and anonymous, with their careful intelligence reports providing information but seldom suggesting directions for policy. The British agents were always anxious to influence policy decisions and sought to do so not only in their official reports, but perhaps with even more effect in books and articles. In these works, they were concerned with reaching a small but influential audience in India and England, and they wrote with great frankness. As Edward Thompson put it, in this period, 'when no one ever thought of any public but a British one, criticism was lively and well-informed, and judgment was passed without regard to political exigencies' (Thomson and Garratt 1934, 665).

Malcolm was an archetypal representative of the early nineteenth-century generation of administrators who, quite self-consciously, set out to be soldiers and scholar–statesmen. His ambition marched with his achievements as he became governor of Bombay, conqueror of Central India, and author of widely read books on India and Persia. A passionate defender of Wellesley's expansionist administrator, he was convinced that the political horizon of India must be somewhere in the northwest mountains, not, as was still the official policy in 1800, in the Gangetic plain. In the 1760s, Oudh had been seen as the necessary buffer state, but in 1806 Malcolm was speaking of Persia as 'the barrier to India' (Kaye 1856, 397, 'Malcolm to Lord Minto, November 23, 1806').

Malcolm's mission to Persia in 1808 was part of an exercise in diplomacy that constitutes a landmark in the history of the development of modern India's relations with the whole northwest area, including Persia and the Persian Gulf area, Afghanistan, Sind, and the territories of Ranjit Singh in the Punjab. The sending of envoys with plenipotentiary powers to negotiate treaties was an indication, almost unnoticed at the time, that the Bengal government had become the Government of India in a far more important sense than that envisaged by the Charter Act of 1773, giving the governors general of Bengal control over all foreign relations. Fear of French activity made the question of relationships between India and the northwest area, including Persia, urgent in 1808, but in a broader sense it was the rise of a strong state in India that brought the whole region into the orbit of the Government of India.

Malcolm's voluminous correspondence, which provides one of the earliest statements of the arguments for the inevitability of involvement in the whole area, is completely India-oriented (Kaye 1856). The emphasis was on India itself, not on Great Britain. The argument that the foreign policy of the Government of India during the nineteenth century was dictated to serve British, not Indian, interests is of dubious validity at any time, but it is singularly inappropriate for the events of this period. Malcolm, and the government that he represented, had an almost myopic concentration on India's needs, which they understood in terms of preventing a French invasion. Assuming the reality of the French threat, the force that the British had to oppose was slight: an army totalling about 153,000 men (Foreign Department, 'Report of the Commander-in-Chief, February 15, 1808'). This small army was spread throughout Bengal, Madras, and Bombay, as well as the recently conquered areas of north and central India. Only about one-fifth were actually British soldiers—the rest were Indian mercenaries. The commander-in-chief was well aware of the implications of the proportions, for 'the natives are now in a state of subjugation, or the jealous powers by which we are now surrounded' (Foreign Department, 'Report of the Commander-in-Chief, February 15, 1808').

The first problem was to find a political solution that would not require the commitment of the army outside of India while preventing a hostile force from reaching India. This immediately raised a second issue: the location of the boundaries of India in the northwest. Malcolm's main interest was in the first problem, but his answer partially covered the second one: India must find 'frontiers of influence' that were in no sense part of territorial India.

For Malcolm, as for almost all the British in India in 1808, the question of French intentions to invade India through Persia was not a matter for debate. Agents in Persia and Turkey were busy intercepting French correspondence that pointed in this direction, but the most obvious proof was the imposing embassy that Napoleon had sent under General Gardane to the Persian court with instructions to find a road to India (*Foreign Department*, 'Malcolm to Minto Correspondence no. 10', 1 May 1808 and 15 August 1808). Although this does not mean that an invasion was actually planned—the difficulties in such an undertaking were perfectly obvious to the French—it indicates Napoleon's interest in the possibility of an attack by land in India (quoted in Colebrooke 1884, 191, 'Correspondence from Napoleon, May 10, 1807'). French enmity for Great Britain was, however, in itself a sufficient motivation for an invasion and underlying this, Malcolm was convinced, was Napoleon's dreams of an eastern empire. Since France could not hope to invade by sea, the road to India had to be through Persia, and the task of the French was to win the Persians over as allies. At first, according to Malcolm's informants, they had hoped to do this by promising help in driving the Russians out of Georgia and other territory they had taken from the Persians. When the Treaty of Tilsit had made Russia into their ally, the French had to shift their ground; they now had to persuade the Russians to make a common cause with their old enemies. The most likely invasion route was by the Mediterranean, through Syria, along the Euphrates, and finally to Persia, where the advance to India would be made with Persian and Russian cooperation. Malcolm was one of the very first to see a possible threat to India from Russia, having discussed the matter in a memorandum in 1801, but he had concluded that there was no real danger, since the risks involved were too great for the advantages to be gained (*Foreign Department*, no. 10 'Letter and Memorandum from Malcolm, August 15, 1808'). Malcolm knew that an invasion would take three or four years of preparation, and that would require enormous organization, but he saw no intrinsic impossibilities in such an undertaking.

Given that the wisest policy was the one that 'seeks to fight the Battle of India on the banks of Euphrates', what was the best strategy? To begin with, every effort should be made to convince the Persians that while France could help them, the British, operating from India, could cause them irreparable harm. The British could cut off the lucrative trade between the Persian Gulf and India. In arguing that this would persuade the Persians to drive out the French embassy, Malcolm expressed one of the most characteristic of nineteenth-century Indian attitudes towards neighbouring states: the idea that friendship with India meant exclusion of the representatives of all powers suspected of being unfriendly to her. (*Foreign Department*, no. 10, 'Letter and Memorandum from Malcolm, August 15, 1808'). Such an argument would have been unlikely in a

European setting, or in reference to an Indian ruler even a few years earlier, but it reflects the changed situation in power relations. For Malcolm,
as for Wellesley, the Asian states did not have the same quality of sovereignty as European ones and required different treatment.

As in other Asian countries, according to Malcolm, patriotism
was unknown in Persia, where the ruler acted on despotic impulse,
not principle. Since this was so, if the Persians refused to dismiss the
French embassy, and there was evidence of preparation for an Indian
invasion, their government should be subverted. Through alliances with
disaffected groups, it would be possible, Malcolm argued, 'to promote
plunder and prevent tranquility in the countries our enemies must pass
or occupy' (*Foreign Department*, no. 10, 'Letter and Memorandum from
Malcolm, August 15, 1808'). In mitigation of this ruthlessness, it must
be remembered that Malcolm was speaking of an alternative to war, having concluded that India had to be defended at the Euphrates and that
it would be impossibly expensive for the Indian government to dispatch
an army to seize and garrison Persia in the event of a French attack. The
logic of his position, based on the conviction that Indian defence began
far beyond the actual borders of administration, remained a central
premise of political thinking in India throughout the nineteenth century.
Its implication for the neighbouring countries was that their independence depended upon coming to terms with the strategic needs of Indian
defence. This search for frontiers did not threaten them because the rulers of India were greedy for more territory—there is very little evidence
of this anywhere along the borders—but because their independence
was perceived as a source of weakness in the defence of India.

It was this understanding of frontier relationships that focused attention on the northwest borderlands in 1808. Sind, Afghanistan, Ranjit
Singh's kingdom in the Punjab—all had to be fitted into the defence
needs of the power that now dominated the subcontinent (Grewal 1980).
That this power was the British, and that at this particular moment
the threat to its security was posed by another European nation, the
French, obscures the situations, suggesting that the issues at stake were
European (Singh 1980). It was, in fact, the existence of a strong *Indian*
power that posed the threat to the countries of the borderlands, and one
can fairly safely conjecture that their fate would not have been markedly
different if that power had been Indian in origin, not European.

The immediate need was for contact with the rulers of the great arc of territory stretching from Karachi at the mouth of the Indus, through the hills to Kabul, and back again to Lahore at the apex of the Indian plains. The envoys sent to the region were also instructed to find out as much as they could about the region, for almost nothing was known about it; James Rennell, the first of the great geographers of India, had taken most of his information about the area from Ptolemy and the Greek writers (Rennell 1788). Sind was of particular interest because of the report that the French were arranging for cooperation in case they wanted to invade India from Persia along the coast. Since no one was certain about the feasibility of such a route, the main task was to make a map showing 'every object which can render it useful in a military point of view, giving the road passes, defiles, fortifications, and faces of the county' (quoted in Phillimore 1950, 168).

Establishing diplomatic relations with Sind was not easy, since, as in many of the border areas, there was no single centre of authority. The lower Indus valley had never been very firmly controlled by the Mughals, and the local chieftains who replaced them in Afghanistan were not any more successful than the Mughals in establishing authority over their regions. At the end of the eighteenth century, the chieftains (or *amirs*) of a Baluchi tribe, the Talpurs, had gained control. The amir of Hyderabad was acknowledged as the chief of the family, but his relatives, especially his three brothers, had more or less equal rights in their own territories. The evaluation of their rules by contemporary travellers as anarchical and oppressive, destructive of both agriculture and commerce, is fairly unanimous, but it is difficult to get much sense of social and political realities from these accounts (Pottinger 1816; Burnes 1831; Bonomy 1830). The events of the past hundred years had changed patterns of trade in the whole area, and some of the poverty must have been due to this as well as to the misrule of the amirs. Moreover, as elsewhere in the border regions, as new rulers they had scarcely time to establish themselves when they were faced with the challenge of the rise of an expansive power in India. Lacking the political or material resources to deal with this challenge, they took refuge, as had many Indian rulers, in evasion, aggression, and an attempt to withdraw from formal contact with the foreign power.

Since the amirs would naturally object if they knew his real motivation for coming, the agent was to represent that his mission was to collect indemnity for losses suffered by the Company's previous agent when he had been compelled to leave the area in 1800 (*Foreign Department*, no. 1, 14 March 1808). Commercial interests were secondary in 1808 as they had been in 1799, when Wellesley had ordered the establishment of a Company factory as a cover for political activities (Wellesley 1836, 518, 'Wellesley to Jonathan Duncan, April 7, 1799',). Double dissimulation was involved in these activities: through arguing that the missions were for trade, they hoped to fool not just the amirs of Sind, but also the directors of the Company in London, who looked with great suspicion on the diplomatic activities of Indian officials (Embree 1960). The amirs were not taken in, and in 1808, as in 1800, they assumed British intentions were at the establishment of political influence (see Huttenback 1962).

The agents and the local authorities in Sind, as everywhere in the border regions, spelled out these intentions long before the central authorities in Calcutta were willing to recognize them. The reports from Sind in 1800 by Nathan Crow, the first official agent, presented the same arguments for making Sind a frontier of British power in India that were used for forty years before finally being annexed. Direct access would be provided to Afghanistan, he argued, making easier both military action and internal subversion; foreign influence could be excluded; and trade could be expanded into the interior (Huttenback 1962). Mountstuart Elphinstone, who had been sent at the same time as envoy to Kabul, suggested that it might be a good idea to buy Sind from the Afghans. Although they claimed it as part of the general Afghan confederacy, they did not control it, so such an arrangement might be regarded by them, he thought, as both profitable and face-saving (*Foreign Department*, no. 4, 13 May 1809). At the back of these proposals was the assumption that the political system of Sind did not entitle it to be considered as a self-existent sovereign entity. The treaty that was signed in 1809 pointed in the same direction, even though the Governor General went out of his way to speak of the state of Sind in his communications with the ruler (*Foreign Department*, no. 7, 10 October 1808). It was essentially an unequal treaty, with the amirs of Sind agreeing to keep out not only the envoys of France, but also those of the Marathas (Aitchison 1912, 317). This is one of the earliest and clearest indications of those fundamental principles of foreign policy of the Government of India in the nineteenth century: no genuinely independent state would be allowed to exist on the border of India and, beyond the actual borders of contact, in the borders of influence, the presence of foreign states would be excluded whenever possible. The working out of these principles depended upon internal political conditions and the counter-interests of other powers as well as geographical location and previous relationships of the border states to the eighteenth-century Indian state system.

Sind was important for foreign relations because it was seen both as a buffer between India and Afghanistan and a possible channel of communication. Afghanistan was still regarded as a threat in itself, so potent was the memory of the invasions in the eighteenth century, not, as later on, largely as a buffer against a possible Russian attack. Since almost nothing was known of its internal political conditions, it was assumed that the ruler, Shah Shuja, controlled the vast territories conquered by the Durannis forty years before. Mountstuart Elphinstone, who was just beginning his influential career in Indian administration, was instructed to make a defensive treaty with him against the French and Persians. Elphinstone soon discovered that Shah Shuja had not the slightest interest in a defensive alliance against external invaders; his only concern was maintaining a precarious hold on his power against the chieftains who were the effective rulers throughout the region. As a Central Asian traveller put it, 'The king has enough to do to look sharp after his own head, instead of troubling himself with the affairs of other states' (Colebrooke 1884, 195). Although he assumed that the British were really only interested in gaining territory either from him or the Sikhs, he agreed to sign a treaty of friendship promising him money to help him repel a French attack on Afghanistan, in return for which he was to exclude all French influence from his kingdom forever (Forrest 1884, 347; and *Foreign Department*, no. 6, 'Correspondence between Elphinstone and Minto, April 29, 1809'). In his desperation, he hoped that the British would see the advantage of supporting him on the throne, rather than let him be overthrown by his enemies, even though Elphinstone lectured him and his ministers rather self-righteously on the need for the Afghans to settle their own affairs, since the Indian government would not interfere in Afghanistan's internal politics. But no help was forthcoming when within a month of the signing of the treaty he was driven into exile by his enemies.

More important than the treaty were Elphinstone's reports and memoranda on Afghan politics and society, which became basic information for subsequent foreign policy decisions (Elphinstone 1819; *Foreign Department* 1809). Eighty years later, his report was still described as 'the only standard work we possess regarding the countries which form the Afghan monarchy' (quoted in Colebrooke 1884, 195). His proposals for a settlement of the northwest frontier, while addressed to the immediate situation—the fear of a Franco-Persian alliance—were a tentative formulation of the classic nineteenth-century understanding of the area as a constant tension zone.

For Elphinstone, the Indus was 'the boundary of India', and he is one of the first writers to emphasize the need for 'natural' frontiers with the neighbouring countries (Elphinstone 1819, 41). But they envisaged the Hindu Kush and the other mountains of the north as forming a natural boundary enclosing the dominions of the king of Kabul and India, so that Indus was an internal frontier within a subcontinental region that included the Afghan plateau. The Indus, in other words, might become a frontier of administration for the Government of India, but the frontier of influence would be the mountains beyond the plateau. This geographic understanding was behind his elaborate proposals for financial support to be given to maintain Shah Shuja as ruler of Afghanistan (*Foreign Department*, no. 4, 'Elphinstone to Minto, May 13, 1809'). The advantages that would follow from the political ascendancy such help would purchase were tantalizing: command of the northern routes from Persia to India; the control of the navigation of the Indus; and influence in Seistan and the other mountain regions between the Indus and Afghan territories. His suggestion for the purchase of Sind was part of this general scheme of securing all the country between the Indus and Persia to British influence as it would prevent invasion from the south while providing bases for defence.

Part of Elphinstone's blueprint was fulfilled through the conquest of Sind, and the search for methods of establishing influence in the Afghan plateau remained as perhaps the single most important aspect of the foreign policy of the Government of India until 1947, when once more the Indus valley passed from control of a power based in the internal Indian heartland. In 1809, however, Elphinstone's argument for control of the northwest through subsidies and the purchase of Sind was not received in Calcutta with enthusiasm. The payment of subsidies by Great Britain to control governments in Europe, it was pointed out, had uniformly failed (*Foreign Department*, no. 6, 'Elphinstone to Minto, May 13, 1809'). In no cases had subsidies won loyalty or gratitude, even though they were usually solicited, but instead had produced 'sentiments of disgust and jealousy in the power that has accepted them'. And instead of helping rulers to defend themselves, the subsidies had been looked upon as a right, carrying with them the implication that all defensive measures were to be carried out at British expense. Nothing could be worse than that Britain's reputation in Europe as a giver of subsidies should be transferred to India, so that 'Asiatic states should learn to attach the condition of pecuniary aid to every effort ... to make ... concert with us' (*Foreign Department*, no. 6, 'Elphinstone to Minto, May 13, 1809'). As for his suggestion of purchasing Sind, while it was true the king of Kabul claimed authority over it, in fact it was an independent government whose legitimacy was founded on the same basis as that of other states which have been formed by 'the revolution of Empires and Kingdoms'. In this reversion to the pre-Wellesley position of regarding the Indian states as genuinely independent entities, Minto, the Governor General, emphasized that the kind of transfer of power Elphinstone proposed was equivalent to direct and unqualified projects of conquest and usurpation (*Foreign Department*, no. 6, 'Elphinstone to Minto, May 13, 1809'). The best defence was the distance separating India from the dominions of the king of Kabul, with rulers of the Indus valley and Punjab acting as buffers.

Since the necessity of control of the northwest approaches to India became such a pervasive and enduring doctrine, it is worth emphasizing that, like so much else that is regarded as integral to Indian political history, it is essentially a product of replacement in the eighteenth century of the multi-state system by the new pattern of administrative unity. The metaphor of continual waves of invaders sweeping into India from the northwest mountains is a product of nineteenth-century British historiography, not of the Indian historical imagination or memory. For the Mughals, the Afghan plateau and the mountains were neither a frontier nor a potential invasion route, but a part of their particular dynastic concern because of its links with their original homeland in Central Asia. More remotely, during the thirteenth and fourteenth centuries,

North India had been subjected to the ferocity of Mongol incursions, but this was a fate shared with much of Western Asia, particularly Iran. The knowledge of earlier invasions by other Central Asian peoples, sun as the Huns, scarcely survived in historical memory except in the references in Puranic literature, but even in these the emphasis was not upon the geographic origin of the despoilers, but their destruction of the order of society.

For Elphinstone and those who followed him either in fact or in imagination to the northwest, the primary problem for the Government of India in the area was to prevent any foreign power from gaining influence in the area. This was not just a question of preventing territorial control or the acquisition of any kind of special position by a foreign government, but the exclusion of all forms of diplomatic and commercial contacts. Thus, in the case of Sind, not only were the French excluded by the treaty made during war time in 1809, but also, along with other Europeans and Americans, in the one made in 1820 under Elphinstone's influence when he was governor of Bombay (Aitchison 1912, 318). Elphinstone's suggestion for persuading the Afghans to agree to a policy of exclusion that in itself had no advantages for them was through the payment of subsidies that would make them dependent upon the Government of India. As for the actual frontiers of India, Elphinstone was among the earliest to argue that the Indus, not the mountains, should be made the boundary. Backed by the deserts of Rajasthan, it would provide both defence from invasion and an area of separation from the hill tribes (Colebrooke 1884, vol. 1, 193–4).

The northwest would have entered the Indian political orbit to some extent because of the fear of the French at the beginning of the century, but it was almost certainly the acquisition of Delhi and the surrounding districts during the Second Maratha War that made relations with the whole area, and particularly the Sikh territories in the Punjab, of overriding importance. Up till then, there had been little thought of expansion towards the northwest, with Oudh being accepted as a buffer for the Bengal territories. But the annexation in 1801 by Wellesley of the fertile lands in the Doab, the area between the Ganges and Jamuna rivers belonging to Oudh, changed the picture: the Company's frontiers now marched with those of the Marathas, without any intervening territories to lessen the likelihood of conflict. When war broke out with the

Marathas in 1803, Delhi at once became the focus of attention, falling to the British armies within a few months. By the treaty of Surji–Arjangaon signed on 30 December 1803, Scindia, who had controlled the area for thirty years yielded Delhi and all the land they controlled between the Jamuna and the Ganges to the British (Aitchison 1912?).

The significance of Delhi in Indian history is surprisingly hard to assess. Despite the romantic myths of its antiquity, it was neither a very old nor a famous city when the Turkish conquerors selected it as their capital at the end of the twelfth century. It has nothing of the natural setting possessed by dozens of great fortresses in India, such as Chitor, Mandu, or Gwalior, but is on an open plain that, as Sir James Craig had told Wellesley, was without any easily defensible line. But this, in fact, seems to be the key to Delhi's importance: its possession was a committal to the control of Punjab, the Gangetic plains, and at least eastern Rajputana. The seeming impregnability of the magnificent hill fortresses scattered with prodigal profusion throughout India was probably a major source of weakness to the rulers who possessed them, because they always suggested the possibility of a retreat, even if the control of the countryside was lost. Furthermore, while some of the great fortresses commanded the most accessible routes from one part of the county to another, in general they were on the fringes of the most valuable areas. They dictated the location of the political power, rather than serving it. Delhi, in contrast, compelled its possessor towards expansion. This was the case in 1800: its acquisition meant an almost automatic widening of political horizons.

Three parties were involved in the frontier problem created by the change in control of Delhi: the British themselves; the small Sikh principalities east of the Sutlej river; and Ranjit Singh, who had only recently established himself as an undisputed ruler of the northern Punjab, with his capital at Lahore. By 1808, the issue had become acute, with Ranjit Singh's agents in Delhi trying to find out what the British regarded as their boundary in the north, on the west bank of the Jamuna (*Foreign Department*, no. 30, 21 March 1808). This was a vital matter for Ranjit Singh, because if the British claimed all the territory up to the Sutlej, then he would not be able to force the Sikh chieftains to the east of the river to pay tribute to him. That he was so uncertain about the British claims is an illustration of the point made before about the external boundaries of Indian states: they were not defined with any exactitude, nor were rulers anxious to define them, as this was a self-limitation on the collection of revenue.

For the Cis-Sutlej chieftains, as they were referred to at the time, the extension of British power into the Delhi area had a very different meaning: their possible salvation from Ranjit Singh's intention of bringing all the Punjab under his control. When representatives of the four most important of the chieftaincies—Patiala, Jind, Nabha, and Kaithal—met the Company's resident in Delhi in 1808, their ostensible purpose was to discuss an impending visit of Ranjit Singh to the great Hindu pilgrimage centre of Hardwar. But their real concern was to persuade the resident to place their territories under British protection. Their possessions, they argued, had been held since ancient times, with 'particular advantages and disadvantages' from the masters of Delhi. Having given allegiance to the Mughals when Ahmad Shah Duranni had captured Delhi, they acknowledged his lordship; then when the Marathas took over, they transferred their allegiance to them; and, finally, when Scindia's general, the Frenchman Ferron, held Delhi, they looked to him 'from [their] ancient dependence on him who held the supreme authority at Delhi' (*Foreign Department*, no. 8, 18 April 1808). Now as the masters of Delhi, the British had the duty and the right and claim to this same allegiance; on their part they had the right to expect protection. They summed all this up in a verse:

> What can he fear from the falling wall
> Who hath a prop like thee?
> What danger from the waves of the sea can he have to dread,
> Who hath Noah for his pilot? (*Foreign Department*, no. 8, 18 April 1808)

No Vicar of Bray could have put his case more coolly than this and the Cis-Sutlej chiefs were not alone in insisting that the possession of Delhi carried with it the duty to accept the allegiance of client states in the area and to provide protection to them from powerful enemies. The ruler of Bikaner, one of the more important of the Rajput chieftains, had expressed similar sentiments to Elphinstone, and like the Sikh chieftains, saw such lordship as a guarantee of their independence, not as its abrogation (Elphinstone 1819, vol. I, 21). Their political memories and experience was of the multi-state system of the eighteenth century, in which allegiance to a central power at best implied the right to ask for assistance and at worst, the payment of tribute.

But the new rulers of Delhi were not willing in 1808 to accept these implications of its possession. A claim to the country up to the Sutlej could have been made good without much difficulty, but this would have meant, however, a common frontier with Ranjit Singh, 'a neighbor of a most ambitious and annoying character'. Archibald Seton, the Delhi resident, suggested to the Governor General that Ranjit Singh be persuaded to agree that his border was the Sutlej, while that of the British was in the Karnal district, with the Cis-Sutlej chiefs acting as a buffer between the two states (*Foreign Department*, no. 30, 21 March 1808). The Calcutta Council decided not to act at that moment on deciding the location of the northern boundary; instead they ordered that Seton's dispatch 'do lie for consideration' (*Foreign Department*, no. 8, 18 April 1808; Bhuyan 1972, 177).

A more positive action was taken in sending an envoy to Ranjit Singh's court at Lahore. The head of the mission was Charles Metcalfe, one of those young men, like Elphinstone and Malcolm, who was then finding in India an opportunity for the exercise of power and initiative, perhaps unequalled anywhere else in the contemporary world (Panigrahi 1968). The problem of the location of the northern frontier and relations with Ranjit Singh offered an especially attractive field for diplomatic initiatives, which Metcalfe exploited with enthusiasm. Remarkably little was known of the Sikh kingdom at this time, despite the large number of European officers in Ranjit Singh's army, and, as with Afghanistan, there was a tendency to overrate its power, so that Ranjit Singh was treated much more as an equal than any of the other Indian ruler of the time. The stereotype of the Sikh national character was also being formed at this time, with a young English traveller to Amritsar reporting in 1808 that the Sikhs were much like British sailors, 'spending their money as fast as they get it on the pleasures of women and wine' (*Foreign Department*, no. 13, 11 July 1808). He also reported with enthusiasm that the women of the Punjab were 'far superior in symmetry of person and beauty of countenance to those of any other part of India'. Perhaps this light-hearted approach convinced the Sikhs that the British were no danger, for when a fakir warned Ranjit Singh that the consequences of letting the English traveller seeing his dominions would be the arrival in a short time of two or three regiments, he laughed at him and told him he was a fool (*Foreign Department*, no. 13, 11 July 1808).

In the long run, of course, the fakir was right, for a clash with the British was inevitable. Their idea of the independent Sikh chiefs providing a buffer between their boundary north of Karnal and the Sutlej was illusory as it ran counter to the fundamental basis of Ranjit Singh's kingdom—a union of all the Sikh chieftains in the Punjab, coupled with expansion to the west and southwest against the Afghans. Not the least of his achievements, however, was to postpone the clash during his lifetime. The first crisis occurred in 1808 when the decision was finally made by Calcutta, after considerable pressure from Metcalfe and the local military commanders, to assert British authority over the Sikh chieftains in the area between the Jamuna and the Sutlej. The establishment of a military post at Ludhiana in 1809 made British intentions clear to both the chieftains of the area and to Ranjit Singh (Hasrat 1968, 82–102). Metcalfe's legitimization of the takeover on the grounds that the British were the legatees of the Marathas, the previous rulers of the area, did not impress Ranjit Singh; but no one knew better than him that the only validation of territorial claims was the ability to hold them (Hasrat 1968, 89). The three central figures in the movement towards the Sutlej were local officials—Metcalfe, who was the agent at Lahore; Seton, the Resident at Delhi; and David Ochterlony, the commander of the military forces. Calcutta was uneasy about their activities, afraid that they might provoke a war with Ranjit Singh, but forced to acquiesce for lack of immediate information.

Their gamble that Ranjit Singh would not risk a war with the British to prevent the extension of their frontier to the Sutlej paid off, and in April 1809, he signed a treaty of perpetual friendship with the British at Amritsar (Aitchison 1912, vol. VIII, 144). From Ranjit Singh's point of view, the treaty seemed advantageous because while it prevented his expansion across the Sutlej, it promised that the British would have 'no concern with the territories and subjects of the Raja to the northward'. In effect, this was a recognition of the conquests he had already made, and a tacit admission of his freedom to expand westward against the Afghans. But despite the treaty, this political settlement was basically unstable. It was based on the supposition that the Sutlej was a clear-cut line of demarcation between two sovereignties, when in fact, as in other areas both in Europe and India where boundaries were drawn through territories and complex relationships existed between petty chieftains and more powerful ones, there were many ambiguities. Thus, Ranjit Singh had given the territory of Wadni, south of the Sutlej, to his mother-in-law in 1808, but when he imprisoned her in 1822 during a quarrel, he reclaimed the land. This made him a chieftain within the territory protected by the British, while at the same time they acknowledged him as a sovereign ruler (Hasrat 1968, 114). This was only one of many similar cases, making the Sutlej a far less useful border than it had originally seemed (Farooqui 1941). Above all, 'a nation in arms'—which was what the Sikh kingdom essentially was, a federation of chieftains held together by the discipline and profits of war—was not likely to be able to live long in peace with a neighbour whose frontiers were equally fluid, and whose leadership was subjected to strong internal pressure to follow an expansionist policy.

This pressure is one of the basic facts of Indian political life in the early years of the nineteenth century. Ever since Wellesley's administration, it had been almost unremitting, coming not from Great Britain, as it should have in any classic model of imperialism, but from the local officials. Metcalfe's views are representative of the prevailing mood. Intoxicated at first by the possibility of playing a role in the destiny not only of the Punjab, but also the whole of the Northwest through to Central Asia, he had gone to Ranjit Singh's court at Lahore expecting the rituals and ceremonies of contemporary European diplomacy, but found instead of an organized state a form of personal power that had no analogy in Western political experience (Kaye 1854; 1856, vol. I, 249–54, Metcalfe's 'Memoranda'). Romanticism was soon replaced by a hard-headed approach for reality, in which the question of frontiers became paramount. He reminded the Governor General that 'our policy in India rests upon our military superiority. It has no foundation in the affections of the people' (Kaye 1854, vol. I, 342, 'Paper to Lord Moira'; Blackwood 1857, 660). The implications of this fact for frontier policy were plain, he told another friend. 'I remember the time,' he wrote in 1814, 'when the advancement of our influence on the Sutlej was reprobated even by Lord Wellesley.' Then his mission to Lahore saw the triumph of his own views on the matter, and now there was general recognition that this was only a temporary halt. Metcalfe, like most of his generation, was doubtful about the permanence of the empire the British had created in India, but he was convinced that the best chance of preserving it was through expansion: 'making ourselves strong by all just means' (Kaye 1854, vol. I, 394–5, 'Metcalfe to Richard Jenkins, November 3, 1814'; Blackwood 1857, 660).

That the Sutlej remained the frontier during Ranjit Singh's life was partly due to his willingness to compromise and to achieve his ends whenever he could by political means. This was how he had won his kingdom because, as Metcalfe pointed out, despite his formidable army, most of his conquests were bloodless, brought about by waiting for a moment of weakness in an opponent and then applying pressure through a combination of threats and concessions (*Foreign Department*, no. 1, 5 December 1808). His military success in the areas where the British had agreed not to interfere undermined the stability of his kingdom. After the Treaty of Amritsar had deflected his attention from the Sikh states between the Sutlej and the Jamuna, he had turned to the west and north. The Kangra hills were taken in 1811 and Kashmir in 1819. Attock—the fort that guarded the great crossing of the Indus, the key to an advance towards the Afghan possessions in Peshawar and the hills— fell in 1813. The capture of Multan in 1818 gave him control of upper Sind, while the capture of Peshawar in 1823 from the Afghans brought him face to face with the challenge of penetrating into mountains.

The general result of all these conquests was probably not seen at the time by either the Sikhs or the British: the elimination of the boundaries that had emerged during the previous century between the powers based in the Indian plains and those in the mountains. What the Sikhs had done was to return the area to somewhat the same political condition in which it had been under the Mughals, but without any of the administrative structures that had made it possible for the Mughals to integrate it, at least partially, into their Indian empire. The whole vast area of the Punjab, upper Sind, and much of what was later to become the Northwest Frontier Provinces, was thus thrown into one political unit, but with only nominal overall control. The search for a frontier in this unstable political milieu that remained for almost a century a major concern of the Government of India was thus a direct legacy of ten years of expansion by Ranjit Singh. The Sikh kingdom was similar in this respect to the other border states, especially Nepal and Burma, where dynasties with strong expansionist ambitions created unstable conditions in the boundary zones with British India. Both had been quiescent for some time, but coincidental with the expansion of the Sikh kingdom they entered a new phase in their internal histories that brought them in conflict with British power.

That the tensions created by the movement of their frontier to the Sutlej gave the British a new area of contact with the Nepalese is the point of a question Metcalfe asked a friend in 1814: 'Are you acquainted with the plans of Government regarding Nepaul?' (Kaye 1856, vol. I, 295, 'Metcalfe to Richard Jenkins, November 3, 1814'). Along the original areas of contact—the northern districts of Bihar—fairly satisfactory arrangements had been worked out between the Company's Bengal government and the Nepalese by 1800, even though the boundary had not been demarcated. But first Wellesley's new acquisitions west of Oudh in the Delhi region and then the advance to the Sutlej had greatly increased the points of tension.

No other war that the Government of India fought with its neighbours was more clearly a 'border war' than with Nepal in 1814–16. The Governor General had argued for intervention in the Himalayan area on the grounds that it 'would be conductive to the success of any commercial objects which our improved intercourse with these mountain districts might open to the enterprise of our merchants' (quoted in Sanwal 1965, 130), this echoing the dream of trade through the mountains that had so fascinated Warren Hastings and his generation, but there is little stress on this in the contemporary records. The emphasis is always either on the intrusion of the Nepalese into the older possessions of the Company along the Bihar frontier or the dangers likely to arise from their expansion westward through the mountains. As with most wars, there was little dispute over the facts, only over their interpretation. As noted above, the Permanent Settlement in Bengal and Bihar required closer definition of land rights in the border districts than had existed before. The issue was not to whom the peasants paid rent for their lands, but to which government the zamindars paid their dues. The result was a series of disputes, with appeals to past precedents, most of which were vague and ambiguous, over the revenues from the fertile terai lands, which were of great importance to Nepal. Disputes of quite another kind arose along the new frontier that had been created by the British assertion of authority from the Jamuna to the Sutlej. Here, as elsewhere along the northern mountains, chieftains had held land in both the plains and the hills, acknowledging the suzerainty of the rulers of the Punjab for their lands in the plains, but maintaining their independence in the hills (Vogel and Hutchison 1933).

The simultaneous emergence of British power in the plains and Nepalese power in the hills ended this loose but workable arrangement. As elsewhere, the appearance of the British with a system of administration that demanded fixed boundaries created new tensions, for as the Gurkhas moved westward through the mountains to the Sutlej, they conquered territory belonging to the Sikh chieftains whom the British had taken under their protection. The Nepalese claimed that their conquests in the hills entitled them to the attached lands in the plains, since plains districts such as 'Punjore, Narayan Garh, and Lahurpur—had always belonged to whoever possessed Sirmur and Hindur' in the hills (Nepalese Commander Amar Singh Thappa to General Ochterlony, quoted in Samwal 1965, 122). David Ochterlony, who had been appointed the Governor General's agent in the Jamuna–Sutlej area, was the most vigorous proponent of the need to meet this new situation with a carefully worked out border policy. The Calcutta government had already laid down a policy that the Nepalese would 'not be permitted to extend their conquests to the districts below the hills' (Nepalese Commander Amar Singh Thappa to General Ochterlony, quoted in Samwal 1965, 120). Ochterlony was quick to point out that however useful foothills might seem as a boundary in theory, in practice they provided very little clear delineation, since the hills were cut by valleys leading into them from the plains. Thus, to admit the foothills as the legitimate boundary of Nepalese claims meant opening up the plains to them.

Ochterlony's solution was a variant of the one that was to be so often suggested for India: the creation of a buffer between the actual Indian borders and those of Nepal. It would be easy, he thought, 'to throw a boundary line of petty states which should be independent of both Governments and prevent all future collisions' (Nepalese Commander Amar Singh Thappa to General Ochterlony, quoted in Samwal 1965, 129). Dehra Dun, the valley between the Himalayas and the Shivaliks, was an example of the kind of buffer state he had in mind. But since such a scheme would have implied recognition of the Nepalese conquests in the hills, the government rejected it. The Governor General insisted on the restoration of the power of the hill chiefs conquered by the Nepalese arguing that this would be relatively easy since the hill chieftains would have the active support of their people, and once they were restored, the chieftains would show their gratitude to the British by giving them ascendancy in their councils (Nepalese Commander Amar Singh Thappa to General Ochterlony, quoted in Samwal 1965, 131). Probably Ochterlony's buffer states would not have worked, but neither would the Governor General's plan, for it required the Nepalese to give up the territory they had conquered in the mountains to the west of their original territory as well as the lands they claimed along the Bihar frontier. The situation had reached an impasse. As the Raja of Nepal wrote to the Governor General, 'The land which is disputed is by right mine; you will not be satisfied without war' (Rajah of Nepaul 1824, 384), for it was, of course, precisely the British refusal to recognize his right that made a settlement without war impossible.

The war, which began late in 1814 and lasted until early 1816, was the most difficult the British had fought in India up to this point. Although the British had more men under arms, the Nepalese made skilful use of their mountain terrain and difficult climate, forcing the British to recognize that anything like a complete capitulation could not be hoped for. For their post, the Nepalese did not want to continue the war, as the raja recognized how ruinous it was to his kingdom, with its heavy independence upon the lowlands for revenue. But when he suggested making concessions along the disputed frontiers, his ablest military commander, Amar Singh, argued that Tipu Sultan's fate showed how little use it was to try to placate the British: give them what they ask, and they will then make higher demands (Prinsep 1825, vol. I, Appendix B, 'Amar Singh to the Raja of Nepal, March 2, 1815'). Amar Singh pinned his hopes for a successful end of the war on that dream that inspired many of the Indian rulers at the time: a union of the rulers against the British. Why would Ranjit Singh, he asked, not join the Nepalese in crushing the British, when he himself was so hard-pressed by them (Prinsep 1825, vol. I, Appendix B, 'Amar Singh to the Raja of Nepal, March 2, 1815')? One answer was that Ranjit Singh may have known that the raja of Nepal had proposed to the British that a solution of their difficulties over boundaries would be a joint expedition against the Sikhs, with a division of their territory to satisfy the needs of both the Nepalese and Indian governments. The British were not interested in the proposal, and having recorded their balance after early repulses, forced the Nepalese in 1816 to accept a treaty ending the war (Aitchison 1829, vol. II, 173–4).

The contrast between the Treaty of Sagauli and such early documents as the one signed in 1772 with Koch Bihar is striking, with its recognition of the need to compromise and to treat Nepal as a genuinely sovereign state. Reading the treaty, one is tempted to see, especially in the emphasis on the careful definition of boundaries, the explanation of Nepal's survival as an independent state when others—seemingly in the same category, such as Sikkim—passed into the control of the Government of India. The only major exception to the treatment of Nepal as an equal state is the article that prevented the raja of Nepal from taking into his service any European—including British—or American subject, but this in itself was a kind of guarantee against future British interference, and one that probably did not press very hard on the Nepalese, as they had already begun their policy of excluding foreigners.

Nepal lost to the British all its recent conquests in the western hills including Kumaon and Garhwal in the Himalayas and Dehra Dun, the great sweep of fertile valley land between the Himalayas and the Shivaliks. This gave the British what they had not possessed before: territory in the mountains, beyond the Gangetic plain. The Kali river was made Nepal's western boundary, ending further controversy over the borders between the foothills and the plains, but not over the limits of British power into the interior towards Tibet. This was not, however, a matter of much concern at the time: not for nearly a century and a half would such points in the then undefined frontier as Shipki Pass become of importance for the Government of India. But this deep down intrusion into the mountains nonetheless made the Bengal government what it had not been before—a Himalayan power, with possibilities of political contacts along new frontiers.

The Treaty of Sagauli gave India her first clearly defined external boundary. In the original draft of the Treaty, most of the terai lands had been taken from Nepal, but in a subsequent modification, those lying in the areas between the Kosi, Gandak, and Rapti rivers were restored, with the exception of areas over which the Bengal government had long asserted a claim. Most significantly, provision was made for a survey for arranging 'a well-defined boundary' acceptable to both countries, 'with a view to the distinct separation of the respective territories of the British Government to the south and of Nepal to the north' (Aitchison 1829, vol. II, 175–7). A provision was made that if there should be any indentations in the straight line of the new frontier, an exchange of lands would take place. This appears to be the earliest treaty in India that makes such specific provisions for what would later be called a demarcated border, and it is interesting that the line to be drawn was to be an 'artificial' frontier, not one dependent on natural features, such as river. Even where rivers did provide a useful boundary line, the surveyors were careful to put up boundary posts, since the Himalayan rivers frequently changed their courses (*Foreign Department Miscellaneous Records*, vol. 138, 135–9, 'Correspondence from W. Clark to the Government of Bengal, December 4, 1817').

This was, on the whole, the most successful of all the boundaries, for while there were frequent disputes over minor sections, there were no further major crises. The demarcation of this boundary, along with a survey of the new Himalayan territories, was one of the first great achievements of the men who were laying the foundation for the organization that became the Survey of India (Phillimore 1950, vol. III, 19–29). With almost fanatical enthusiasm, the surveyors struggled through the unknown territory, driven by a desire to get to the source of the Ganges and Jamuna and to reach the areas beyond the mountain crests. One of the most remarkable of them, J.A. Hodgson, who was in charge of the survey in the Himalayan area between the Sutlej and Nepal, complained that the work was done at 'the risk of breaking one's neck, or being starved for frozen to death', but he managed to cover most of the area (Phillimore 1950, vol. III, 31).

The settlement that followed the end of the war was not confined to the Nepal frontier, but to a remarkable degree the whole stretch of mountain territory from the Sutlej river to the eastern borders of Sikkim assumed a political stability that lasted for the next 130 years. There was, however, no uniformity in the arrangements that grew out of the Treaty of Sagauli, but in their variety they illustrate most of the solutions for frontier problems that were formulated during the century. Kumaon, the territory west of Nepal, between the Kali and Alaknanda rivers was brought under the direct administrative control of the

Bengal government. Aside from preventing future Nepalese expansion, this outright annexation was justified on the grounds that the hills contained iron and copper, and also, it was thought, might provide trade routes to China (*Papers Respecting the Nepaul War*, 566, 'Correspondence of Lord Hastings to Secret Committee, June 1, 1815').

Beyond Alaknanda, up to the Sutlej, the territory was returned to the hill chieftains who ruled it before the Nepalese conquests. The most important of these was the chief of Garhwal, whose lands had included much of the annexed territory of Kumaon. The status of Tehri–Garhwal was the same as that of the princess in the interior who had through the years accepted British paramountcy, forging all independence in their foreign relations in return for a large measure of internal autonomy and guarantee of their power (Atkinson 1884). Beyond Tehri–Garhwal, up to the Sutlej, was the hill state of Bashahr, with a similar status. The northern boundary of both the annexed territory of Kumaon and of the hill states of Tehri–Garhwal and Bashahr was simply 'the snowy range' separating them from Tibet. As late as 1909, this boundary was shown as undefined on official maps (*Memorandum on Native States* 1909, vol. II, 'Maps' section). The hill states, in contrast to the administered territory of Kumaon, which was not geographically or culturally much different, illustrate what Sir Alfred Lyall saw as the function of such protected states, 'a convenient method of extending various degrees of power, of appropriating certain attributes of sovereignty, without affirming full jurisdictions' (Lyall 1891, 312).

Sikkim was an example of a third kind of political arrangement to meet this need. Threatened by Nepal ever since the rise of the Gurkha power in the 1760s, it was protected from further Nepalese expansion in the Himalayans by the Treaty of Sagauli, which specified that any disputes between Nepal and Sikkim would be arbitrated by the British, with the Nepalese bound to accept the British award (Aitchison 1892, vol. II, 174). By the Treaty of Titalia in 1817, the Sikkim ruler accepted this same condition, along with the exclusion of Europeans and Americans and the promise to give military aid to the Indian government in case of need (Aitchison 1892; 1876–1933 (1931 edition), vol. XII, 58–9). This was an 'unequal' treaty, but it was by no means an assertion of paramountcy of the kind found in the treaties with the rulers of internal states of the other border areas and states, Bashahr and Tehri–Garhwal. H.H. Risley in his introduction to *The Gazetteer of Sikkim* is surely in error when he says that the Treaty of Titalia granted anyone paramountcy (Risley 1894, iii). That Sikkim retained throughout the nineteenth century, and even after 1947, its special status was probably due in part to its function as, in effect, an administered zone between India and its neighbours to the north. Either directly administered territory or a princely state with a more precise acknowledgement of British paramountcy would have had difficulty in maintaining the special relations that existed between Sikkim and Tibet. While these relationships were defined in religious, not in western political terms, their political significance was indicated by the fact that the raja of Sikkim's capital during much of the first half of the nineteenth century was actually at Chumbi in Tibet (Risley 1894, iii). Such imprecision in political relations, including the undefined boundaries between Tibet and Bhutan, was only possible because of Sikkim's peculiar status which was located in the Indian political spectrum somewhere between actual sovereignty and dependency. It is noteworthy that the Treaty of Titalia in making over to Sikkim terai lands taken from Nepal speaks of the 'full sovereignty' of the Sikkim raja.

The fourth kind of border arrangement is seen, of course, in Nepal itself, which was by no means a dependency of India, but which was very clearly within the British sphere of 'influence'. More than any other area on the Indian perimeter, Nepal was a buffer state, effectively separating India from immediate contact on a long border from China. It probably would have been possible in 1815 to have completely defeated Nepal, resulting in a treaty that affirmed British paramountcy, if not outright annexation. According to the Governor General, this was not done because the objectives of the war were better served by continuing the existence of a weakened, but still independent, country. 'We should have had infinite trouble,' he explained to London, 'in the formation and maintenance of any other Government, and we might also have dissatisfied the Chinese, by setting up a dependent of our own' (quoted in Ramakant 1968, 36, 'Correspondence of Lord Hastings to Chairman of East India Company, August 6, 1816'). The function of Nepal was thus not to separate India from a dangerous neighbour, for there was no fear of China at this time, but rather to strengthen good relations with China, which at this point the Company ardently desired.

During the early years of the nineteenth century, the frontiers of Bengal attracted little official attention, but after the Nepalese War they once more assumed the importance they had held briefly in the 1770s and 1780s. The climax of this interest was the First Burmese War from 1824 to 1826. The standard explanation of the war, and the consequent enormous expansion of territory controlled from India, drew upon the classic late nineteenth-century understanding of the nature and function of the frontiers: since 'there was no natural barrier of mountain or river to the province of Bengal upon the east', it was impossible to confine British power (Roberts 1967, 294). But as had already been shown along the Nepal border, and as was to be made amply clear for the rest of the century in the northwest, neither rivers nor mountains in themselves provide boundaries that in anyway impede expansion, or at least lessen the likelihood of war.

Then, as now, political conditions, not natural frontiers, determined the relations between India and adjoining powers, and by the early 1820s these made for an unstable frontier in the northeast. On the one side was the British power in Bengal, committed to a quest for internal stability and emphatic on its need to prevent any intrusion into its territory. On the other side was Burma, with a dynasty no less desirous of asserting its internal authority and jealous of any restriction on its sovereignty. In such a situation, it was not the lack of natural frontiers but the existence of intervening territories with weak governments—Assam and the conglomeration of hill states of indeterminate political status—that led to conflict. The refusal of Burma to have normal trading relations, which was perhaps the major cause of the Second Burmese War in 1852, was not a significant factor in the 1820s. Economic considerations find virtually no mention in the contemporary records. The emphasis is on borders, and the problem generated by what the British, from their point of view, regarded as the aggressive expansion of the Burmese, and the Burmese, from theirs, saw as a refusal by the British to acknowledge these legitimate spheres of influence.

The reactivation of the eastern frontier began in 1811 when Chin Byan, a leader of the refugees who had fled into British territory when Burma conquered Arakan, invaded Arakan from Chittagong. Since there was no question that Chin Byan was based in Bengal, and furthermore was probably receiving arms from British merchants, the

Burmese court assumed that the attacks on their territory had been instigated by the British (Banerjee 1964, 176). As on previous occasions, the Calcutta authorities denied the charge, but while promising to prevent raids in the future, refused to extradite the refugees. The British were, in fact, in the same situation that their own neighbours along the Indian borders were to find themselves in throughout the nineteenth century: they were unable to assert effective control over the behaviour of frontier areas, thus permitting their territory to be used for intrusions across the border. Southern Chittagong was still virtually unknown territory, and the vagueness of the frontier—despite the insistence by the Bengal government that the Naf river was the boundary—was shown when the Chittagong magistrate at first argued that the land occupied by Chin Byan in Arakan was really in Bengal (Hall 1945, 100).

Chin Byan's death in 1815 lessened the friction over the raids, but sporadic attacks from Chittagong continued to irritate the Burmese authorities, leading them to demand the right to send armies into Bengal if the Calcutta authorities were unable to police the frontiers they claimed with such persistence. It was the failure of the Calcutta authorities to prevent the raids that led the Burmese in 1818 to make a claim for the Bengal districts of Ramu, Murshidabad, and Chittagong (quoted in Harvey 1967, 292–3, 'Letter from the Raja of Ramree to the Governor-General, 1818'). The claim was no more absurd than many others made by governments both in Europe and Asia, being based on the facts that rulers of Arakan had, in previous centuries, controlled these areas for at least brief periods, and the Burmese, by their conquests, had become the legatees of the Arakan kings. By permitting the raids on Burmese territory, the Bengal authorities, according to the Burmese, had given proof of the illegitimacy of their occupation.

This letter has been often quoted as an example of Burmese bombast, but it can also be read as a product of the despair that often drove Indian and other Asian rulers to acts of desperation when confronted by Western power. The Burmese historian Maung Htin Aung is, perhaps, correct when he argues that so far from being contemptuous of the British, the Burmese realized how strong they were, and could not believe they were unable to control a rebel such as Chin Byan (Aung 1965, 26).

Along the Chittagong–Arakan frontier, it was the Burmese who were the aggrieved party, threatening war if the Bengal government did not control the inhabitants of the territories over which it claimed jurisdiction. Along the main eastern frontier, however, it was the British reaction to Burmese expansion and their control of frontier areas that was important. There were two areas of friction: the central region where the hill states of Manipur, Chachar, and Jaintia separated Bengal from Burma, and the northern section where the border was with the ancient kingdom of Assam. Here, there was quite a well-defined border formed by river Manas, and although there had been border incidents through the years, on the whole, the area had not attracted much attention since the 1790s. Its return to prominence as a problem frontier began in 1817 when the Burmese became involved in the complex internal power struggles that had left Assam almost without an effective government for two generations. (For an overview of the historical literature of this period, see Bhuyan 1932, 291–5.) The pattern was one that had become familiar through the years in Indian politics: a claimant to power appealed for outside help, which when given was a prelude to a loss of independence. Badan Chandra, who had been ousted from the office of Bar Phukan, governor of the western part of Assam, fled to Calcutta to seek support from the Bengal government; when it was refused, he turned to the Burmese (Sen n.d., xiii). The Burmese responded by sending an expeditionary force in 1817 that put their own nominee on the throne as a puppet for the time being; but they returned as a permanent occupying force two years later. According to Htin Aung, the Burmese king Bagyidaw (1819–37) did not take this action because he had dreams of an expanding empire, but because he had concluded that unless Assam was annexed by the Burmese, the British would use its internal troubles as an excuse for taking it over, thus adding to their power in the area (Aung 1965, 29). It is an argument that the British had frequently used for their own conquests and, from the Burmese point of view, it was probably genuine.

The most important British response to the Burmese annexation of Assam came from David Scott, who as magistrate at Rangpur was the chief British official in the border area. It was his report that provided the Calcutta government—and beyond it, London—with information, and his interpretation of the significance of the Burmese presence on the Bengal frontier largely determined the policy followed in subsequent years. In general, Scott's attitude was similar to that of other local officials in the frontier area. Sensitive to changes taking place in his area, and possibly magnifying their importance, he urged the Calcutta officials of the necessity of measures which they at first regarded as unwise but eventually accepted as inevitable. By 1822, it was clear to him that the Burmese were in control of Assam and had made it a province of their empire. This, Scott insisted, had radically altered the whole political situation in the area with Bengal now having as a neighbour a powerful and warlike country instead of the feeble Assamese administration (*Foreign Political Consultations*, no. 50, 26 July 1822, 'Correspondence of David Scott to Council, July 11, 1822'). A larger force, he pointed out, would now have to be stationed on the frontier than would have been needed a few years previously to have taken over the whole of Assam. Scott saw the shape of things to come in an incident in 1822 when the Burmese set a precedent they would be quick to follow (*Foreign Political Consultations*, no. 50, 'Correspondence of David Scott to Council, September 27, 1822').

The Calcutta government, at first, was not inclined to accept Scott's reading of the frontier situation. They saw no reason for making an issue of the Burmese occupation of the island in the Brahmaputra on the Assam border or for acceding to Scott's suggestion for an elaborate system of beacons to be built on the hilltops to be lighted in case of a Burmese invasion (*Foreign Political Consultations*, no. 69, 'Correspondence of David Scott to Council'). Despite all rumours of impending trouble on the Assamese border, Lord Hastings, the Governor General, was still convinced in 1822 that there was 'not the remotest apprehension of a rupture'. Instead of worrying about a Burmese invasion, Hastings' own solution was to reinforce the guards along Bengal's six-hundred-mile frontier with Assam to prevent the intrusion of the marauding parties that led to friction between the two states (*Foreign Department*, nos 673 and 659, 'Letter from Lord Hastings, July 27, 1822').

Scott's argument was that such a defensive posture left untouched the problems created by the existence of a strong power on the other side of the Bengal border; what was needed was a forward movement into the whole area from Assam itself through the eastern hill states. The simplest way of doing this was by offering help in driving out the Burmese to the Assamese leaders who had fled for refuge to Bengal

(Banerjee 1964, 208). This policy might lead to war with Burma, but Scott felt that the possibility of driving out the Burmese and restoring a weak, and presumably grateful, government on a vulnerable frontier was worth the chance.

While the authorities at Calcutta were unwilling to move towards a confrontation with Burma in Assam, the logic of Scott's position became more attractive when, concurrent with their annexation of Assam, the Burmese moved against the hill states of Manipur, Cachar, and Jaintia. Manipur had been subjected to Burmese intrusions as early as the 1760s with the establishment of the Alaungpaya dynasty, but new pressures had made its rulers virtually vassals after 1812 when a defeated claimant for power Marjit Singh sought Burmese help (Harvey 1967, 283). The parallels to the Company's accession to power in Bengal was deepened when Marjit Singh was deposed and he fled to the neighbouring state of Cachar, where along with other Manipuri refugees, he seized control of the government. The resulting turmoil in Cachar gave the Burmese an opportunity to intervene in its affairs. At the same time, they asserted a claim over the neighbouring hill state of Jaintia on the basis of their position as successors to the Ahom kings of Assam, who had once controlled the area. The Bengal government was thus faced with the likelihood of having Burma as an immediate neighbour on an undefined and vague frontier in the eastern hills as well as in Assam. For this reason, Scott urged that the Bengal government should work for the establishment of regimes in Cachar and Jaintia that would be independent of both the Burmese and the British, thus providing a neutral buffer zone between the two states. Coupled with this was his conviction that the people of Cachar, as of Assam, would rise in support of any attempt to overthrow the Burmese (*Foreign Department*, no. 660, 'Letter from Lord Amherst to Select Committee, February 23, 1824').

This belief in the possibility of establishing states that would be committed to friendship with India, but accepted by other powers as genuinely independent, is one of the most persistent of political ideas in nineteenth-century India, appearing again and again in the context of frontier policy. It would be difficult to imagine a situation in Indian frontier history where its application would have been practical; and certainly as Lord Amherst, the new Governor General, recognized, there was nothing in the events of recent years that suggested that the Burmese would have been willing to agree to the neutralization of a frontier zone. His own solution for the problem of the hill states was to declare Cachar and Jaintia to be a 'protected state', wholly within Bengal's 'general system of defensive arrangements for the frontier' (*Foreign Department* no. 660, 'Letter from Lord Amherst to Select Committee, February 23, 1824'). The frontier of eastern Bengal as it had been under the Mughals and during the early years of Company rule, the eastern edge of Sylhet district, was now thrust deeply into the hills.

By bringing itself into contact with the Burmese along a much longer, an even more undefined, border than had existed previously, the Bengal government increased both the points of friction and the fears of the Burmese. Contemporary British accounts make much of the warlike mood of the Burmese, insisting that everyone from 'the king to a Beggar (the Burmese) were hot for war. ... They thought that all the world ought to be slaves of the king of Ava' (quoted in Harvey 1967, 363). This may have been so, but it more likely reflects the widespread British view that the Burmese, in Lord Amherst's words, were 'the most barbarous and sanguinary of all Eastern nations' (*Foreign Department*, no. 660, 'Letter from Lord Amherst to Select Committee, February 23, 1824'). The actions of the Burmese in this period are more likely to have been the product of growing desperation as the British thrust into areas such as Cachar and Jaintia, which they regarded are their own sphere of influence.

The situation was thus tense all along the eastern frontier when the Burmese laid claim to the island of Shahpuri, which, according to the British accounts, was wholly on the Bengal side of the Naf river, which has long been accepted as the boundary in that area (*Foreign Department*, no. 660, 41–9, 'Letter from Lord Amherst to Select Committee, November 21, 1823'). A series of skirmishes took place, with some loss of life on both sides. The local official, as was usual in such cases, in his reports to Calcutta stressed the need of holding the disputed territory and of teaching the Burmese a lesson. Added to the frequent case for an open declaration of war now seemed overwhelming to the Calcutta authorities, and on 5 March 1824 the Governor General formally announced that the approach of the Burmese armies towards the borders of Bengal as well as the maintenance of national honour required an appeal to arms 'against the insults and aggression which the arrogance and grasping spirit of the Burmese Government' had caused (quoted in Banerjee 1964, 241). However hypocritical this may sound, there is nothing in the records to suggest that it was not quite sincerely meant; the Bengal government was conscious of its own rectitude in having sought an adjustment of the border dispute over Shahpuri with the Burmese, and in having given help to the rulers of the hill states, whose people, men such as Scott were convinced, hated the Burmese (*Foreign Department*, no. 662, 169–72, 'Secret Department Correspondence, February 23, 1824').

How the acquisition of new frontiers on the eastern border was largely the product of forces within the Bengal government itself is shown by the reaction of the London administration of the Company to the reports of events during 1823 and early 1824. They accepted the necessity of standing firm on the island of Shahpuri, worthless though it was from either a commercial or military point of view, because this touched 'the national honor and character of [the Burmese] government'. But involvement in the hill states was another matter; the Burmese could hardly have been expected not to object to their virtual annexation by Bengal. The argument that Cachar has to be taken because it commanded the passes through which Burma might invade Bengal seemed to them particularly weak. 'This may be said,' they pointed out, 'of any petty state lying between our frontier and the territory of any considerable power' (*Foreign Department*, no. 680, 1–9, 'Extract from Dispatch from Select Committee to Governor-General, August 4, 1824'). The best way of avoiding disputes in this situation was to not get involved in the politics of the intermediate country. But as had happened before, and was to happen many times again, the London administration could do little more than protest the acquisition of territory and the declaration of war. The reversal of forward movements of frontiers was seldom a political possibility.

From the very beginning of its territorial involvement, the problem of defending and defining frontiers had moved the Company towards the assumption of the role of an Indian power. The pressures came from within the context of Indian political life, and were not an extension of interests of the British government. The whole sequence of events leading to the war with Burma demonstrated how far the Bengal government had moved in the direction of becoming an autonomous entity, motivated by the same political impulses that characterized any independent state.

The concern with frontiers at one level can be seen as a problem in defence of the interests the Company had built up in Bengal, but there is more to it than this. The reactions of the officials and the arguments they used were those of the defenders of a nation state, with such abstractions as 'national honor' being applied to their conduct. No other issue in sixty years of British rule pointed so clearly to the development of what can only be called a national consciousness, however incipient, as did frontier problems. It would be difficult to demonstrate any significant difference between the attitude of the foreign rulers of Bengal in the 1820s and those of the Indian nationalists in the 1960s in relation to borders and frontiers.

The conventional judgement on the Burmese war, which lasted two years, is that it was badly managed by the Indian government. Aside from the war with Nepal, however, this was the first time British power in India had confronted what was in effect a national government, and even more than in the case of Nepal, a government that was fighting for survival and knew it. The Treaty of Yandabo signed in 1826 was much harsher than the Treaty of Sagauli, and was much more concerned with providing defined borders acceptable to both states; it was a treaty clearly imposed by the victors. At the outbreak of the war, the emphasis was on security for the eastern frontier, and it was assumed that this would be achieved through reinstating the old rules in Assam, continuing the protected status of the hill states of Manipur, Cachar, and Jaintia, and along the Chittagong frontier, separating Arakan from Burma, with some member of the old ruling family in charge (*Foreign Political Consultation*, no. 1, 'Memorandum of the Governor-General, February 20, 1824'). By the end of the war, there was less certainty about the creation of the ring of buffer states, with quasi-independent status. Since the beginning, Scott had thought the 'imbecility, cowardice, and treacherous principles' of any of the Assamese princes made them unlikely candidates for the guardians of the frontiers against the Burmese (*Foreign Department*, no. 662, 'Letter from David Scott, February 23, 1824'). From Chittagong, the same kind of advice went to Calcutta from the local officials. Arakan, it was argued, should be taken from Burma and brought under Indian rule. Only then could there be peace on the frontier. 'We must have the mountains as a barrier between us and you,' the British agent told the Burmese commissioners sent to arrange the treaty, 'to prevent the recurrence of war' (quoted in Banerjee 1964, 342).

The result was a treaty that reduced Burmese power and gave control of the territory to the Bengal government that had never before been under the direct control of an India-based power (Aitchison 1892, vol. 1). The Arakan district, along with the coastal islands, was annexed, with the Arakan Mountains providing a boundary from the north down to Cape Negrais in the south. As was usual with mountains, this boundary was much less defined in practice than it seemed in the vague maps of the period, but after the troubles along the Naf it promised a considerable degree of isolation from the main Burmese territories. Pegu and the other districts of the Irrawaddy delta were not annexed, although some of the local officials, especially the army officers had urged that it either be made a buffer state under some representative of the old dynasty, or that it be annexed (Banerjee 1964, 347). It was recognized that the Burmese would have been unwilling at this time to sign a treaty that gave up Pegu, but furthermore its acquisition would have led to new frontier problems, for the delta was entirely open to the north. It was decided, however, to annex Tenasserim and the associated territories of Ye, Tavoy, and Mergui. The Salween river demarcated the boundary with Pegu, with the Pakchan river marking the southwards extension of the territory and the Bilauktaung Mountains providing an interior boundary with Siam. This new boundary, which was intended to lessen old frictions, quickly gave rise to new ones.

From the beginning there was never much enthusiasm either in Calcutta or London for Tenasserim. Not only was it soon apparent that the revenues would not cover the costs of occupation, but its possession created a new series of border problems by making Indian territory, for the first time, contiguous with that of Siam. As traditional enemies of the Burmese, the Siamese had welcomed the war with Burma, but when its conclusion made the British their immediate neighbours, they felt threatened and friction developed on the new frontier. British officials in the area began to report to Calcutta that the Siamese were hostile, and they urged that preparations should be made to impress them with British power (Foreign Committee, no. 671, 'Letter from Lord Amherst to Governor of Prince of Wales Island, July 23, 1821').

This militant anxiety of local officials, so familiar a feature of frontier life, was not shared in Calcutta. In a very shrewd analysis of the situation created by the contact of British power with Siamese, Lord Amherst pointed out that far from underestimating British power, and therefore needing to have it demonstrated to them by a display of military might, the Siamese were acting out of extreme dread of what might happen to them (*Foreign Committee*, no. 671, 'Letter from Lord Amherst to Governor of Prince of Wales Island, July 23, 1821').

To prevent border incidents and at the same time to encourage trade and friendly relations, 'our only rational object of policy hereafter in relation to the Siamese should be to allay their jealousy of our ultimate views ... by striving to cultivate a friendly understanding with the Court and its provincial governors in our neighborhood' (*Foreign Committee*, no. 671, 'Letter from Lord Amherst to Governor of Prince of Wales Island, July 23, 1821').

This exchange is reminiscent of many border problems that ended, despite the cautions of Calcutta and London to the local officials. That this did not happen in Tenasserim with a drive against Siam, was only partly because of the restraints imposed by Calcutta. The internal situation in Siam, along with the French presence in Southeast Asia, turned British interest back towards Burma itself (Klein 1968).

It is hard to say how much significance these acquisitions along the eastern coast of the Bay of Bengal had for India. The whole of the bay was now fringed by Indian territory, making the Government of India what it had never been before, a Southeast Asian power. This statement presupposed the correctness of the interpretation of George Coedes, that the Indian cultural presence in Southeast Asia was not the result of political control (Coedes 1968). But the involvement was always curiously formal, and the area did not generate any of the same interest in India as did the connection with Central Asia through the northwest, despite the large Indian migration into Southeast Asia. Lord William Bentinck summed up the generally ambiguous attitude to India when he wrote in 1829, shortly after becoming Governor General, that 'there must always be an apprehension whether these provinces while they divert a portion of our force from the general defense of our Empire may not subject us to the additional risk of war with our new and uncivilized neighbors' (*Foreign Committee*, no. 671, 887, 'Minute of Lord William Bentinck, February 19, 1829'). It was not until 1833 that the annexation of Tenasserim was finally accepted by the Court of Directors (Banerjee 1964, 353).

In addition to the coastal annexations, the war with Burma brought large new area under Indian control along the eastern frontier north of the old Bengal district of Chittagong. In the Treaty of Yandabo, these annexations were defined in a negative fashion: 'The king of Ava renounces all claims upon, and will abstain from all future interference with, the principality of Assam and its dependencies, and also with the contiguous petty states of Cachar and Jyntea.' Beyond this exclusion of Burmese influence, there was no agreement as to the actual political arrangements for the area. The great increase in expense for defence of the new territories, which were generally not very productive and returned little new revenue, was one of the main arguments against their acquisition.

The most interesting solution to this problem came from Scott, who urged the establishment of military colonies in the temperate hill zones (*Lord William Bentick Papers*, no. 2791, 'Letter from David Scott to Lord William Bentick, July 21, 1830'). British troops could be settled in an area like the Khasi Hills, and be given military service in return for their land. Nothing came of his proposal, but it is one of the very few examples of serious thought being given to the creation in India of a resident British military class. At the outbreak of the invasion, Scott had issued a proclamation announcing that the Burmese who had invaded Assam, slaughtering 'Brahmins and women and cows', were to be driven out and in their place a government would be established 'adapted to your wants, and calculated to promote the happiness of all classes' (*Foreign Department*, no. 662, 173–4, 'Proclamation to the People of Assam'; Wilson 1827, 35). But Scott already had doubts about the wisdom of attempting to restore the ruling family in control of the whole of Assam, and it was soon decided to bring Lower Assam—the valley areas to the west of Bishnath—under direct British control.

The rest of the valley was restored to a member of the Ahom dynasty in 1833 but was annexed in 1838. The hill areas between Burma and the valley were left in control of tribal chieftains who agreed to maintain peace with the British territories; the hill areas to both sides of the Brahmaputra were not concerned in these transactions (McKenzie 1884, 5). In the other direction, Manipur was brought into the circle of protected states, with the Indian government being given the right to station troops there against Burmese intrusions (43). As for a border where Burma and Bengal did meet, in the hills beyond Cachar and Chittagong, the watershed seemed to provide a wholly satisfactory line. A few years after the Treaty of Yandabo when Lord William Bentinck was sending a mission to Burma, he warned them that there was no need to meddle with any border questions, as 'the mere fact of the streams running towards the Irrawaddy or to the Burrampooter [Brahmaputra] sufficiently marking the right of the lands through which they travel [*sic*]' (*Foreign Miscellaneous Reports*, no 261, 'Minute by Bentinck June 20, 1831'). This is one of the earliest references to the watershed as an Indian frontier, which was to receive its most vigorous statement eighty years later on the McMahon Line. There is no evidence that the Burmese in 1831, any more than the Chinese in 1914, shared this almost mystic fate in the watershed as a determinant of borders.

The Burmese War by no means established the eastern frontier: the annexation of Burma itself took sixty years, and along the rest of the new frontier there were few years where an agreed boundary could be found. But all the main lines of frontier advance had now been laid down, and commitments made that would be fulfilled during the next century. These acquisitions in 1824 were not the product of impulse. The annexation of Assam in some form had been urged by local Company officials since the early 1790s, and rejected then and later by Calcutta and London. In the case of Manipur, the first treaty of the Company with a country on the borders of India had been with it in 1762: it had not been put into effect, but its provisions were not unlike those made in 1833 and 1834. Even the advance into Burma was an echo of the events of 1759 when the English merchants were massacred at the Burmese port of Negrais, when the Company had not been strong enough to take revenge. The expansion of British rule on the eastern frontier, as elsewhere, was thus neither very rapid nor planned. It is true that at no time was there a policy of frontier expansion laid down either in London or Calcutta, except the proscription in the 1784 Act of all acts of conquest. But within the Company's administration there were always those who argued, and, what is more important, worked on the frontier itself, and then ratified in Calcutta and London after events had forced a decision. Belief in expanding imperialism planned and directed from the metropolitan centres is possible in this instance only if one concentrates on the materials relating to final decision and to justification of acts that had already taken place.

The passing of the Charter Act by Parliament in 1833 confirming the Company's administrative control in India for another twenty years is a significant landmark in the making of modern India. The change in name of the chief official in the Company's administration from 'Governor General of the Presidency of Fort William in Bengal'—the title he had held since the Regulating Act of 1773—to 'Governor General of India' was more than a formality; it was evidence of the change that had taken place in the power structure in India.

Up to the end of the eighteenth century, Bengal had remained what it essentially was in 1765 at the time of the transfer of the diwani: one Indian power among many. Beginning with Wellesley's administration, the multi-state system of eighteenth-century India had been replaced with the overwhelming predominance of the Bengal-based British power. The expansion and definition of external frontiers had made the Government of Bengal into the Government of India. The old presidencies of Madras and Bombay, which had retained some measure of autonomy, were brought under complete control of the Governor General. Now they were not, as the viceroyalties and provinces of previous Indian empires has been, reduplications of the central authority, linked to the imperial institutions largely through the governor, but integral units of a central authority. Where there was no actual administrative control, as in Central India and Rajputana, the princes had been brought into the new structure through an acceptance of British paramountcy. Outwardly, their status was not unlike that enjoyed by their counterparts, and in many cases, their lineal predecessors, under the Mughals; but in fact it was quite different. They were not, as under the Mughals, imperial appointees, part of the central administrative structure, deriving their status from their position as military commanders and revenue officials. Under the new system, the princes had more of the symbols but less of the substance of power, with pressure continually being exerted to bring their administration in line with that existing under the Government of India. By 1833 the multi-state system still existed only in the areas of the Punjab under Ranjit Singh's control and in an attenuated form, in Sind. Beyond them was Afghanistan and Central Asia, occupying analogous political positions as Nepal and Burma on the eastern frontier. The definition of their relationships with the Government of India, which formally came into existence with the Charter Act of 1833, was to be the dominant theme in frontier history during the next thirty years.

Bibliography

Aitchison, Charles Umpherston. 1829. *East India Company*, vol. II.

———. 1892. *Lord Lawrence*. Ann Arbor: University of Michigan Press.

———. 1912. *A Collection of Treaties, Engagements, and Sanads Relating to India and Neighbouring Countries*. Calcutta: Government of India.

——— (ed.). 1876–1933. *A Collection of Treaties, Engagements, and Sanads Relating to India and Neighbouring Countries* (with Index compiled by Manuel Belletty); revised edition, 7 vols; 3rd edition, 11 vols; 4th edition 13 vols; 5th edition, 14 vols. Calcutta.

Amherst, William Pitt. 1824. 'Indian and Colonial Intelligence'. *The Oriental Herald: and Journal of General Literature*, vol. 2.

———. 1825. 'Papers Laid before Parliament'. *The Oriental Herald: and Journal of General Literature*, vol. 5.

Atkinson, Edwin T. 1884. 'The Himalayan Districts of North Western Provinces of India'. In *The Gazetteer*, vol. XI. Allahabad: Northwest Provinces and Oudh Government Press.

Aung, Maung Htin. 1965. *The Stricken Peacock: Anglo-Burmese Relations 1752–1948*. The Hague: Martinus Nijhoff.

Banerjee, A.C. 1964. *The Eastern Frontier of British India 1784–1826*. Calcutta: A. Mukherjee.

Bhuyan, Suryya Kumar. 1972. *Anglo-Assamese Relations 1771–1826*. Gauhati: Lawyers Book Stall.

———, ed. 1932. *Asamar Padya Buranji*. Gauhati: Department of Historical and Antiquarian Studies.

Blackwood, William. 1857. 'Our Indian Empire'. *Blackwood's Edenborough Magazine*, vol. 82.

Bonomy, James. 1830. *A Memorandum on the Northwestern Frontier of British India*, vol. 205. New Delhi: Government of India National Archives.

Bowring, Lewin. 1899. *Haidar Alí and Tipú Sultán, and the Struggle with the Musalmán Powers of the South*. Oxford: Clarendon Press.

Brittlebank, Kate. 1999. *Tipu Sultan's Search for Legitimacy*. Delhi: Oxford University Press.

Burnes, James. 1831. *A Narrative of a Visit to the Court of Sinde*. Edinburgh: Stark.

Coedes, George. 1968. *The Indianized States of Southeast Asia*. Honolulu: University of Hawaii Press.

Colebrooke, Sir Edward. 1884. *Life of the Honourable Mountstuart Elphinstone*, vol. 1. London: John Murray.

Cox, J.L. 1824. *Papers Respecting the Nepaul War*. The British Library: East India Company.

A Descriptive List of Vakil Reports Addressed to the Rulers of Jaipur, vol. 1, in Persian. 1967. Bikaner: Rajasthan State Archives, Government Press.

Elphinstone, Mountstuart. 1819. *An Account of the Kingdom of Cabul*, 2 vols. London: Longmans.

Embree, Ainslie T. 1960. *Charles Grant and British Rule in India*. New York: Columbia University Press.

Farooqui, Mian. 1941. *British Relations with the Cis-Sutlej States*. Lahore: Punjab Government Record Publications.

Foreign Department Papers Respecting the Nepaul War, 1815. New Delhi: Government of India National Archives.

Foreign Department Secret and Separate Proceedings, 1798, 1808, 1809. New Delhi: National Archives, Government of India.

'Foreign Political Consultations 1596–1859'. *A Descriptive List of the Vakil Reports Addressed to the Rulers of Jaipur*, vol. 1 (in Persian). 1967. Rajasthan State Archives

Foreign Political Consultations and Miscellaneous Records of the Foreign Department, 1596–1859. New Delhi: National Archives, Government of India.

Foreign Political Proceedings. 1796? New Delhi: National Archives, Government of India.

Foreign Secretary Correspondence, June 12, 1800, number 38. New Delhi: Government of India National Archives.

Forrest, George, ed. 1884. *Selections from the Minutes and Other Official Writings of the Honourable Mountstuart Elphinstone*. London: Richard Bentley.

Grewal, Jagtar Singh. 1980. *Maharaja Ranjit Singh and His Times*. Punjab: Guru Nanak Dev University.

Hall, D.G.E. 1945. *Europe and Burma*. London: Oxford University Press.

Harvey, G.E. 1967. *History of Burma*. London: Frank Cass.

Holdich, Sir Thomas. 1916. *Political Frontiers and Border Making*. London: Macmillan.

Hutchins, Francis G. 1967. *The Illusion of Permanence*. Princeton: Princeton University Press.

Huttenback, Robert A. 1962. *British Relations with Sind, 1799–1843*. Berkeley: University of California Press.

Harrington, Jack. 2010. *Sir John Malcolm and the Creation of British India*. New York: Palgrave Macmillan.

Hasrat, Bikrama Jit. 1968. *Anglo-Sikh Relations, 1799–1849*. Hoshiarpur, Hasrat Publication.

Heatley, D.P. 1894.'British Protectorates and Jurisdiction'. *Scottish Geographical Magazine*, vol. 10.

Jenkins, Herbert. 1914. *The Wellesley Papers: The Life and Correspondence of Richard Colley Wellesley*. London: Herbert Jenkins Limited.

Kautilya. 1960. *Arthashastra*, translated by R. Shamasastry. Mysore: Mysore Publishing House.

Kaye, John William. 1854. *The Life and Correspondence of Charles, Lord Metcalfe*, vol. 1. London: Richard Bentley.

———. 1856. 'Malcolm's Journal'. In *The Life and Correspondence of Major-General Sir John Malcolm*, vol. 1. London: Smith Elder and Company.

Klein, Ira. 1968. 'The Diplomacy of British Imperialism in Asia, 1880–1914'. Unpublished PhD dissertation, Columbia University.

Lord William Bentick Papers. 1733–71. Nottingham: University of Nottingham.

Lyall, Sir Alfred. 1891. 'Frontiers and Protectorates'. *The Nineteenth Century*, vol. 174.

Malcolm, Sir John. 1826. *A Political History of India*, vol. 1. London: John Murray.

Martin, M. 1836a. The Despatches, of the Marquess Wellesley K. G. During His Administration In India London: John Murray

———. 1836b. 'To Sir J. H. Craig'. The Despatches, Minutes and Correspondence of the Marques of Wellesley During His Administration in India, vol 1.

Martin, Montgomery. 1837. *Despatches, Minutes and Correspondence of the Marquis Wellesley*, vol. 1. London: W. H. Allen.

McKenzie, Alexander. 1884. *History of the Relations of the Government with the Hill Tribes of the North East Frontier of Bengal*. Calcutta: Home Department Pres.

Memorandum on Native States in India, 1909, vol. II. 1909. Calcutta: Superintendent of Government Printing.

Metcalfe, Charles Theophilus. 1858. *The Life and Correspondence of Lord Metcalfe*. London: Smith and Elder Company.

Panigrahi, D.N. 1968. *Charles Metcalfe in India*. Delhi: Munshiram Manoharlal.

Pearce, Robert Rouiere. 1846. *Memoirs and Correspondence of the Most Noble Richard Marquess Wellesley*. London: R. Bentley.

Phillimore, R.H. 1950. *Historical Records of the Survey of India*, multiple volumes. Dehra Dun: Survey of India.

Poona Residency Correspondence, vol. I. 1936. New Delhi: Government of India National Archives.

Pottinger, Henry. 1816. *Travels in Beloochistan and Sinde: Accompanied by a Geographical and Historical Account of Those Countries; with a Map*. London: Longman, Hurst, Rees, Orme, and Brown.

Prinsep, H.T. 1825. *History of the Political and Military Transactions during the Administration of the Marquess of Hastings*. London: Kingsbury.

Rajah of Nepaul. 1824.'Instructions Given by the Rajah of Nepaul to Chunder Sekker Opadeea for Negotiating with the British Government'. In *Papers Regarding the Administration of the Marquis of Hastings.*

Ramakant. 1968. *Indo-Nepalese Relations.* Delhi: S. Chand.

Renick, M.S. 1987. *Lord Wellesley and the Indian States.* Agra: Arvind Vivek Prakashan.

Rennell, James. 1788. *Memoir of a Map of Hindoostan.* London: M. Brown.

Risley, H.H. 1894.'Introduction'. In *The Gazetteer of Sikkim.* Calcutta: Bengal Secretariat.

Roberts, P.E. 1929. *India under Wellesley.* London: George Bell & Sons.

———. 1967. *History of British India under the Company and the Crown.* London: Oxford University Press.

Sanwal, B.D. 1965. *Nepal and the East India Company.* Bombay: Asia Publishing House.

Sardesai, G.S. 1935.'Marathi Riyasat'. In *A History of Modern India,* vol. 2.

Sardesai, Govind Sakharam. 1946. *New History of the Marathas: Sunset over Maharashtra, 1772–1848,* vol. III. Bombay: Phoenix Publications.

Sarkar, Jadunath and G.S. Sardesai (ed.). 1936–51. *English Records of Maratha History: Poona Residency Correspondence,* 15 vols.

Sen, S.N. (ed.). n.d. *Prachin Bangala Patra-Sankalon.* Calcutta: Calcutta University.

Singh, Harbans. 1980. *Maharaja Ranjit Singh.* New Delhi: Sterling.

Thomson, Edward, and G.T. Garratt. 1934. *Rise and Fulfilment of British Rule in India.* London: Macmillan.

Torrens, William McCullagh. 1880. *The Marquess Wellesley: Architect of Empire.* London: Chatto and Windus.

Varma, Birendra. 1968. *English East India Company and the Afghans.* Calcutta: Punthi Pustak.

Vogel, J.P., and J. Hutchison. 1933. *History of the Punjab Hill States,* 2 vols. Lahore: Superintendent, Government Printing.

The Wellesley Papers: The Life and Correspondence of Richard Colley Wellesley. 1914. London: Herbert Jenkins.

Wellesley, Marquess Richard. 1836. *The Despatches, Minutes, and Correspondence of the Marquess Wellesley.* London: G.J. Murray.

Wilson, Horace Hayman. 1827. *Documents Illustrative of the Burmese War.* Calcutta: Government Gazette, by G.H. Huttmann.

4 *Frontiers and the Mountain Wall, 1833–57*

During the first 70 years of British territorial control in India, the northwest mountain perimeter, which dominated the foreign policy of the Government of India in the late nineteenth century, was of little consequence. The mountain ranges to the east and northeast of Bengal had attracted much more attention, although even there the general assumption was that the foothills defined the limits of expansion. The deep thrust into the Himalayas between the Sutlej and the Kali rivers at the conclusion of the war with Nepal was an important exception, but because of political conditions in Tibet as well as the physical nature of the terrain, no immediate political consequences followed from its annexation. In the east, the extension of political control over Cachar, Jaintia, and Manipur was not so much concerned with the special problems involved with mountain frontiers as a completion of the plan to exclude Burmese influence in the whole area from the Bay of Bengal into Assam. The settlement after the Burmese war that brought this territory under Indian control left untouched the future of the hill country to the north of the Brahmaputra as well as the unknown country in the tangle of hills beyond the extreme eastern end of the Assam valley.

In the northwest, the situation was somewhat different. The relation of the new British power with its base in Bengal to the mountain areas of the northwest had been raised at an early stage of the establishment of British power, first by the Afghan invasions of North India and later by the threat of a French intrusion during the Napoleonic wars. With the cessation of these specific threats, the northwest mountain areas tended to disappear from official concern, for the Company's government, even after Wellesley's conquests, remained largely an eastern Gangetic power. The acquisition of Delhi had, however, made a basic change in power relationships within India, even though this was not immediately discerned by either Calcutta or London. With the advance of the frontier to the Sutlej, involvement with the politics of western Punjab and the Indus valley, and through these areas with the northwest mountains, was a foregone conclusion. The British would discover what conquerors coming from the northwest had always known: the mountains are a transitional zone into India, not a barrier. Power in the past had generally flown downward from the mountains into the plains, finding ready access through the passes after the establishments of bases on the Afghan plateau; now the movement was to be in the reverse direction.

By 1833, at the time of the formal creation of a Government of India, this process was already under way, with Lord William Bentinck's administration showing a renewed interest, after the hiatus that had followed the activity during the Napoleonic wars, in the search for frontiers in Sind and Punjab. During the next thirty-five years—a period defined by the India Act of 1833 at the one extreme and at the other, the ending of Sir John Lawrence's administration (when relations with Afghanistan changed considerably)—the frontiers reached their approximate limits but were not very precisely demarcated nor was there even a general agreement as to what the limits of actual territorial control would be. During the next period, roughly from actual 1870 to 1914, the first actual demarcation of boundaries in the mountains, as distinct from the demarcation along the mountain edge that had taken place after the war with Nepal, was carried out. Even then much remained vague, but as far as British power in India was concerned, this marked the end of over a century of debate and negotiation.

The explanation that has seemed most satisfactory to historians, as it was for contemporaries, of the shift in interest that took place in the 1830s toward the northwest is that it was the product of fear of Russian expansion through Central Asia towards India. Whether this fear was a cause or an effect of the Russophobia, which was a characteristic attitude in Great Britain at the time, is uncertain, although the fact that it was more pervasive and dominant in official thinking in India than it was in Britain suggests, if not an Indian origin, at least one that was peculiarly relevant to the Indian situation. In the formulation and execution of British foreign policy, Russian intentions were one among many factors that had to be considered, while in India Russia was the only great power that had to be taken into serious consideration throughout most of the nineteenth century. It is noteworthy that many of those in Great Britain who were early advocates of a policy that would prevent Russian expansion were men with Indian connections such as Wellington, whose personal and family connections with India were intense and of long duration, or Ellenborough, who was president of the Board of Control, the Cabinet's link with the Indian administration (see Norris 1967). The way in which fear of Russia, or perhaps more exactly, the desire to prevent Russian expansion into areas where the Government of India was considered to have special interests, preoccupied the thinking of officials in India is easy enough to document; the printed literature is vast, and the unpublished records provide almost inexhaustible sources for an explication of 'the Great Game in Asia' (Davis 1927; Ewans 2004).

But despite the seemingly overwhelming evidence for giving fear of a Russian invasion the dominant place in any explanation of the foreign policy of the Government of India, and hence of the definition of frontiers, this was not the only, perhaps not even the major, determinant in the fascination the northwest exercised over so many minds. Some importance must be given to the old expectation for trade through the mountains to Central Asia. As has already been emphasized, this expectation was a lively element in the efforts by Warren Hastings and his contemporaries to forge links with Tibet, and it was given renewed life after the close of the Napoleonic wars as England sought new markets, especially for cotton goods (Redford 1934, 108–26; Ingram 1980). That later knowledge proved these hopes illusory does not, however, detract from their reality. When Lord William Bentinck, as Governor General, spoke as late as 1831 of the need for information about the countries between the Indus and Caspian 'in aid of war or commerce' (Bentinck 1831a; Ludlow 1858). This equal emphasis on the two factors of trade and defence against Russia was probably justified. For men like Bentinck, to explain imperial territorial expansion in terms of expanding trade was not to give away a guilty secret, but to provide it with a kind of moral justification.

Policy relating to frontier expansion and trade was given historical continuity at this point by the appointment of Lord Glenelg as president of the Board of Control. He was the son of Charles Grant, who, as a dominant power in the Company for thirty years, had opposed all territorial advances, arguing that British interests could be best served through trade, not conquest (Embree 1962). Echoing that position, Glenelg now reminded the Indian government: 'our motive is to extend our commerce, and only our commerce, along the waters of the Indus' (Norris 1967, 46). But this warning was made with some pessimism, for Glenelg, perhaps recalling the many speeches in which his father had denounced the course of expansion, noted that war and conquest 'seem almost invariably to follow the extensions of our commercial interests with the natives of the East'.

An important aspect of the Government of India's preoccupations with Russian expansion in Central Asia was fear of the effect it might have on India. References to 'public opinion' are few in state papers meant for public circulation, as the Government of India neither then nor later wished to give any indication that it was responsive to public criticism; but, in fact, there was widespread anxiety not to arouse in any way the antagonism of the people. This was not, as is sometimes suggested, an attitude that developed as a result of the 1857 uprisings. The Company's opposition to missionary work, for example, was largely based on the fear of a hostile reaction in India (Embree 1962, 239–52). The great danger, according to a Government of India memorandum in 1831, was the 'moral effect' Russia might have on the people and princes of India. Continual talk of the Russian danger, it was feared, might tempt Indians to a reassessment of British power and the possibilities of seeking assistance from Russia (Bentinck 1831). The British assumed that many people, especially in the princely states, were waiting for an opportunity to undermine their rule, and nothing was more likely to provide this than an awareness by Indian powers of the presence of a hostile country on the frontiers. So, the implications of the Russian advance into central Asia were political in the deepest sense. What was urgently needed, in modern terminology, was a policy of containment.

There is still another factor in northwest frontier policy that must be taken seriously, even though it is more intangible, and less amenable to definition and documentation. This is 'the challenge of the frontier'— the attitude, briefly noted in the first chapter, of which Curzon in Great Britain and Turner in the United States of America were the historians and eulogists. 'The challenge of the frontier' is a jejune explanation, but it at least suggests something of the compelling appeal enticed by unexplored regions, particularly mountains, on the periphery of known territory. Two quite separate facets of the meaning of this challenge are recognizable in the Indian situation, one personal, related to the individuals involved, the other political, part of the historical experience of the Government of India as an Indian power. The personal element included the appeal that the unknown and dangerous has always made to some people. Scarcely separable from this was the impulse towards geographical exploration that remained an abiding British passion. Intermingled with both was the shrewd assessment that reports from areas such as Afghanistan and Central Asia might prove useful in advancing one's career (Phillimore 1945–50).

The element rooted in the Indian historical experience is more complex and tenuous: it depends upon the argument that strong powers in India move towards completion of territorial control of the whole subcontinent. Boundaries of Indian kingdoms, it was argued earlier, were always essentially unstable, with the possession of power carrying with it almost a compulsion to expansion (Phillimore 1945–50). In the 1830s, as in the 1760s, there were strong arguments for a policy of consolidation rather than expansion, with men such as Metcalfe arguing that the Sutlej and the Indus should mark the limits of westward and northward expansion (Kaye 1854, vol. II). But there was always a sense of incompleteness of empire, of a need to find frontiers where power could rest with the assurance that it had reached its logical limits. The mountain wall seemed a far more certain line of definition than did the rivers of the Punjab plains. Even before they were reached, it was argued that the frontier must be found beyond the mountains, or in the great plateaus beyond.

In the search for frontiers in the northwest, these four determinants—the fear of Russia, the hope for trade, the fascination of the unknown, and the impulse for expansion built into the Indian historical experience—were intertwined. They reinforced each other, but very often in official writing one was frequently emphasized to the exclusion of the others. This was the Russian danger, which seemed to provide the clearest justification for either actual territorial conquest or radical political intrusion. In fact, the more potent impulse was coming from within India itself, from the almost compulsive movement to make political control march towards what were conceived to be the natural frontiers of an Indian government.

The search for a 'buffer state' in the northwest was the result. With his long experience in Delhi, Metcalfe had argued that the Sutlej was the true northern frontier of India, with the Sikh kingdom of Ranjit Singh, and to a lesser extent the territories of the Amirs of Sind, providing all that was needed by way of a buffer. But by the 1830s, the durability of the Sikh kingdom was being questioned, and the political structures of Sind were regarded as confused anachronisms. Thus, young Alexander Burnes, on his historic voyage up the Indus in 1831 at a time when Ranjit Singh's power was at its height, shrewdly suggested that with his death his kingdom would collapse. The very source of Ranjit's strength—the feuds between his chieftains and their complete dependence on him—meant there would be no strong group to hold power after him, and the ties with the Army were purely personal (Burnes 1831). The obvious answer was to look beyond them to the Afghan country, to find in the mountains and plateaus a barrier to the Indian plains through forming connections that would, in Sir Alfred Lyall's terms, create a buffer state that would be placed under 'political taboo as far as concerns rival powers whose hostility may be serious' (Lyall 1891, 313), and which by reciprocal understanding would be guaranteed against foreign aggression. There were two possible general lines of action that might be taken in the creation of a client state: through subsidies and guarantees to make the acceptance of client status worthwhile to an incumbent ruler; or overthrow a ruler and replace him with someone with claims to legitimate succession. The decision was finally made in favour of the second expedient, but it was preceded by a decade of activity and debate in which those other determinants of frontier policy—trade and the challenge of the unknown—reacted with the policy of containment.

Reliable political and geographical information was needed before any major decisions could be made on frontier policy, and an attempt to meet this need was made through the famous episode of the gift of dray horses to Ranjit Singh. The belief that the Indus was navigable, and that it could provide an entrance into the heart of Central Asia, had been urged for a decade, but surveys of the river were impossible because of the distrust of the Amirs of Sind, through whose territory it passed; like Lord Glenelg, they were aware that commercial enterprise had often been followed by war. It was apparently Lord Amherst who suggested as a pretext for a survey that Ranjit Singh be sent a present of horses up the Indus. Henry Pottinger, who had been the Company's agent in Sind, added the suggestion that the gift should include a large carriage; since this would be too big a package to send by land, the Amirs might not be so suspicious (Malcolm 1880). No one was fooled, of course, by this elaborate game, except perhaps the Calcutta government itself, who had little way of checking on the information supplied by Burnes, the young lieutenant in charge of the expedition up the Indus (see Davis 1927, 23–6). The Amirs objected to the barges being sent up the Indus, but they did not possess the power to oppose the thinly veiled reminders that only British power stood between them and their enemies—the Afghans and the Sikhs. As for Ranjit Singh, he was as anxious as the Amirs that the British should not gain detailed information about the Indus and the country beyond it; but having made a career of accommodation and compromise, he was not disposed to raise too many objections to the new British plans for Indus navigation and commerce.

The schemes for Indus navigation in the early 1830s have a special place in the development of the Indian administration, for they provide one of the most striking examples of the change from the rather haphazard methods of the early period to the systematic compilation of reports. In this emphasis on investigation and report, it is tempting to see the influences of Benthamite utilitarianism working through Lord William Bentinck, although this aspect of British intellectual impact on Indian administration has probably been somewhat exaggerated. The two major reports came from Burnes and Charles Trevelyan, with Burnes's based on his voyage up the Indus with Ranjit Singh's horses and

Trevelyan's on information available in the Calcutta secretariat (Burnes 1831; Trevelyan 1835). That both reports were optimistic about the chances of improved trade, the feasibility of using the Indus as a great internal waterway, and the possibility of checking Russian expansion in Central Asia has led some writers, in the light of later developments, to accuse Burnes and Trevelyan of being irresponsible, if not deliberately misleading. But their reports, especially Burnes's, are cautions, emphasizing how partial their information was, and how little was known in detail of either the geography or politics of the regions beyond the Indus. Both drew heavily upon older accounts, with Herodotus and Arrian being frequently evoked. No one who reads the memoirs of the British in India can miss the continual appeal to classical experience. Schoolboy memories of Alexander and of Roman expansion fed the imagination of the young men who looked with restless ambition to the unknown world beyond the Indus.

Burnes especially was drawn to the parallels with Alexander's voyage as he made his way up the Indus; consciously or not, he was linking himself with the romantic dream of Western destiny in Asia. It is at this point that personal involvement and private ambition mingle with the purposes of the state, distorting the weight of evidence to favour the idea of the necessity and possibility of extending the power of the Government of India beyond the Indus. Burnes was perfectly aware, for example, that trade on the Indus was negligible, but he believed this was because the banks were in the control of 'barbarous princes' whose extortions prevented commerce. He knew the Indus was shallow, with constantly shifting channels, but he was convinced that steamships built on the pattern of the flat-bottomed river boats could sail from the Delta to Lahore (Burnes 1831; McCulloch 1849, 23).

While Burnes was fascinated by his role as an explorer retracing, in the reverse direction, the splendours of Alexander's conquests, Trevelyan, the bureaucrat, was no less entranced by the possibilities of expansion. With some sophistry and a considerable degree of historical inaccuracy, he defaced his summary of trans-Indus trade with a careful assertion that the idea for penetration into Central Asia had originated wholly with the authorities in London in 1829. This emphasis is a reminder, in the words of a modern sociologist, that 'social reaction is always influenced by an audience', with the discussion going into decision-making never being just linear between the actual participants (Caplow 1968, v). The audience in the 1830s, as the decision was being made on the location of the frontier, while a relatively restricted one, was heterogeneous. There were the members of Indian administration in London, including the directors of the Company whose influence was dwindling but who were still not unimportant, and the Board of Control, the link with the British government. The actual decision would be made by the Governor General, based on the information coming in from the frontier, sometimes in the form of direct reports from field agents, but more often filtered through the resident at Delhi, the political agents at Lahore, and executives such as Trevelyan in Calcutta.

Information on the northwestern frontier did not come only from Burnes and Trevelyan. Journeys had been made into the area before, and all through the 1830s new facts and speculations met the demand created by the debate over the location of the frontier and the extent to which the Indian government should involve itself in the regions beyond the Indus. The most prestigious of the Company's servants in India, Charles Metcalfe, deplored this interest. He remembered and regretted the enthusiasm of youth which inspired him, twenty years earlier when he had been sent as the envoy to Ranjit Singh's court, to dream of being the agent for expansion into Central Asia. Now, he argued, 'We could do no better than by avoiding forced intimacy, for either our character is so bad, or weaker states are naturally so jealous of the stronger, or our habits are so distasteful, that no native state desires connection with us' (quoted in Hasrat 1968, 123, 'Metcalfe, Minute of October 25, 1830'). But this attitude presupposed a balance of political forces that had vanished with the dominance of British power. It was not a question of 'forced intimacy', but of deciding what relations were essential for the interests of the Government of India, or, as Lord William Bentinck had put it, of relating 'a new era of civilization, happiness, and of blessing to this great Indian world' (Bentinck 1831). In his frontier policy, no less than in such dramatic social measures as the abolition of sati, Bentinck was the authentic spokesman for the new imperialism that combined benevolent paternalism, with a belief in radical social change, and expansionism in one strange amalgam.

The overwhelming weight of opinion inclined towards Afghanistan as the vital area for Indian interests, with the fortress city of Herat at the western end of the Afghan plateau becoming the focus of attention. All invasions of India, it was believed, had come through the passes guarded by Herat into the Afghan plateau, and the threat in the 1830s was that it might fall to Persia, which was coming under Russian domination. This idea that Herat was 'the key to India' occupies an extraordinary place in the thinking of the time, being accepted as a truism demanding no proof. The British agent at Tehran summed up its importance in apocalyptic warning: 'If Persia should succeed in taking Herat, while Russia subdues Khiva, and overawes Bokhara into submission ... it would be hopeless for us to attempt to preserve a footing in Afghanistan or in Persia. Both these countries, in short Central Asia, would be lost to us' (quoted in Norris 1967, 176, 'Sir John McNeil to Lord Palmerston, June 25, 1838').

Criticism of this attitude is easy: the British had never had Central Asia, so could not lose it; the importance of Herat was exaggerated; the influence of Russia in Persia was oversimplified. But reality, at least what is significant, is not what the historian sees later, but what seemed to those involved in the making of decisions as both necessary and prudent, and by the end of the 1830s there was no real question in Calcutta that necessity demanded intervention in Afghanistan that would place the effective frontiers of India at Herat, not at the Sutlej or the Indus. The fear of Russia was fed by reports from India, not from London, which is clear from the hundreds of intelligence reports, almost all emphasizing the influence of Russia throughout Central Asia and the Middle East that were sent from agents, both British and Indian, employed by the Government of India (see, for example, *Foreign Department Political Proceedings*, nos 40–7 [11 February 1835]; nos 29–31 [10 August 1835]). The activities of the best-known Indian agent of the period, Mohan Lal of Delhi, are particularly interesting (see *Political Correspondence*, 1834–6, nos 104–5 [December 31, 1834] and no. 7 [December 5, 1836]; and the expurgated extracts from his journal, Lal 1846).

'I presume to state my opinion,' an agent wrote about the territory between Herat and Kabul, 'that the occupation of these countries is an absolute necessity if there be any danger of an attack on the British possessions from the west or northwest' (Pottinger 1839). The agent at Herat, Sir Henry Rawlinson, used the magic phrase: 'Herat was the key to India.' It and Balkh must be the outworks of the northwest frontier, for there was no other way to prevent a Russian or a Persian advance

(Todd 1839). Burnes, who had been appointed commercial agent at Kabul, filled his reports with accounts of Herat as a trade entrepôt for Persia, Russia, India, and Central Asia. If it fell into Russian hands, he argued, India and Great Britain would lose all hope of participation (Burnes 1839).

Making Afghanistan a buffer state required a ruler who would be at once independent within his country and loyal to the Government of India. That these requirements were contradictory was recognized at times but given the compulsion to make Afghanistan 'the outworks of the northwest frontier', it was hoped that some solution would be found. The obvious choice for a ruler who fulfilled the requirements was Dost Muhammad Khan, who had maintained his rule at Kabul since 1826 and had made a number of overtures towards the British. Burnes was the most enthusiastic proponent of an alliance with Dost Muhammad, arguing that he preferred 'the sympathy and friendly officers of the British to all these offers, however alluring they may seem, from Persia or from Russia' (Kaye 2015, 119). He was, however, ruler of Kabul, not of Afghanistan. The area around Kandahar was in the hands of another member of his family, while the Herat district was controlled by the Sadozai clan, who had been the rulers of most of Afghanistan before the rise of Dost Muhammad and his clan, the Barakzai. In the west, the Afghans had lost Peshawar and its fertile valley to the Sikhs in 1834. It was this last fact that was crucial in the Government of India's relations with Dost Muhammad, for the loss of one of his most important cities had made him the bitter enemy of Ranjit Singh, and an alliance with him would have necessitated a break with the Sikhs, for his price would have been the restoration of Peshawar.

An alternative solution seemed increasingly attractive: an alliance with Shah Shuja, an exiled claimant to the Afghan Kingdom who had obligations both to Ranjit Singh and the British. A member of the Sadozai family, he had taken refuge with the Sikhs after being driven from Kabul by his enemies, the Barakzai. He had been a useful pawn for Ranjit Singh in his own attacks on Afghan territory beyond the Indus, including Peshawar, although the British had always refused to support him in any attempt to recover his throne (*Foreign Department* 1837, nos 11–24, 'Governor-General to Captain Wade'). The decision of Lord Auckland to use him for the establishment of a buffer state in Afghanistan rather than the actual ruler, Dost Muhammad, was based largely on the information supplied by the political agents of the Government of India in the Punjab. Auckland's dependence on reports from the Punjab agents is made especially clear in correspondence between the Government of India and Claude Wade (*Foreign Department*, 1837, nos 11–24, May 15). The case for Shah Shuja was put most forcefully by Captain Wade, who for many years had been the government's chief political agent in Ranjit Singh's territories. He agreed with Burnes and the others that the frontier of India was on the Afghan plateau, but he was convinced that its location there had to come through a strengthening of ties with the Sikh kingdom, not through their being weakened, as would follow from an alliance with Dost Muhammad. Since all the correspondence from the Kabul group passed through his hands, he was in an excellent position to counter their arguments (see Pottinger 1839; Kaye 1878, vol. I, 294). He thought that the creation of a strong Afghanistan with British help through the union of Kabul, Kandahar, and Herat was neither possible nor desirable; the feuds within the Barakzai family were too fierce, and the existence of a powerful Afghan state would be intolerable to the Persians as well as to the Sikhs. The policy of the British government should be to preserve the status quo as far as the division into three states was concerned, but to gain a foothold through supporting Shah Shuja's return to power in Kabul (Kaye 1878, 294–5).

This frontier policy was embodied in the Tripartite Treaty of 1838 between the Government of India, Ranjit Singh, and Shah Shuja, confirming for the Sikhs their possession of the trans-Indus territories including Peshawar and Kashmir, but excluding them from further advances against the Amirs of Sind. For renouncing claims to Sind as well as those to territories in the Punjab once held by the Afghans, Shah Shuja was to be recognized as ruler of Kabul and Kandahar, but not of Herat (Aitchison 1912, vol. VIII, 154). By agreeing not to enter into foreign relations without the knowledge of the Government of India or of the Sikhs, he committed himself to a close alignment with the Indian subcontinent, rather than with Central Asia. In effect, the treaty was intended to make the Afghan plateau once more what it had been under the Mughals—an integral part of Indian political life. Lord Auckland, the Governor General, was aware how high the stakes were, but he was convinced that a friendly power and intimate connection with Afghanistan, a peaceful alliance with Lahore and an established influence in Sind are objects for which some hazard may well be run' (quoted in Dodwell n.d., vol. V, 497, 'Lord Auckland to John Hobhouse, August 23, 1838'). He was insistent that Indian, not European politics, made necessary the extension of the frontiers of influence into Afghanistan, although it was obviously of importance to Great Britain that Russian dominance not be extended throughout the area (Auckland 1838).

When Auckland and others argued that the extension of the frontiers of influence into the Afghan plateau was demanded by Indian politics, they had something more in mind than the protection of the subcontinent from a Russian invasion. Throughout the 1830s, there was a constant uneasiness that an anti-British alliance might still be formed against the British. Nepal, the last genuinely independent Hindu kingdom in the subcontinent, seemed most likely to assume the role of leadership in any such attempt. This view was very forcibly expressed by Charles Trevelyan, one of the most influential members of the inner circle of the Government of India. The Nepalese, he was convinced, were 'much the most formidable enemy we have in India', and were waiting for a chance to renew hostilities (Trevelyan 1838). Numerous reports also came to Calcutta of agents moving between Kathmandu, Lahore, and the capitals of those Marathas princes who had been brought under British protection but whose courts seethed with anti-British feeling (*Foreign Department*, 1837–9, nos 11 and 12, 3 January 1834; *Foreign Office Public Correspondence*, nos 51 and 52, 22 February 1838). Even the Rajput princes, who by this time were beginning to be regarded as the most loyal of the Indian rulers, were receiving embassies from Nepal (*Foreign Department*, 1837–9, nos 35–7, 1 August 1838). On the eastern frontier, Burma was far from reconciled to the great losses she had suffered during the war. Within the territories under the direct administration of the Government of India, there were also signs of potential trouble, notably from the Muslim, groups identified by the British as Wahhabis (*Foreign Department*, 1837–9, nos 20–5 [10 July 1839]; nos 29–32 [14 August 1839]). Though these Muslim groups had no direct affiliation with the Wahhabis of Arabia, the term was applied to any Muslim group hostile to British rule and centred in the mosques both of North India and Hyderabad.

Any revival of the power of Islamic countries on the Indian border-lands would obviously inspire such groups, as well as provide possible sources of support for an uprising in India. As Brian Hodgson, the very knowledgeable agent of the Government of India, saw it, there seemed every likelihood of the border countries and the groups within India itself 'getting clubbed together against us' (*Foreign Department*, 1837–9, nos 124–8, 'Brian Hodgson to H. Prinsep, May 29 1839', 26 December 1839). Failure to act decisively on the northwest frontier, quite apart from threat of invasion, would, it was widely believed, suggest to the Indian powers that the Government of India was weak. Trevelyan summed up the implications of the situation for frontier policy: 'The snowy range of the Himalayas is the great frontier of India. We are not safe until we reach it and as an European people we ought to cling to it in order to secure our dominions in the plains' (*Broughton Papers*, MS 36,469, vol. XIV). Just as it was necessary for India's security to move into Afghanistan, so, Trevelyan argued, it was necessary to consider the whole border situation in terms of India's needs. This meant, he was convinced, a renunciation of the treaty of Sagauli in 1816 with Nepal in which Nepal had been recognized as an independent nation. This was a self-denying ordinance on the part of the Government of India, which accorded Nepal an international status it had not formerly enjoyed. Trevelyan's argument on this point is of great importance for under-standing a significant segment of official thinking in the Government of India in regard to the border nations.

Nepal was something less than a genuine nation because, according to the Trevelyan argument, the present rulers, the Gurkhas, had never been heard of until the middle of the eighteenth century, when they conquered the petty Himalayan states of the Kathmandu Valley. At the end of the century, after their defeat in the attempted invasion of Tibet, they had been forced to acknowledge Chinese supremacy, although this was rarely exercised in any direct fashion. The generosity of the Government of India at Sagauli had strengthened the Nepalese instead of weakening them, for they had lost their least defensible territories while retaining those that permitted them to build up a strong military power, independent of both China and the Government of India. The result was that 'we have an enemy in our house who is ready to stab us in the back the moment we put ourselves in a posture of defense against other enemies' (*Broughton Papers*, MS 36,469, vol. XIV). Trevelyan's solution was to find an opportunity for doing what was left undone in 1816—the complete subjugation of Nepal. China was in no position to object, and India would be left with a northern frontier of hundreds of miles of mountain boundaries safe from all attack. At the same time, the threat of an alliance between Nepal, the Burmese, Ranjit Singh, and the Marathas would be ended forever.

The internal political situation, quite as much as the fear of a Russian invasion, was thus a determining factor in the decision to extend the frontiers of influence to the borders of Persia and the Central Asian kingdom. Rightly or wrongly, it was believed in 1839 that Indian needs dictated the definition of new frontiers. Lord Auckland mobilized an army which took Kabul in July 1839, and Shah Shuja was restored to the throne which he had lost thirty years before.

Auckland's frontier policy seemed a complete success, justifying both the approval it had received from the British cabinet and the enthusiastic optimism of the chief political agent of the expedition that 'for all the fighting we are likely to have, half a brigade would be more than enough' (MacNaughten 1839; Norris 1967, 207–30). From the vantage point of Kabul, the extension of influence to Herat and beyond into Central Asia seemed easy, and there was talk of occupying the country up to the Amu river. Another idea put forward at this time was the creation under British influence of a union among the Uzbeg states of Central Asia that would be a buffer against further Russian expansion. The principal exponent of this visionary scheme was Arthur Conolly, who had made journeys into the Khanates of Central Asia, and who, as part of his programme for a united Central Asia, had written what must be the first historical work to show that the British in India had a special regard for their Muslim subjects ('Captain Arther Conolly to William MacNaughten, December 26, 1840', in MacNaughten, vol. II, no. 47). Stories had been spread among the Muslim rulers—possibly, he thought, by Hindus—that the British aimed at overthrowing them or that they had overthrown the Muslim rulers in India; so he prepared a historical sketch showing how well, in fact, Muslims in India were treated. As for the Khanates of Central Asia, the only interest the Government of India had in them was in 'the existence of strong and friendly states between its borders and the frontiers of those countries' ('Captain Arther Conolly to

William MacNaughten, December 26, 1840', in MacNaughten, vol. II, no. 47). But as Harold Nicolson said of European foreign policy, the part played by 'planned intention' is 'infrequent and adventitious', and 'seldom is the course of events determined by deliberately planned purpose' (quoted in Marshall 1954, 10).

Disaster struck in December 1841 when an uprising against Shuja Shah drove the Indian army out of Kabul, utterly destroying it as it retreated towards the Khyber Pass. Auckland's reputation was also destroyed, for he was the official spokesman for an adventure in imperialism doomed to failure because of its basic presuppositions but made more contemptible by bad planning and incompetence. 'Jesus of Nazareth, what disgusting stuff is this!' was the comment of General Charles Napier, the conqueror of Sind, on an attempt by one of the officers of the campaign to justify the losses suffered by the Indian army. 'With the exception of women, you were all a set of sons of bitches' (quoted in Norris 1967, 450, Napier's 'Marginal Comments on Vincent Eyre's *Military Operations at Kabul*'). Less profanely, this was also the interpretation of Sir John Kaye's monumental work on the war, one of those historical studies which becomes a part of history itself, shaping subsequent events by its definitiveness and authority, as well as by its assertion of a point of view that reflects the spirit of the age (Kaye 1878). Kaye's condemnation of the war combines the curious blend of moralism and realpolitik that characterizes so much of nineteenth-century British writing on India. Kaye castigated Auckland for an act of unprovoked aggression, but one senses behind this judgement another one—Auckland's major perspective of time, the policy that had led to the war was a logical, but incautious, extension of the search for defensible frontiers that had dominated official thinking for sixty years.

This is because the failure of the Afghan adventure did not mean the abandonment or even the substantial modification of the policy on which it was based, but rather a redefinition of where India's northwestern frontiers should be located. The Indus once more became the focus of attention, with Sind and the Sikh kingdom becoming the areas to be brought either directly or indirectly under the control of the Government of India. By 1841, the absorption of both in some form was almost a foregone conclusion; the decisions that had to be made were in regard to timing, methods, and formal relationships. The Afghan debacle hastened the process, for all the arguments that had been used for expansion of the frontiers of influence beyond the mountain ranges had even greater validity for the territories between them and the existing frontier of the Government of India.

By the 1840s, the idea of 'natural boundaries' had begun to assume a central importance in foreign policy discussion, with 'natural' being used to indicate not just well-defined physical features but, more importantly, to carry a political meaning. There were limits to sovereignty, it was implied, which had been decreed by Providence. Lord Ellenborough provided an interesting example of this usage in 1842 when, as the newly appointed Governor General, he said that the Government of India was 'content with the limits nature appears to have assigned to its Empire' (quoted in Huttenback 1962, 69, 'Indian Secret Letters, April 30, 1842'). That within a year he was the enthusiastic supporter of the annexation of Sind does not indicate either a reversal of his former position or, as his opponents argued, hypocrisy and lack of judgement. The natural boundaries of 1842 was the great desert that stretched to the east of the Indus valley and Sind. This is the boundary, more or less, that now exists between India and Pakistan. The one, without too much straining of historical imagination, was the successor state of Ellenborough's Government of India; the other was the kingdom of the Muslim Amirs. What changed the situation was not a new perception of geographic reality but of a political fact: the British presence in Sind made untenable the continuance of the old system of government.

The annexation of Sind in 1843 followed logically from the treaty forced on the Amirs during preparations for the Afghan war in 1838. The main demand made by the Government of India was for the appointment of a resident in Sind, with all the attendant power, however ill-defined, to interfere in the internal politics of the area. Two worlds were meeting, and they could not accommodate themselves to each other. Pottinger, the resident in Sind, admirably expressed the Government of India's case against the Amirs when he reported that they 'one and all, publicly give out that they do not want to amass money, or to improve their territories' (Cox 1843, 64). The familiar pattern of charges and counter-charges of broken faith and treachery followed, with increasing demands from the Government of India driving the Amirs to desperation.

When the war finally came, Sir James Outram, who had been the previous resident in Sind, protested violently, for he could argue that it had been brought about by the inability of the Amirs to rule in a way that was alien to them. Their personalistic autocracy, modified by the clan system of the tribal peoples to which they belonged, could not adjust to the bureaucracy of the Government of India. Outram may have been right that until the British entered Sind 'all classes were as happy as those under any government in Asia', and the annexation was 'most tyrannical—positive robbery' (Goldsmid 1881, 314). But there was no way to undo the pressures that had built up against the Amirs over the years. This was the point made by Outram's opponent Sir Charles Napier, the strange neurotic who was commander of the Company's armies. He had no illusions about who had broken the treaties that led to the war, but, as he sardonically put it, that 'we break treaties ... is not a reason for letting others do the same' (Napier 1857, 196). One of the Amirs put this in a different way when he said that Napier was declaring that the British had conquered the rulers of Sind, while, in fact, the Amirs were already tributaries and subjects of the British when the war began (Khan 1844, 546).

More clearly than any of the other participants, Napier realized why the creation of a powerful state had transformed the frontiers of all the neighbouring kingdoms. Beyond the existing political frontiers of the Government of India were, he argued, natural boundaries: in the northwest, the Indus; in the north, the Himalayas; and in the East, the Brahamputra. The space between was filled by 'weak, uncivilized nations' (Napier 1857, 346) which not only had the folly to insult the British, but, quite as demanding of retribution, they opposed commerce and left idle great tracts of land which could have yielded crops and a great river which could have been a highway for trade. This argument—that a nation by refusing to trade was acting in defiance of the law of nations—was often heard later in the nineteenth century, and found notable expression in Commodore Perry's mission to Japan. In India, it was combined with the idea of natural frontiers. A powerful state did not even necessarily have to advance to its natural frontiers, but, in Napier's metaphor, a natural law was demonstrated as 'the larger body attracts the smaller' (Napier 1857, 346). In another physical science, he found further proof and justification for extending the frontiers. There is also as it were a chemical affinity to the larger one, for the people of Sind, 'one and all, are our own in their hopes and aspirations' (Napier 1857, 346). This had a curiously modern ring, for in the early years of expansion in India, the argument, so familiar in later boundary discussions, that ethnic and cultural similarities of peoples should be considered in boundary making was not often heard. Such arguments fleshed out Napier's famous epigram: 'We have no right to seize Sind, yet we shall do so, and a very advantageous, useful, humane piece of rascality it will be' (Napier 1857, 218). Napier had been content to find the natural boundaries of India on the Indus itself, but a few months later the Governor General discovered a new 'ultimate boundary'—the chain of mountains beyond the Indus (quoted in Huttenback 1962, 69, *Ellenborough Papers*, no. 77).

There are very few references in early nineteenth-century discussions to the ethnic, linguistic, or even economic characteristics of a region as factors to be considered in deciding frontiers, but, rather surprisingly, involvement in Sind elicited such a concern. By one of those curious ambiguities with which British rule in India is associated, it was Ellenborough, the model imperialist, who seems first to have seen that the choice of frontiers had implications for the development of India as a national unit. The new boundaries that were the legacy of the annexation of Sind would, he insisted, embrace all the peoples of India, giving them a new unity through freedom of internal trade and a uniform currency. A careful regard for the interest of the people, 'not the pecuniary advantages of the nation of strangers', could, he said, give India a future of limitless prosperity (Colchester 1874, 65). The contradictions between such sentiments and the aggression that ended in the annexation of Sind were resolved by the larger union of the Indian peoples that would follow from the introduction of the mundane instruments of internal free trade and a uniform currency. 'I ought to look only to India,' he told the Queen. 'I must ... act in the spirit of a native, not a foreign, governor' Colchester 1874, 65, 'Ellenborough to Wellington, March 22, 1843').

In territorial terms, the vision of India that was emerging out of the expansionism of the 1840s was not bounded by the Kirthar range immediately beyond the Indus: it included the whole territory between the Hindu Kush, the Indus, and the sea. Perhaps Ellenborough did not realize the full implications of his idea, as his knowledge of the geography of the area was hazy. But sixty years later, Sir Thomas Holdich, an authority on the area, argued that the natural frontier of India was far into Afghanistan—a line formed by the Hindu Kush and its extensions to the hills near Herat (Holdich 1909 [2012], 373). The mountain ranges that seemed to provide such satisfactory natural frontiers here as elsewhere were as unstable and as ill-defined as the edge of the desert had been when the movement against Sind had started.

By the time Sind was finally annexed, a number of surveys of the Indus and the principal land routes had been carried out, but they were not very accurate. In the years immediately before the takeover, the surveyors had been compelled to camouflage their activities, making their observations by the stars rather than the sun, since the people became suspicious when they saw the Englishmen measuring and calculating the land (Phillimore 1945–50, vol. IV, 243). The correspondence from Calcutta following the annexation emphasizes the importance of maps of the new conquests, with the Governor General showing special concern for an early decision on the boundaries of the new conquest (*Alphabetical Catalogue* 1931, 337–8, 411–14). The basic issue was the extent of territory to be taken on the western bank of the Indus. Where was a line to be placed that would be suitable for defence while at the same time not lead to further westward expansion (quoted in Lambrick 1952, 179, 'Letters from Ellenbrough to Napier, March 6, 1843')? Little consideration was given to the Indus itself as a frontier, partly because of the belief that it would become a highway for steamships was still maintained by the Government of India. Shallow draught steamships would, it was believed, soon be sailing up the Indus into the Sutlej; the dependence on the Ganges as the gateway to the north would be lessened; and, as momentous political consequence, Delhi could soon become the capital of the Government of India. 'To have in our hands the ancient seat of empire, and to administer the government from it, has ever seemed to me to be a very great object,' Ellenborough wrote to the Duke of Wellington (Colchester 1874, 309, 360). Expansion towards the limits of the Mughal Empire brought with it dreams of Mughal grandeur.

In lower Sind, river Hab formed the boundary of Karachi district, which had passed under British rule in 1899. The Kirthar range continued the line beyond the Hab. On the Indus, Kashmir was the northernmost point in the annexed territories. From here to the Chandia hills in the west were over a hundred miles of desert, without any kind of boundaries (Lambrick 1952, 275). Sovereignty over the area north of Kashmir including the hill country was claimed by the Sikhs, on the ground that the territory had belonged to the previous Afghan rulers of Lahore to whom they were the successors as well as through actual conquest and occupation (Singh 1963, vol. I, 201, 280). But their actual control over the region did not extend far beyond the right bank of the Indus at the point where their territories met with the Sind annexations.

With the acquisition of this undefined territory on the western bank of the Indus began the northwest border problems that were to remain with the Government of India over a hundred years until they became part of Pakistan's inheritance in 1947. The basis of the frontier problem was that the many tribes inhabiting the great belt of mountains that stretches over 1,200 miles from the extreme north of India to the Arabian Sea were, for all practical purposes, independent of the rulers of either the plateaus to the west or of the Indian plains to the east. The familiar description of these tribes as predatory, for whom plundering raids to the Indians plains were part of their way of life, is probably fair enough, but the nature of the political society existing in the area had made possible adjustments that made these raids endurable to the peoples of the plain. It was the new forms of administrative power represented by the British that made the continuance of the old relationship between the hills and the plains untenable, as demonstrated by the Sind Government's decision to put down the tribal incursions along the northern borders of Sind (Lambrick 1952, 275–98).

The stabilization of the areas occupied by the Baluchi tribes was a slow process, beginning in 1843 and not really completed until the 1890s. Throughout the years, the reports from agents and officials restate the familiar theme: the inability of the rulers to control their border people. Here, as elsewhere, the conjunction of the territories of the Government of India with tribal peoples who had utterly different concepts of territorial control and administration led to endless quarrels. Unable to meet the demands of the Indian authorities to keep the border raiders in check, and faced with intrigues and intra-tribal rivalries, the most important of the Baluchi chieftains, the Khans of Kalat, lost internal control (*Alphabetical Catalogue*, 1931, 352–3). The solution to what later writers were fond of summarizing as 'a condition of anarchy, chaos, and civil war', was not, as elsewhere, annexation of the whole area, but only of a narrow strip of territory on the north and northwest that isolated the Baluchis from contacts with outsiders. Sir Thomas Holdich, one of the ablest of the frontier officials in the late nineteenth century, analysed the difference between the Baluchistan area and the Northwest Frontier Province:

> It could be traced to the difference of our actual position in reference to the borderland. In the north we were in front of the border tribes—we are so still; in the south we were both in front of them and behind them. There were no back doors on the Baluchistan frontier for comfortable and timely retreat should matters go badly in front—no hidden means of communication with unseen supporters in the vast upland plains which stretched away to Kandahar and Kabul. (Holdich 1909 [2012], 187)

The search for a frontier in upper Sind had been begun almost before the war ended, with the initiative not coming from Calcutta but from the local military commander, John Jacob, and, to a lesser extent, from Napier. Insofar as the Government of India has a frontier policy for Sind, it was to maintain the power of the Khan of Kalat over the mountain territories to the west of Sind. In return, the Khan would restrain the tribes from invading Sind. In general, this was the view of the people with long experience in India and with deep attachment to the old order. Napier's judgement on it was succinct: the 'set of old bitches ... do not see that the interest of every Prince within our frontier is to send us to hell' (Shand 1900, 125). Working within Napier's picaresque framework, Jacob evolved a plan of action that was to lead to a frontier quite different from that existing anywhere else along the Indian perimeter.

The first stage in the evolution of the frontier in the Sind region came from Jacob's rejection of defensive border posts. A frontier cannot be secured by such posts, unless, he said, 'like the Romans in Britain, you can afford to build a wall from end to end' (Shand 1900, 133). Existing defensive works were to be destroyed, with their place taken by troops always on the offensive, 'seeking out the foe, not waiting for an attack'. Jacob pushed his outposts into the hills, striking terror into the area, and disregarding the fact that the hill country belonged to the Khan of Kalat, not Sind. 'The loss of life has been terrific,' he wrote after a raid, 'but it is satisfactory to know that the slain men were robbers and murderers' (Shand 1900, 140). Jacob claimed that this policy of terror was really humane; since once force had been shown to be effective, it would 'excite men's better natures, till all men, seeing that your object is good ... join heart and hand to aid in putting down violence' (Lambrick 1960, 170). The rhetoric may not carry conviction to the modern reader, but with one exception, the frontier between Sind and the territories of the Khan of Kalat was stabilized by the treaty in 1854 and demarcated in 1862.

The exception related to the other aspect of Jacob's border policy, his conviction that the security of India depended upon the military occupation of Quetta, with its command of the Bolan pass. Military occupation would require some form of civil government, and this meant sovereignty. 'The red line of the map would be pushed farther westward, and without finding so good a resting place as now.' The immediate return from the possession of Quetta would be greater control over the Baluchis, but beyond this were two more enticing possibilities. One was an advance into the Afghan plateau. The other was the fulfilment of that old dream of trade through the mountains. The Bolan Pass, he believed, was 'the natural outlet to the ocean of the commerce of a very large portion of Central Asia' (Lambrick 1960, 306).

These arguments were not acted upon in Jacob's lifetime, but Quetta was finally acquired in 1876 by treaty from the Khan of Kalat (Aitchison 1912?). Over the next twenty years, more territory was acquired—from Afghanistan, the Khan, and the tribal chiefs in the Zhob river area. This created a narrow stretch of frontier under the Government of India that cut off Baluchistan from direct contact with both Afghanistan and the tribal peoples in what was to become the Northwest Frontier Province. This frontier policy initiated by Jacob to a very considerable extent determined the location of the northwestern boundary by the Government of India at a later period. In the 1860s, its general location seemed to be an open question. Where was the best stopping place? The left bank of the Indus; the foot of the hills beyond the Indus; some point within the mountains; or, as many insisted, a line on the far edge of the Afghan plateau?

In fact, the options were not as open as they seemed. The conquest of Sind had foreclosed the possibility of the Indus as the frontier. The movement into the Baluchi hills made it unlikely that the line would stop at the foothills at any point along the northwestern ranges. And the first Afghan war had shown how difficult, if not impossible, it would be to maintain Indian hegemony, after the Mughal fashion, over the Afghan plateau.

The annexation of Sind, more than any previous acquisition, demonstrated that territorial sovereignty implied a large measure of autonomy for the Government of India. There was a special irony that this should have taken place when Ellenborough was Governor General, for as president of the Board of Control he had insisted that London must not only define policy for India but control the details of its execution. It was his aim, he had said in 1829, to make 'every public servant in India feel that he was at all times under the eye and within the reach of the British Government' (Philips 1940).

After Ellenborough had gone out to India, Sir Robert Peel reinforced this view by stating that, with the improvement of communication, Parliament would take a greater interest in Indian events, especially when they were as questionable as they seemed to be in Sind (Peel 1899, 6 June 1843). But as Peel acknowledged, the lapse of time, the difficulty in getting accurate information about local conditions, the need to act quickly, all meant that the Indian authorities had to act on their own (Peel 1899, 6 April 1842). Furthermore, the office of Governor General had a different meaning in Calcutta than it had in London. In Calcutta, the intoxicating idea occurred to Ellenborough that he could make the Government of India as potent a power as the Mughal Empire had been under Akbar. This meant, as he succinctly put it, he must 'act like Akbar' (quoted in Law 1926, 64). 'I must write and act for India, not for England,' he said on another occasion, indicating, perhaps unconsciously, how governors general became rulers of India, not remaining mere agents of the British Cabinet (Peel 1899, 24 March 1843). In light of this identification with India, another statement of Ellenborough's takes on new meaning. Now that Sind had been acquired, careful military and political planning, he argued, would lead to the acquisition of the Punjab, Kashmir, and Peshawar, everything within the circle of the mountains. And then, long antedating Disraeli's action, he envisioned this process of territorial gains terminating with 'the assumption of the imperial title by the Queen', with all the chiefs of the region becoming the feudatories of the Empire (in Peel 1899, MS 40475).

This enthusiasm for conquest fits the conventional stereotype of the imperialist, but it is also a by-product of expansionist nationalism, with its search for national identity and its fulfilment of manifest destiny. Since Ellenborough and his lieutenants were British, their expansionist policy was not seen as nationalism, but any ruler of a strong Indian state might have acted in a very similar fashion. It was only accidental that it was the British who reactivated that dream of an empire encompassing the whole of the subcontinent that had haunted the political conscious-ness of Indian rulers since the age of the Mauryas. Ellenborough's evocation of Akbar was more than bombast; it was a claim for territorial sovereignty that would define a nation.

The public reaction to this new extension of the frontiers of admin-istration demonstrated the ambiguity of the status of the Government of India. Although nothing as yet can be identified as Indian nationalist opinion on an issue of this kind, two sets of responses may not unfairly be labelled as 'Indian', in the sense that they are analogues of attitudes that became familiar at a later date. One is the response of the Amirs and chieftains of Sind, as revealed in the petitions for redress of the grievances they addressed to the new administration as well as in the administrators' defences of their actions (*Alphabetical Catalogue* 1931). They resented, of course, the loss of personal power that followed their defeat in battle, but they also spoke for those who felt that old ways were threatened by the intrusion of alien thinking and behaviour. It was this same inchoate resentment that a decade later was to find expression in the upheavals of the mutiny of 1857. Perhaps more significant was a response voiced not by Indians but those who regarded themselves as surrogates for India within the Government of India. For this group of people, Outram was spokesman and symbol. For them the extension of the frontier was a ruthless exercise of power, justified neither by the requirements of defence nor the possibilities of trade. Their attitudes and arguments were those that were to be used forty years later by Indian nationalists against the annexation of Burma and the wars on the Afghan frontier. Perhaps the major difference is that opponents of expansion in the 1840s gave more weight to the wrong done to the con-quered people than did the nationalists in the 1880s.

In England the reaction to the extension of the northwestern fron-tiers of India was also similar to what would have been expected from an articulate public opinion if it had existed in India. The spokesman for the official responsible government position was the Duke of Wellington. Any public criticism of Napier or Ellenborough, he insisted, would endanger the solidarity needed to maintain power in India (in Colchester 1874, 369–80, 'Wellington to Ellenborough, April 5, 1843'). But even Wellington's magisterial intervention could not silence the criticism evoked by the Government of India's action. A powerful denunciation of the annexation came from the directors of the Company, the body that historically had opposed territorial expansion. By 1843, the directors had little of the influence they had once enjoyed, but their opposition to annexation was embarrassing to a government that was an unenthusiastic supporter of the action (Ripon n.d., 322–5, 'Ripon to Wellington, September 25, 1843'). The directors' arguments were similar to those that had been used by their predecessors forty years earlier against the expansionist policies of Wellesley: the ruinous expense of wars, the added cost of administering new territories, the deflection of energy from the central problems of the Government of India (Colchester 1874, 369–80; *Parliamentary Debates*, 3rd series, 1844, vol. 72, col. 555, Speech by R. Mangles, 12 February). The conservative humanitarian response to the annexation found a fitting spokesman in Lord Ashley, the great reformer. Echoing the argument that Burke had made in his attack on Warren Hastings' treatment of Indian rulers, Ashley said the Amirs of Sind were part of 'a fraternity of crowned heads' who had entered into a treaty relationship with the British that had been callously abrogated by the Government of India. He was able to quote the judgement of Pottinger, one of those who had been most instrumental in persuading the Amirs to sign the treaties, that this act had been 'the most unprincipled and disgraceful that has ever stamped the annals of our Empire in India' (*Parliamentary Debates*, 1844, vol. 72, col. 343, Speech by Lord Ashley, 8 February).

But such passionate denunciations of the annexation did not lead to its reversal. The participants in the debate were concerned with the personal wrongs done to the old ruling classes in Sind, or with the acrimonious dispute between Napier and Outram, rather than with the implications of the extension of the frontier to the Indus and beyond it to the mountain ranges. The only comparable territorial gains since the decisive movements in the 1760s were those of Wellesley in the early years of the nineteenth century when British hegemony over the interior of India had been so unmistakably asserted that it had been impossible to reverse the process, even though this had been desired by the most influential figures in the Company (Embree 1962). The extension of the frontier meant that the Government of India would be directly involved in the complex politics of Central Asia and the Afghan plateau. More immediately, it hastened intervention in Sikh politics, for it gave the Government of India a new frontier with the Sikh kingdom, and one that was peculiarly unstable and ill-defined.

The Government of India's intervention in Punjab followed what had become the classic pattern. Following Ranjit Singh's death in 1829, there was a struggle for the succession, with factions within the palace and the army seeking alliances that would make it possible to establish a viable government. Such struggles were familiar—perhaps necessary—features of traditional Indian politics. Aurangzeb's wars with his brothers for the Mughal inheritance is the most famous of the wars of succession, but on a smaller scale, and with less drama, they could be duplicated in the history of most Indian courts, whether Hindu or Muslim. In a formal sense, the Government of India has no direct concern with the internal struggles of the Sikhs, and it might have remained aloof during the inter-regnum, waiting for one faction to emerge victorious with whom it could then negotiate. But two features of the struggles in the Punjab made the Government of India see them as a threat to its own fragile stability. Both has to so with the maintenance of the existing frontiers. In the Punjab itself, as a result of the relaxation of the Lahore government's control, there were a series of border incidents that the British saw as deliberate provocations, preludes to Sikh incursions across the frontier. In addition, rumours of plans for alliance between the Sikhs and neighbouring states were continually being reported to the Government of India by its agents. What the government feared, and what seemed inherently probable to many observers, was an alliance between the Sikhs and a Hindu power, either Nepal, where there were groups known to be hostile to the British, or Gwalior or Indore, whose rulers had still not abandoned hope of regaining their independence. In this situation, the existing frontiers appeared increasingly vulnerable.

As events in Punjab pointed to a collision with the Sikhs, the Government of India strengthened frontier posts, increased the garrisons in the north, and kept a careful check on the activities in the Lahore court. Joseph Cunningham, the British agent who watched these developments with great sympathy for the Sikhs, noted that while these steps seemed fair and moderate to the British, the Sikhs took a different view of the relative condition of the two states. Aware of their own weaknesses, Cunningham (1918, 248) observed, 'They feared the ambition of their great and growing neighbour, they did not understand why they should be dreaded when intestine commotions had reduced their comparative inferiority still lower; or why inefficiency of rule should be construed into hostility of purpose.'

Cunningham's analysis of the anatomy of imperialist expansion has the great merit of stressing the psychological reaction of the weaker border power. Convinced that British activity on the frontier could only be preparation for invasion, they began responding in a fashion that made invasion inevitable, given the presuppositions of the Government of India regarding the behaviour to be expected from an Indian power.

Before the outbreak of the first war with the Sikhs in 1845, the advantages and disadvantages that would accrue to the Government of India from intervention in Sikh affairs had been considered at all levels of the Indian administration, and it had been generally recognized that control of the Punjab would present the government with frontier problems of a new dimension. As already noted, elated by the acquisition of Sind, Ellenborough had argued in 1845 that careful military and political planning could bring 'everything within the mountains'—the Punjab, Kashmir, and Peshawar—under Calcutta, thus terminating the process begun in the 1760s (Peel 1899, ms 40, 475, 'Ellenborough to Hardinge, April 15, 1845').

When the war ended with the virtual defeat of the Sikhs in 1846, there was widespread disappointment among the administrators and military officers, especially the younger ones, that the government did not annex the whole of the Punjab (*Broughton Papers*, MS 36,475, 'Hardinge to Hobhouse, September 2, 1846'). They wanted the Indus to be the frontier, marking, they were convinced, the natural boundary of the empire they had helped create in the subcontinent. Instead, in 1846, Ranjit Singh's descendants were left in Lahore, and the frontier was pushed only from the Sutlej to the Beas, with the addition of the hill territories of Kashmir and Hazara between the Beas and the Indus.

Of this area, the land from the Indus to the Ravi was assigned to Gulab Singh. Although, as Raja of Jammu, he was a subordinate to the Lahore government, he had made an alliance with the British during the war, and the acquisition of Kashmir was his reward (Aitchison 1912). The treaty with Gulab Singh speaks in one place of his 'independent possession' of Kashmir but this meant internal control, not territorial sovereignty. Its significance for the search for frontiers is indicated by its special clauses relating to the border. The eastern borders of Gulab Singh's territory would be defined by commissioners appointed for the purpose. He was to make no changes in his borders without the consent of the paramount power, which would also mediate disputes with neighbouring states.

These provisions look back to events that had taken place before the war in 1845. They were a precaution against the kind of border problems that had been precipitated in 1841 when Zorawar Singh, a military commander from Jammu, led an army into western Tibet, an action that reactivated Chinese interest in the area. The ostensible justification of this invasion was based on the claim that Ladakh, over which the Sikhs asserted suzerainty, had authority over the whole area of the Sutlej basin up to Mansarovar Lake (*Foreign Proceedings Secret Correspondence*, September 1841, nos 99–100). The Government of India had supported the Sikh claim to Ladakh, but they did not want a Sikh advance beyond the mountains to the borders of Nepal. Aside from the dislocation this would have caused in the wool trade that passed from Tibet through Bushair into India, there would be dangerous political implications in a link between the Sikhs and the Nepalese, the last two independent Hindu kingdoms (*Foreign Proceedings Secret Correspondence*, 28 August 1847, nos 139–83). The Government of India's pressures forced the recall of Zorawar Singh's army, but the Chinese sent troops to occupy Ladakh as evidence of their authority there.

The British were uncertain as to the political status of Ladakh, but the best information was that the ruler of Ladakh acknowledged the authority of both the Sikhs and the Chinese although the actual power in Ladakh had been held by the Sikhs since 1834 (*Foreign Proceedings Secret Correspondence*, 22 June 1842, nos 40–9). The Chinese were anxious to drive the Sikhs south of the Himalayas and to prevent them from making any kind of claim over Ladakh and the neighbouring regions, but despite what a British agent called their tendency to 'arrogate to themselves a superiority no doubt of long standing', the Chinese had too few troops in Lhasa to make an effective occupation of Ladakh. Instead, they withdrew their forces, contenting themselves with the promise that the Ladakh Buddhist leaders would continue sending presents as evidence of Chinese suzerainty. Ladakhi leaders appealed to the Government of India through the frontier agents for protection against both the Sikhs and Chinese, but they were put off with a deliberately ambiguous promise that if they were treated badly by either the Sikhs or the Chinese 'that which is good, will be done' (Foreign Proceedings Secret Correspondence, 22 June 1842, nos 40–9). This was the origin of the long drawn attempt to find some frontier in the northern area that would be acceptable to the Chinese.

The formal search for a northern frontier between India and China began with an attempt by the Government of India to set up a commission which would include representatives from the Chinese authorities. For the Calcutta authorities, dependent on the reports that had been coming in from their agents in the area for the past twenty years, the definition of the frontier was a simple issue. Writing from the Residency in Lahore, Henry Lawrence declared that the boundary between Ladakh and Chinese territory was well-known and undisputed, although he admitted his agents Vans Agnew and Alexander Cunningham had not actually made contact with any Chinese authorities (Foreign Proceedings Secret Correspondence, 28 August 1847, no. 153, 'Letter from Henry Lawrence, May 20, 1847'). On the basis of this information the Governor General made his report to London. There could be no quarrel with the Chinese, the Governor General argued, since the boundary between Ladakh and Tibet had been 'laid down by nature'—a line formed by the Karakoram mountains, the Pangong Lake, and the hills to the South (Foreign Proceedings Secret Correspondence, July 1847, no. 48). Henry Lawrence had enunciated the principle that was to have such a fateful history in Indian frontier disputes: the boundary followed the crest of the hills. While there might be uncertainty about the line in some places, the country was so desolate that neither would suffer any territorial disadvantage, even if errors were made (Foreign Proceedings Secret

Correspondence, August 1847, no. 153). The Boundary Commission could also engage in good works, taking medicines to the inhabitants of the remote areas, collecting scientific information, and studying the religion and customs of the people. There would be no need for the Commission to travel the whole length of the border, but they could trace a satisfactory line on a map at their first meeting. Then when the Chinese realized that the Government of India was not 'actuated by any spirit of political aggression, but solely by a desire to participate in and extend the blessings of commerce', they would begin to feel 'more gratified than alarmed at the extension of our influence to the farthest boundary of their empire' (*Foreign Proceedings Secret Correspondence*, 28 July 1847, no. 153).

The sincerity of this statement was matched by its obtuseness. The Chinese had little interest in either of the two major British motivations for defining the border—preventing Gulab Singh of Kashmir from expanding his dominions and encouraging the growth of trade between India and Tibet. They undoubtedly preferred dealing with Gulab Singh, rather than the British, and as for trade, they had been forced by the Treaty of Nanking to open up five ports, more than adequate for any trade China desired with India. The Canton authorities, who handled the negotiations for the Chinese, summed up their position in what the Indian Government regarded as a characteristic piece of Oriental evasion. The boundaries between the empire and the neighbouring rulers (who acknowledged their relationship to the emperor through the sending of tribute) 'have been sufficiently and distinctly fixed, so that it will be best to adhere to this ancient arrangement and it will prove far more convenient to abstain from any additional measures for fixing them' (*Foreign Proceedings Secret Correspondence*, 28 July 1847, no. 153).

The Chinese refusal to define the boundaries of their empire did not lead the Government of India to abandon its search for a northern frontier. So certain were its agents that a boundary 'laid down by nature' existed in the area that they continued the work of definition on their own. To preclude, as they put it, any possibility of further dispute, they proposed as a boundary 'such mountain ranges as form watershed lines between the drainages of different rivers' (quoted in Lamb 1964, 67, 'Correspondence from A. Cunningham, July 23, 1846'). This was not, of course, what the Chinese had meant by the 'ancient arrangement', which had to do with customs duties and tribute, but it made possible the virtual completion of a border in the north that satisfied the Government of India. The border problems involved in the arrangements for Kashmir and the hill country made with Maharaja Gulab Singh had, from the point of view of the Government of India, been relatively simple. Aside from the evasiveness of the Chinese, the difficulties in defining the limits of control were physical, not political.

In the Punjab itself, the situation was quite different, with the decisions on defining a frontier being intimately related to the complexities of the Indian political situation. There was, first of all, what the reports described as a strong Sikh 'national feeling' to be taken into account. This interesting phrase occurs in a letter of the Governor General in 1846 explaining why he had resisted the pressure from civilian and military officials for annexation. It is one of the rare cases when the Government of India considered national consciousness or ethnic differences, rather than defence, in its search for a workable frontier (in *Broughton Papers*, MS 36,475, 'Lord Hardinge to Sir J.C. Hobhouse, September 2, 1846'). Extension of the frontier would bring into the territory not only a discontented ruling class, but also a peasantry that having prospered under Sikh rule, would resent the change. Related to this was the Government's belief that the Sikhs would provide a bulwark against Muslim enemies both within and without India. With their fanatical hatred of the British, the Muslims of India would be ready to make common cause with the Afghans or the Persians, and a Hindu power would have a stake in opposing them on the frontier and would gain the sympathy of Hindus throughout India (in *Broughton Papers*, MS 36,475, 'Lord Hardinge to Sir J.C. Hobhouse, September 2, 1846').

The role envisaged for the Punjab in 1846 was thus quite different from that which had been assigned to Kashmir or Nepal. They were to be political vacuums, with their external borders defined to prevent them from coming in conflict with China. What was sought was stability, with the presumption that trouble was more likely to come from the aggressively expansionist policies of a Gulab Singh rather than from China. The Punjab, on the other hand, would be a bulwark against invasion since the Sikhs—in common with the Hindus in the rest of India—had a stake in keeping out the Muslim peoples of Central Asia (in *Broughton Papers*, MS 36,475, 'Lord Hardinge to Sir J.C. Hobhouse, September 2, 1846').

Annexation of the Punjab, it was argued in 1846, would not only deprive India of this defence, but the creation of a new frontier 400 land miles beyond the present line would impose new strains upon the Government's resources. The present arrangement cost the Government nothing, but with a new frontier resting on the mountains or the Indus, troops would have to be stationed in a line from Lahore to Peshawar. Six months of the year these troops would be isolated by the rains, since by now it was known that the Indus was not navigable. Added to the enormous increase in cost was a political consideration; the Bengal army would not want to serve a thousand miles from home. Since the mutinies in the spring of 1844 were caused by the antipathy to troops serving in Sind, this was a warning to the government of the tenuous base of its military power, and how a new frontier to be guarded might tip the balance.

But there was a possible escape from this dilemma: recruitment from the local population. Perhaps if the frontier were extended, the Governor General suggested, an army might be raised made up of Sikhs and Muslims. Their natural antipathies could thus be counterbalanced, and they might be willing to exchange national independence—the phrase is Lord Hardinge's—for the security of a military service (in *Broughton Papers*, MS 36,475, 'Lord Hardinge to Sir J.C. Hobhouse, September 2, 1846'). This suggestion for the control of the northwest marchlands is of particular interest as it closely foreshadows the general policy followed with considerable success in the second half of the nineteenth century.

Reading the Government of India's defence of its policy in not annexing the Punjab in 1846, but with the hindsight provided by the events of the next few years, it is easy to assume that the arrangements were regarded as interim, and that there were plans to move towards absorption of the area as soon as gains had been consolidated. The enthusiasm of the pro-annexationists in the administration—'the young civilians and the gallant officers'—certainly supports this reading of events. But at higher levels the conviction that the northwest frontiers had been stabilized at a minimum cost to the Government of India seems to have been quite genuine. As late as April 1847, the Governor General concluded on the basis of the intelligence reports coming to Calcutta from Lahore that 'the Punjab was never so quiet in the memory of man' (*Broughton Papers*, 20 April 1847, MS 36,475).

That a year later another Governor General, Lord Dalhousie, had decided that the time had come to extend the boundaries of India by annexing the Punjab, despite the plausible arguments of his predecessor against such a policy, reflects not so much the duplicity of an expansionist power as changing factors in the political situation. Quite simply, the Government of India's perception of events in the Punjab was that the Sikhs had broken their part of the bargain, and they no longer provided a stable frontier (in *Broughton Papers*, MS 36,475, 'Lord Dalhousie to Sir J.C. Hobhouse, August 15, 1848'). The judgement of British observers at the time who were sympathetic to the continuance of the Sikh kingdom as well as of later Sikh historians was that the Lahore court was goaded to desperation—as it had been in 1845—by a combination of factional struggles at the court and pressures from the Government of India's officials in the Punjab. On another level, government officials were disturbed by intelligence reports that noted that rumours were being spread in the bazaars that the British were cow killers, and that the faith of the Guru was in danger. The importance of the chain of information for decision making at this time is clear. The reports of Sikh activities came from the young military and civilian officials who, as Lord Hardinge had noted, were enthusiastic for annexation.

The old belief that the Punjab could serve as a buffer state between India and Afghanistan faded before the palpable weakness of the Sikh kingdom. A vague humanitarianism and a nostalgia for the old ways could not counter the realities of self-interest as perceived by the Government of India. 'Old women and young ladies' opposed annexation on moral grounds, according to Governor General Lord Dalhousie, and in those categories he included the resident at Lahore as well as many members of the British Cabinet. But the logic of events pointed to the necessity of bringing the whole of the Punjab completely under control of the Government of India. The troubles in the Punjab which the resident and the commander-in-chief saw as merely local rebellions were, he insisted, massive insurrections by the whole Sikh kingdom that could only be ended by annexation (in *Broughton Papers*, MS 36,475, 183–220, 'Dalhousie to Hobhouse, August 15, 1848'). The armies were mobilized, and by the end of the rainy season in 1848 they moved against the remnants of the army that Ranjit Singh had created. By the end of March 1849, the war was over, with almost all of the subcontinent once more under the control of a single power.

The process of annexation of the Punjab demonstrated once more two of the essential features of the expansion of the Indian borders. One was the dependence of the Government of India officials in Calcutta on their intelligence gathering service. The other was the autonomy of the government from effective direction by the authorities in London. To see the annexation as 'British imperialism' is to misunderstand the inner nature of the search for borders. The imperialist expansion that ended in the conquest of the Sikh kingdom was only 'British' in the sense that the officials in Calcutta and their agents in Punjab were British citizens. The impetus to expansion came not from London but from Calcutta and from the agents of the Government of India in the Punjab. These agents—not Resident Henry Lawrence, who opposed annexation—were young military and civilian officials who, as enthusiasts for a showdown with the Sikhs, supplied the Governor General and his council in Calcutta with the information on which they based their decision for extending the administrative frontiers of the Government of India beyond the Indus. The reports of the agents can be followed in detail in the records of the Foreign Department and Dalhousie's letters also make it clear that he accepted the reports of the agents, disregarding the cautionary comments on them made by the resident at Lahore. Two of the best known of the frontier agents, Herbert Edwardes and James Abbott, acted so independently of the resident at Lahore, their superior, in initiating actions that were calculated to antagonize the Sikhs and force them to behave in a manner that the Governor General would construe as rebellion, that a modern historian has suggested that they were acting under secret orders from the Calcutta Government (Hasrat 1968, 320).

But a conspiracy is not necessary to explain the congruence of the activities of the frontier agents with the Governor General's conviction that the Punjab should be annexed. Agents such as Edwardes and Abbott saw the possibility of the destruction of the Sikh kingdom, and this possibility became a moral imperative for action. In his diary, Edwardes contrasts conditions in Lahore before and after its occupation by the British, nothing that 'so shameless and abandoned a city was supposed not to exist in Asia.' It was filled, he said, with courtesans;

the Sikh soldiers spent their time gambling; above all, there was everywhere a lack of order, and 'if there is any one thing which more than another characterizes the Anglo-Indian government, it is method and regulation'. What the Sikhs had to learn, he suggested, was that the day of license had departed, even though this was as 'galling to them as it was beneficial to the country' (Edwardes 1963, 174). 'Method and regulation' were synonyms for morality and virtue for men such as Edwardes, as they were, in a somewhat more sophisticated sense, for Lord Dalhousie. When, for example, Edwardes used Muslim mercenaries from the hills instead of Sikhs to put down an uprising in Multan, the Sikhs saw this as an attempt by the British to subvert their power and destroy their religion. Dalhousie accepted Edwardes' interpretation that the protests of the Sikhs were signs of a general insurrection against the Government of India. Even if proof of a widespread conspiracy could not be found, Dalhousie speculated, the willingness of the Sikhs to believe in one would justify annexation (in *Broughton Papers*, MS 36,476, 195, 'Dalhousie to Hobhouse, August 15, 1848'). This, in turn, justified the expansion of the borders of the modern South Indian nation states.

Bibliography

Adye, John. 2017 [1897]. *Indian Frontier Policy: A Historical Sketch*. London: Leopold Classic Library.

Aitchison, Charles Umpherston. 1912. *A Collection of Treaties, Engagements, and Sanads Relating to India and Neighboring Countries*. Calcutta: Government of India.

Alder, G.J. 1974. 'The Key to India? Britain and the Herat Problem, 1830–1863'. *Middle Eastern Studies*. London: Taylor & Francis, Ltd.

Alphabetical Catalogue of the Contents of the Pre-Mutiny Records of the Commissioner in Sind, 1857. 1931. Karachi: Commissioner's Printing Press.

Auckland, Lord George Eden. 1838. 'Auckland to Hobhouse, November 15, 1838'. In *Broughton Papers (Letters and Papers of John Cam Hobhouse, Lord Broughton)*, vol. XIV, MS 36,473. London: British Library.

Bentinck, William. 1831a. 'A Few Minutes of Lord William Cavendish Bentinck and a Memorandum of Information Regarding Afghanistan and Central Asia', 23 August 1831. *Foreign Miscellaneous Records*, no. 262. Delhi: Government of India, National Archives.

———. 1831b. 'Minute by Bentinck', 20 June 1831. *Foreign Miscellaneous Records*, no. 261. Delhi: Government of India, National Archives.

————. 1831c. 'Secret Letter to Bengal, July 29, 1831'. In *Bentinck Papers* , no. 2677. Nottingham: University of Nottingham.

Brendon, Piers. 2010. *The Decline and Fall of the British Empire, 1781–1997.* New York: Vintage Books.

British Parliament. 2009. *Accounts and Papers of the House of Commons.* Oxford: Oxford University Press.

Broughton Papers (Letters and Papers of John Cam Hobhouse, Lord Broughton), vol. XIV, MSS 36,473–6. London: British Library.

Burnes, Alexander. 1831. 'A Geographical and Military Memoir on the Indus'. *Foreign Department Secret Proceedings,* no. 21, 25 November 1831. Delhi: Government of India National Archives.

————. 1838. 'Alexander Burnes to W.H. MacNaughten, October 20, 1837'. *Foreign Department Political Correspondence,* no. 38, 31 January 1838. Delhi: Government of India National Archives.

————. 1839. *Reports and Papers, Political, Geographical, & Commercial.* Calcutta: G.H. Huttmann, Bengal Military Orphan Press.

Caplow, Theodore. 1968. *Two against One.* Englewood Cliffs, NJ: Prentice Hall.

Colchester, Reginald Charles Abbot. 1874. *History of the Indian Administration of Lord Ellenborough.* London: R. Betley and Son.

Cox, J.L. 1843. 'The Resident in Sinde, to the Secretary with the Governor-General, Hyderabad, October 9, 1838', *Correspondence Relative to Sind, 1836-1843.* London: J.L. Cox.

Cunningham, Joseph Davey. 1918. *A History of the Sikhs: From the Origin of the Nation to the Battles of the Sutlej.* Oxford: Oxford University Press.

Dalhousie, Lord James Andrew Broun-Ramsay. 'Dalhousie to Hobhouse, August 15, 1848'. In *Broughton Papers.*

Davis, H.W.C. 1927. *The Great Game in Asia, 1800–44.* London: Oxford University Press.

Dodwell, H.H. n.d. *Cambridge History of India.* Delhi: S. Chand.

Edwardes, Herbert E.B. 1963. *A Year on the Punjab Frontier in 1848–49,* vol. I. Lahore: Government of West Pakistan.

Ellenborough, Lord Edward. 1899. 'The Standard: Lord Ellenborough on India and Egypt'. *Notes and Queries July 29, 1899.* London: John Francis.

Embree, Ainslie. 1962. *Charles Grant and British Rule in India.* London: George Allen & Unwin.

Ewans, Martin. 2004. *The Great Game: Britain and Russia in Central Asia.* London: Routledge.

Farwell, Bryon. 1988. 'Charles Napier'. In *Eminent Victorian Soldiers: Seekers of Glory.* New York: W.W. Norton and Company, p. 85.

Foreign Department Political Correspondence. 1834–6. Delhi: Government of India National Archives.

Foreign Department Secret Correspondence. 1837–9. New Delhi: Government of India National Archives.

Goldsmid, Sir Frederic John. 1881. *James Outram: A Bibliography.* London: Smith and Elder & Company.

Gommans, Jos. 2018. *The Indian Frontier: Horse and Warband in the Making of Empires.* London: Routledge.

Hanifi, Shah Mahmoud. 2012. 'Shah Shuja's "Hidden History" and Its Implications for the Historiography of Afghanistan'. *South Asia Multidisciplinary Academic Journal* (Online), Free Standing Articles.

Hasrat, Bikrama Jit. 1968. *Anglo-Sikh Relations.* Hoshiarpur, Punjab.

Hobhouse, John Cam (Lord Broughton). *Broughton Papers (Letters and Papers of John Cam Hobhouse, Lord Broughton)*, vol. XIV, MSS 36,473–6. London: British Library.

Hodder, Edwin. 2014. *The Life and Work of the Seventh Earl of Shaftesbury, K.G.* Cambridge, Cambridge University Press.

Holdich, Thomas Hungerford. 1909 [2012]. *The Indian Borderland, 1880–1900.* London: Methuen.

Huttenback, Robert A. 1962. *British Relations with Sind, 1799–1843.* Berkeley: University of California Press.

Ingram, Edward. 1980. 'Great Britain's Great Game: An Introduction'. *The International History Review.* London: Taylor and Francis.

Jones, Stephen B. 1959. 'Boundary Concepts in the Setting of Place and Time'. *Annals of the Association of American Geographers.* London: Taylor and Francis Ltd..

Kaye, John William. 1854. *Charles, Lord Metcalfe: Unpublished Letters and Journals*, 2 vols. London: Richard Bentley.

———. 1878. *History of the War in Afghanistan.* London: William H. Allen & Company.

———. 2015. *History of the War in Afghanistan.* London: William H. Allen & Company.

Khan, Mir Nasir. 1844. 'Correspondence of Mir Nasir Khan to the Court of Directors'. *Parliamentary Papers, 1844*, vol. 36. Delhi: Government of India National Archives.

Lal, Mohan. 1846. *Travels in the Panjab, Afghanistan, and Turkistan.* London: W.H. Allen.

Lamb, Alistair. 1964. *The China–India Border: The Origins of Disputed Boundaries.* London: Oxford University Press.

Lambrick, H.T. 1952. *Sir Charles Napier and Sind.* Oxford: Clarendon Press.

———. 1960. *John Jacob of Jacobabad.* London: Cassell.

Latīf, Muḥammad. 1891. *History of the Panjáb from the Remotest Antiquity to the Present Time.* Calcutta Central Press.

Law, Sir Algernon. 1926. *India under Lord Ellenborough.* London: John Murray.

Ludlow, John Malcolm. 1858. *British India, Its Races and Its History.* Cambridge: Macmillan.

Lyall, Sir Alfred. 1891. 'Frontiers and Protectorates'. *The Nineteenth Century,* August.

Lyall, Sir Alfred, Romesh Dutt, Vicent Smith, Stanley Lane-Poole, Sir Henry Elliot, Sir William Hunter. 1907. 'The British Dominion in Asia'. In *History of India,* edited by A.V. Williams Jackson. New York Grolier Society.

MacNaughten, Sir William. 1839. 'Sir William MacNaughten from Kandahar, Secret Newsletter July 1, 1839'. *Foreign Department Miscellaneous Records,* vol. 331. New Delhi: Government of India National Archives.

Malcolm, Sir John. 1880 'Minute of Sir John Malcolm, August 9, 1880'. In *Bentinck Papers.* Nottingham, UK: University of Nottingham.

Malleson, George Bruce. 1878. *History of Afghanistan, from the Earliest Period to the Outbreak of the War of 1878.* London: William H. Allen & Company.

Marshall, Charles Burton. 1954. *The Limits of Foreign Policy.* New York: Henry Hold.

McCulloch, John Ramsay. 1849. *A Dictionary Geographical Statistical and Historical, of the Various Countries, Places and Principal Natural Objects in the World.* Cambridge: Harvard University.

Moran, Arik. 2019. *Kingship and Polity on the Himalayan Borderland.* Amsterdam: University of Amsterdam Press.

Mount, Ferdinand. 2015. *The Tears of the Rajas: Mutiny, Money and Marriage in India 1805–1905.* New York: Simon and Schuster.

Napier, Sir William Francis Patrick. 1857. *The Life and Opinions of General Sir Charles James Napier, G.C.B.* London: John Murray.

Nicolson, Harold. 2000. *The Congress of Vienna: A Study in Allied Unity, 1912–1822.* New York: Grove Press.

Norris, John A. 1967. *The First Afghan War 1838–1842.* Cambridge: Cambridge University Press.

Parliament of Great Britain. 1909 [1881]. *Hansard's Parliamentary Debates.* Great Britain: Hansard.

Peel, Sir Robert. *Peel Manuscripts,* MS 40,471. London: British Museum.

———. 1899. *Sir Robert Peel: From His Private Papers.* London: John Murray.

Perry, James M. 2005. *Arrogant Armies.* Edison, New Jersey: Castle Books.

Philips, Cyril Henry. 1940. *The East India Company 1784–1834.* Manchester: Manchester University Press.

Phillimore, Reginald Henry. 1945–50. *Historical Records of the Survey of India, 4 vols: 18th century; 1880–1815, 1815–1830, 1830–1843.* Government of India: Surveyor-General of India.

Pottinger, Sir Henry. 1839.'Memoir of the Country between Herat and Cabool, the Parapamison Mountains, and the River Amoo'. In 'Kabul Papers', *Foreign Department* vol. 1, no. 1. Delhi: Government of India National Archives, December 3.

———. 1843.'Correspondence Relative to Sinde: Henry Pottinger to Governor-General, 8 October'. In *Parliamentary Papers*, vol. 39. Delhi: Government of India National Archives.

———. 1844.'Chronicle'. *The Asiatic Journal and Monthly Miscellany*. William H. Allen & Company.

Redford, Arthur. 1934. *Manchester Merchants and Foreign Trade*. Manchester: Manchester University Press.

Ripon, Lord George Frederick Samuel Robinson. n.d. *Ripon Papers*, MS 40,854. London: British Museum.

Sandhu, P.J.S., Vinay Shankar, and G.G. Dwivedi. 1962 [2015]. *A View from the Other Side of the Hill*. New Dehli: Vij Books India Pvt Ltd.

Shand, Alexander Innes. 1900. *General John Jacob: Commander of the Sind Irregular Horse and Founder of Jacobabad*. London: Seeley and Co.

Sharma, Raghav Sharan. 2017. 'Lord Hardinge's Letter to the Directors of the East India Company Explaining the Background of the Boundary Commission of 1847'. In *The Unfought War of 1962*. London: Routledge.

Singh, Khushwant. 1963. *A History of the Sikhs*, 2 vols. Princeton: Princeton University Press.

Syed, Javed Haider. 2007.'The British Advent in Balochistan'. *Pakistan Journal of History and Culture*.

Select Committee of the House of Commons. 1833. *Reports of Affairs of the East-India Company, Minutes of Evidence*. London: Honourable Court of Directors.

Todd, E.H. 1839. 'Memorandum by E. H. Todd', 2 October 1839. *Foreign Department Secret Proceedings*, no. 4. Delhi: Government of India National Archives.

Trevelyan, Charles E. 1835. *A Report upon the Inland Customs and Town Duties of the Bengal Presidency*. Calcutta: Baptist Mission Press.

———. 1838 'Trevelyan to Hobhouse, October 25, 1838'. *Broughton Papers (Letters and Papers of John Cam Hobhouse, Lord Broughton)*, vol. XIV, MSS 36,473. London: British Library.

Afterword

The Continuing Problem of Borders

What are the natural borders of the states of South Asia? As was mentioned earlier in this book, the issue of 'natural frontiers' was raised as early as 1770 when the Company's agents in the northern districts of Bihar and Bengal argued that the 'natural frontiers' of British territory were not the flatlands of the terai beneath the mountains but the foothills of the Himalayas. The issue arose because of the appeal by the ruler of Morang, a 'hill raja' in the vocabulary of the time, to the Company for protection against the Gurkha ruler's incursions.

The Company's agent at its trading post at Purnea, who was in touch with the Morang ruler, argued that an alliance would be much to the Company's advantage, giving access to valuable timber resources and opportunities to send the Company's goods into the Nepal hills; but above all, it would permit the Company to get control of the Morang rulers' territory in the terai. This would give the Company's northern districts a fixed and secure boundary, the 'natural frontier' (Pounds 1951, 146–57) of the Himalayan foothills.

This seems to be one of the earliest usages of the expression 'natural frontiers' which became common in British India. The term originated in France in the late eighteenth century with a quasi-mystical idea that the destiny of the French nation had boundaries designed by nature to coincide with nationality. Obviously, this was not what the Company's agent meant, but rather a boundary supplied by some natural feature, such as a river, a sea, or a mountain range, a feature that clearly demarcated one territory from another and was defensible from intruders. This was what Rennell, the geographer and surveyor, had in mind, as did the other boundary makers in the nineteenth and twentieth centuries such as Durand and McMahon.

The search for 'natural frontiers' in the British usage, not the French, led logically to the states bordering on Nepal, such as Tibet, Bhutan, Assam, and Burma, and the Company took an interest in all of them because it was believed that they offered trading opportunities if boundaries could be satisfactorily defined, while posing security threats if they were not. In addition, some of the Company's officials had begun to develop an interest in Indian culture related to the current intellectual trends in Europe, including science as well as religion and philosophy, even though their stated aim was not to clear a path for knowledge but for trade and administration. Another aspect that emerges in this early search for boundaries was what may be called 'judgmental humanitarianism', one that later would be encountered very frequently to justify expanding the Company's boundaries.

One of the earliest appeals for intervention on such grounds came from Captain Thomas Welsh of the Bengal Army, who had been sent to investigate about rumours of uprisings in Assam threatening the Company's Bengal borders. In his report to Calcutta he argued that 'the ignorance, imbecility, caprice, and execrable cruelty of the government' (Mackenzie 2012, 332) towards the people demanded the British presence to prevent anarchy and to restore the 'the ancient constitution'. By that he meant that the Company's forces should restore the ruler who had been just overthrown in an uprising and remain in Assam until order had been restored. The Governor General from 1793 to 1798, Sir John Shore, who opposed further expansion of British territory, gave a short answer to Welsh's plea: Bring the Company's troops back to Bengal. There was no reason for British power to restore a ruler who, by

Welsh's own account, was deficient in every good quality a ruler needs and 'possesses every vice which is a disgrace to human nature' (H.M. Stationery Office 1813, 553). But Shore thought that an attempt to get the Assamese to adopt any particular form of government and to unite them into anything resembling a state would require perpetual interference and would mean the subjection of the Assamese by the Company. If the British were to place a ruler on the throne, he will be driven out. So, he advised Welsh to reject any thought of taking Assam to serve either as a buffer state or providing a mountain frontier.

In dealing with the Burmese, the British agents occasionally defended them when they crossed into British territory, telling the Calcutta authorities that one chieftain was entirely ignorant of the British understanding of boundaries and the laws and customs of European countries. As one Burmese official put it, 'I now find according to the European custom I have committed an error in crossing the Nef River,' not knowing the British considered it a boundary, and from ignorance he 'crossed the threshold, instead of waiting at the door'. The Burmese, another argued, did not understand the British concern over territorial rights; 'they know only the ruler' rights over his subjects'.

Shore, a long-time official of the Company and the last one to serve as Governor General, was always aware that, while engaged in managing a large political state, the Company was a commercial enterprise, and his policy of non-interference in the internal affairs of neighbouring states, whether within peninsular India or beyond it, both on the northwest and northeast frontiers, was approved by the Company's directors in London. That further extension of territory would threaten the British position in India was acknowledged by Charles Grant, one of the most powerful of the directors. He said it was a 'long received maxim ... which experience has so much justified' that Parliament by the India Act of 1784 forbade any further conquests 'as repugnant to the wish, the honour, and the policy of the British nation' (Morris 1898, 56).

By 1797, however, the letters from Calcutta to the Company's directors in London begin to question the wisdom or feasibility of the policy of non-intervention, given the increasing challenges in maintaining the boundaries of the Company's territories, both within peninsular India and along external frontiers in both the northwest and northeast. The directors, who viewed the policy as sound from a commercial point of view, began to accept the arguments from the Company's servants in India that the fluid boundaries of the multi-state system had to give way to fixed boundary lines demarcated by permanent ones, acknowledged by both parties. They also discovered that this meant compulsion by the British, which is the message behind the seemingly bland assertion of Lyall that up to that line authority had to be extended in some plain and indisputable form.

In other words, the making of boundaries meant war with the states bordering on the Company's territories. Some of the Company's agents saw other possibilities, as did Lieutenant Broughton at Chittagong. Knowing of the great interest that Shore took in the stability of land-ownership for gaining the support of the people, Broughton argued for giving land rights to the Mags, a tribal group living on disputed land between Bengal and Burma. Doing so, he argued, would make them good citizens, grateful to the British, who would provide Bengal with a boundary that was defined and defensible.

In general, reading the correspondence between the Company's servants in India and the directors in London, one gets the sense of unease over the border situation among the Company's servants. The directors had expected that the revenue exacted from the Bengal peasantry would pay for the investment, the goods purchased for sale in Europe, but instead their servants in India were spending nearly 50 per cent of the revenue on the army and fortifications for what they termed 'Public Safety' of Bengal and the other territories. For the safety of the Company's continued profitable existence in India, the officials in India argued, defining the boundaries was the fundamental, but expensive, necessity.

Hence, the idea of firm borders—in the British sense of following natural geographic features—has been part of the understanding of the states of South Asia since the eighteenth century. The frequent border clashes between India and Pakistan, and between India and China, indicate that contested borders continue to be a feature of twentieth and twenty-first-century South Asian political life. The idea of 'natural borders' in the French sense of state borders that expresses the natural social configuration of a national community has also had an expression in South Asian political life. This idea appeared in the writings of Indian nationalists, when it was argued that true nationhood was rooted in a peoples' primordial possession of a land with a cultural inheritance.

Such ideas became associated in the twentieth century with a vigorous Hindu nationalism that sought to exclude other Indian groups such as Muslims and Christians, who, it was argued, had a foreign cultural inheritance that prevented them from sharing in that primordial inheritance rooted in the land. One of the most influential statements of the identity of a nation with territory is found in the writings of V.D. Savarkar, who argued that nation, religion, and language were bounded by natural frontiers—the great arc of the mountains, the seas, and in the northwest the great river Sindhu, later known as the Indus, was the boundary. 'The day on which the patriarchs of our race [the Aryans] had crossed that stream' (Mazumdar 2003, 230), they became reborn as a new people, destined to become a new nation of Hindu or Indians. While associated with nativist, exclusionary religious politics in modern India, it was given expression at a fateful moment in contemporary Indian history. In 1959, Prime Minister Jawaharlal Nehru, a secular socialist, perhaps not knowing its origin, raised this claim when India and China were moving towards war over the issue of where the boundary lay between the two countries. The Chinese had pointed out that the boundary line that the two nations were quarrelling over had been arbitrarily drawn by Great Britain, an expansionist imperial power, when neither India nor China was in a position to negotiate it. Nehru's answer was categorical: The boundary runs 'where it has run for nearly three thousand years' (Fairbank 1987, 8), and the people enclosed by it had always regarded themselves as Indians. This is a long jump between Nepal in the 1770s to South Asia in the contemporary era but it indicates how policies enmeshed in the local commercial concerns of the Company have been linked through the centuries with the nationalist concern with boundaries in the twentieth century that continue today.

Bibliography

Fairbank, John King, 1987. *China Watch*. Cambridge: Harvard University Press.

H.M. Stationery Office. 1813. 'On the East India Company's Affairs'. In *The Parliamentary Debates (Official Report[s])*. Chicago: University of Chicago.

Mackenzie, Alexander. 2012. *History of the Relations of the Government with the Hill Tribes of the North-East Frontier of Bengal.* Cambridge: Cambridge University Press.

Maxwell, Neville. 1970. *India's China War.* New York: Random House.

Mazumdar, Sucheta. 2003. *Antinomies of Modernity: Essays on Race, Orient, Nation.* Singapore: Duke University Press.

Michael, Bernard. 2012. *Statemaking and Territory in South Asia: Lessons from the Anglo-Gurkha War (1814–1816).* London: Anthem Press.

Moran, Arik. 2019. *Kingship and Polity on the Himalayan Borderland.* Amsterdam: University of Amsterdam Press.

Morris, Henry. 1898. *Charles Grant.* Oxford: Oxford University Press.

Pounds, Norman J.G. 1951. 'The Origin of the Idea of Natural Frontiers in France'. *Annals of the Association of American Geographers,* vol. 41.

Index

Kashmir 69, 158–9, 170
Kathmandu, *see* Nepal
Kaye, John 154
Khan, Alivardi 45
Khan, Dost Muhammad 149–50
Khan, Liaquat Ali 16
Khan, Mehdi Ali 98–9
Khan, Murshid Quli 48
Khans of Kalat 159–61
Khasi hills 54, 132
khutba (the Friday sermon) 59
Khyber Pass 154
Kinloch expedition 64–5
Kipling, Rudyard 39
Kitchener, Lord 19
Koch Bihar, kingdom of 23, 54
    Company's intervention in 67
    defiance of conventional political
        classification by 66
    sanction for Bhutanese invasion
        of 67

Ladakh 167–8
Lahore 9, 103, 159, 171
    Afghan power established in 58
    atrocities against Shia population
        in 97
Lawrence, Henry 168, 173
Lawrence, John 35, 140
linear boundaries 20
Lumsden, H.B. 91
Lyall, Alfred 34, 39
    on buffer state 144
    idea of frontiers 34

Madras Presidency 4, 134
Maghna river 54
Mags tribes 182
Malcolm, John 97–102
Malla dynasty 63

Manas river 54, 124
Manipur 124, 126, 129, 132, 139
Mansarovar Lake 167
Marathas/Maratha power 46
    under Bhonsle rule 55
    characteristics of 22
    confederacy 22, 24
    domination associated with
        moving frontier. 26
    semi-permanent frontiers 22
Marshal, P.J. 5–6
McMahon, Henry 3, 18, 28
McMahon Line 2, 31, 133, 180
Metcalfe, Charles 111–14, 143, 147
militarism, in Indian language
    newspapers 15
Monroe Doctrine 30
Mons kingdom 57
Morang hill state 77
    problem of 64
Mughal Empire/power in India 90
    accurate measurement of
        distances 24
    administration of 49
    and administrative control over
        hilly areas 55
    conquest of Islamic missionary
        work. 54
    defeated by Ahom kings of Assam
        54
    European travellers on boundaries
        and end of 21–2
    frontier
        neutrality and non-alignment
            policy in Calcutta and
            London 59
        pattern of 55
    governors 9
    historical characteristic of 23
    imperial institution 8

About the Author and Editor

Author

Ainslie T. Embree (1921–2017) was Professor of History (1958–91) and Professor Emeritus of History (1991–2017), Columbia University, New York, USA. He also taught in Indore, India, served in the US Embassy in New Delhi, and was president of the Association of Asian Studies and the American Institute of Indian Studies, USA. Among his many books is *Charles Grant and the British Rule in India* (1960). He was editor-in-chief of the four-volume *Encyclopedia of Asian History* (1989) and editor of the revised *Sources of Indian Tradition* (1988); *Asia in Western and World History* (with Carol Gluck, 1997), and *India's World and U.S. Scholars: 1947–1997* (with others, 1998).

Editor

Mark Juergensmeyer is Distinguished Professor of Sociology and Global Studies and Founding Director, Orfalea Center for Global and

International Studies, University of California, Santa Barbara, USA. He has previously edited two of Embree's books of essays, *Utopias in Conflict* (1990) and *Imagining India: Essays on Indian History* (1989). He is an expert on religious violence, conflict resolution, and South Asian religion and politics, and has published more than 200 articles and 20 books. Some of his books include *Terror in the Mind of God: The Global Rise of Religious Violence* (2000); *Global Rebellion: Religious Challenges to the Secular State* (2008); and *The Oxford Handbook of Religion and Violence* (co-edited, 2018).